The Three Marias :

Maria Isabel Barreno

Maria Teresa Horta

Maria Velho da Costa

New Portuguese Letters

Translated with a Preface by Helen R. Lane
(prose sections)

Poetry translated by Faith Gillespie
with the assistance of Suzette Macedo

readers international

English translation © Doubleday & Company, Inc. 1975
Poetry translation © Faith Gillespie 1975

1994 edition by Readers International, Inc., USA, and
Readers International, London. Editorial inquiries to
London office at 8 Strathray Gardens, London NW3 4NY
England. US/Canadian inquiries to RI Book Service,
P.O.Box 959, Columbia LA 71418-0959 USA. Published
by arrangement with Doubleday, a division of Bantam
Doubleday Dell Publishing Group, Inc.

The editors wish to thank the National Endowment for the
Arts, Washington DC, for their support. We also gratefully
acknowledge the help of the Canning House Library of the
Hispanic and Luso-Brazilian Council, London.

Cover art, "Evolution" by Piet Mondrian, 1910-1911.
Cover design by Jan Brychta.
Printed and bound in Malta by Interprint Limited.

Catalog records for this book are held by the Library of
Congress and the British Library.

ISBN 0-930523-97-0 Hardcover
ISBN 0-930523-98-9 Paperback

CONTENTS

Translator's Preface

When this book was published in Portugal in the spring of 1972, its three authors were arrested by the authorities, on charges of 'abuse of the freedom of the press' and 'outrage to public decency'. The book was banned, and all copies of it were confiscated. The court proceedings against the 'Three Marias' (as they came to be known) began in October 1972, under the provisions of a new law which made writers, publishers, printers, and distributors legally responsible for the morality of works they put before the Portuguese public.

The trial dragged on for many months, and during this time the cause of the 'Three Marias' was taken up first by women's liberation organizations in many countries, and then by international writers' groups protesting at this pernicious form of self-censorship imposed by the Portuguese law code.

In April 1974, however, the trial was abruptly ended. All charges against the authors were dropped, and the judge proclaimed the *New Portuguese Letters* a work of literary merit and urged the three authors to continue to write. A victory was thus won for freedom of expression, and the *New Portuguese Letters* has become a milestone in the fight for freedom for women.

What has perhaps been obscured amid all the notoriety occasioned by the trial of the Three Marias and their 'pornographic' work is the creative process whereby these *New Portuguese Letters* came into being. In the authors' own words, '*What* is in the book cannot be dissociated from *how* it evolved.'

Two of its authors, Maria Isabel Barreno and Maria Fátima Velho da Costa, were published writers who had been friends since adolescence and worked together as researchers in the Ministry of Economics. They became friends with Maria Teresa Horta, the literary editor of a Lisbon daily and also a writer; one of her volumes of poetry, *Minha Senhora de Mim* (*Milady of Me*)

7

had been banned as 'erotic'. All three women were in their early thirties, all three had been educated by nuns, all three were married and mothers of sons. And all three were eager to use their talents as writers to bring about change in Portugal, a country groaning beneath the dead hand of dictatorship, economic injustice, and stifling repression. The three women decided to have lunch together once a week in a public place, and also to meet one evening a week in private. Their purpose: to examine their similar problems as women and as liberal writers. They found that they were in substantial agreement on the need for reform of social patterns in their country, and they also discovered that they vaguely agreed on the need to put an end to the many forms of discrimination that women suffer in both their public and their private lives. They were not at all in accord, however, as to where the precise roots of the problem lay.

Maria Isabel, the most militant feminist of the three and the most sociologically oriented, insisted that the social institution that oppresses women worst is the role of mother – a role that society idealizes only to mask the slavery of it. Maria Teresa, also an ardent feminist, held that women were generally victimized by society but in addition had very specific aggressors: men – not just any men, but those closest to them: the fathers, brothers, husbands, and sons in their lives. Maria Fátima, on the other hand, had reservations about feminism as an organized movement, finding that in their schism-ridden struggle for women's rights its members often proved just as overbearing as men; she herself was convinced that men and women alike were victims of psychological roles forced upon them by history and society.

They decided that each of them would compose whatever she chose during the week, and deliver to the others a copy of the material. They would discuss it together in detail at that week's evening meeting. Little by little the idea of putting the material together in a book emerged from that shared experience. It was decided that each would also exchange letters with the other two for incorporation within the book. Though unsigned, all these written pieces would be dated, thus giving their collective work a chronological unity as its over-all organizing principle. In order to achieve a thematic unity as well, the women chose the famous *Letters of a Portuguese Nun* as the seed around which their individual contributions would crystallize as a work of literature.

This slim volume, written in the seventeenth century, has long been a classic. Rainer Maria Rilke's *Duino Elegies* were partially inspired by these letters, and his 1913 translation of them is the best known of the many that have been made in the world's major languages. Though the question of their authenticity has never been definitely resolved, it is generally agreed that in the early 1650s a Portuguese girl of sixteen, Mariana Alcoforado, was placed by her widowed father in a Franciscan convent in Beja, a city in the province of Alentejo, south-east of Lisbon, and shortly thereafter took the veil as a nun – not because of a genuine religious vocation, but because this was the fate of girls of her time whose families were unable, or unwilling, to provide their less marriageable daughters with dowries. At the age of twenty-five, Mariana was introduced to a young French officer, Noël Bouton, who had come to the Peninsula with Louis XIV's troops, supposedly dispatched there to help free Portugal from the yoke of Spain, but in reality to further the expansionist ambitions of the Sun King. Soror Mariana fell madly in love with this dashing foreigner, and when he fled to France to escape the consequences of their scandalous relations, tradition has it that between December 1667 and June 1668 she wrote him the five celebrated missives. The letters were first published in French in Paris by the Comte de Guilleragues, director of the *Gazette de France*, in January 1669. Though a Portuguese orginal has never been found, even in translation these letters of Soror Mariana's are an unparalleled combination of searing lyric passion and cruelly lucid self-analysis, 'expostulating her desertion', as she puts it in the language of her century, and detailing her passage from faith to doubt to despair at her abandonment by her French officer-lover. Bouton, that swashbuckling *macho* colonialist whose like history has seen so many times, later became the Chevalier de Chamilly and Marshal of France.

Whether the seventeenth-century letters are genuine or spurious, the choice of Soror Mariana Alcoforado's letters as the inspiration for *The Three Marias: New Portuguese Letters* was a natural one for these three twentieth-century women writers, who in their book have adopted her as their sister in the most extensive connotation of that word. In these *New Portuguese Letters* Mariana's convent becomes the symbol of all the walls within which society continues to confine women: a prison today relabelled marriage, motherhood, or a lifelong feminine docility not far removed from the old religious vows of duty, obedience, and self-abnegation. In the imaginary letters composed by the Three Marias, the relations between Mariana and her French cavalier become the symbol of the deep ambivalence underlying the relations between man and woman in all times and places. In this gloss on her renowned letters, the passion of the original Mariana reassumes its etymological meaning: suffering. In the modern recasting of her story, Mariana suffers not only the humiliating consequences of her self-abandonment as a woman to a man, but also the destructive effects of a kind of female blood curse passed on from hating mother to hated daughter for generation after generation. Other motifs were also implicit in the choice of the seventeenth-century Mariana's letters as a model: in particular, a national and personal sense of isolation and abandonment that her three modern sisters feel is a constant of the Portuguese character.

Gradually, the original *Portuguese Letters* came to serve the Three Marias as a sort of emotional magnet attracting many different kinds of material: poems exchanged between them, suffused with an intimacy mindful of the long tradition of highly charged lyrical poetry in Portugal; prose essays on the condition of woman throughout history; reflections on the many mythical faces men have given her; invented letters to and from a long line of Mariana's female descendants and their lovers, spanning a period of three centuries and calculated to demonstrate the despair concealed beneath sexual passion; and many letters written by a host of fictitious Marias and Marianas and Maria Anas of today. Among these latter are missives from wives forced by the economic necessities of emigration or the military conscription of their husbands to live long years apart from their spouses, lines written by a poor peasant girl sent off by her family to serve as a maid in a rich Lisbon household, and letters from a woman immured in another of our contemporary convent prisons, the mental institution to which she has been committed after being unable to face the role of wife and mother to which husband, family, and society have relegated her.

All the Marias and Marianas and Maria Anas of the book thus become a sort of universal name for woman, and these *New Portuguese Letters* a meditation on the pertinence of the original

Portuguese Letters to the situation of women today. And while the form has deep roots in the country's literary tradition, it also has a collage-like quality, varying as it does in tone from acute intellectual analysis to utterly frank personal revelations, which is close to that of today's 'new novel'.

Both in form and content, this book thus transcends the usual feminist tract. It represents what is perhaps the most penetrating record to date of the process of consciousness raising itself – an experience shared over many months by three women determined to tear down the walls of *their* convent, to break the unconscious male–female covenant leading to mutual repression and exploitation by way of the carnal embrace, to use as a kind of revolutionary explosive the power of the new sexual freedom they were painfully winning, inch by inch, in their personal lives. These *New Portuguese Letters* are the story of a twofold creation – that of a precarious but real sisterhood that has managed to leave room for the passionate emotional interplay of three very different personalities and philosophies of liberation, and of an extraordinary feminine language celebrating, as in religious ritual, the spirit and flesh of all womankind. What they say applies equally to contemporary Portuguese women in a society far more tradition-bound than ours in America, and to women everywhere. Real liberation for all women, their book ultimately suggests, will come only when all separations, both physical and psychological – between the male and female side of the human psyche, between masters and servants, between dominating parents and helpless children, between couples forced apart by economic or political pressures and patterns beyond their control – are done away with by changing not only the consciousness of women but the conditions of a social order that is exploitative to the very core, and in which women remain 'the last colonial territory'. These three sisters of Soror Mariana imply in the end that love in the true sense will become possible only when the enslaving myth of love as irresistible passion is shattered and replaced by a conception of love as comradeship, as a walk hand in hand between the two Pascalian nothingnesses of birth and of death, the human condition shared by all of us regardless of civil status, sex, or country.

The Three Marias: New Portuguese Letters is a book that is pitiless towards man the tyrant but often unforgettably tender towards man the tragic animal who must learn to share both his life and his inevitable death with woman – that creature whom nature has made his partner but history his slave.

'We must change the world,' Karl Marx proclaimed. 'We must change our innermost lives,' Arthur Rimbaud insisted. Even within the most searching recent writing about women by women, books that reveal the dialectical relationship between these two imperatives can be counted almost on the fingers of one hand. Certainly the *New Portuguese Letters* must be included within that tiny number.

Les Eyzies, France   Helen R. Lane
June 1974

First Letter I

... Granted, then, that all of literature is a long letter to an invisible other, a present, a possible, or a future passion that we rid ourselves of, feed, or seek. We have also agreed that what is of interest is not so much the object of our passion, which is a mere pretext, but passion itself; to which I add that what is of interest is not so much passion itself, which is a mere pretext, but its exercise.

Hence it will not be necessary to ask ourselves whether what brings us together is a common passion for different exercises, or the common exercise of different passions. The only question we need ask ourselves is what form our exercise will take – nostalgia or revenge. Yes, it is doubtless quite true that nostalgia is a form of revenge, and revenge a form of nostalgia; in both cases we are searching for something that will not force us to retreat, for something that will keep us from destroying. Nonetheless, passion is still the motive force and its exercise its meaning.

Only out of nostalgia will we make a sisterhood and a convent, Sister Mariana of the five letters. Only out of vengeance will we make an October, a May, and a new month to cover the entire calendar. And of ourselves: What will we make of ourselves?

1.3.71

Second Letter I

More than passion:

its motives; its construction. – Motives that are set into it piece by piece, like a rose window with its transparent images? No – its visceral interior, rather, made of solid glass.

Let us consider the role that joy plays in love: words woven one by one into the magic tapestry of feelings and gestures. With the greatest precision, the hand above the paper sets down ideas in a letter that we write, not so much for another as for our own nourishment: the sweet sustenance of tenderness, of the invention of the past, or the poison of accusations and vengeance, these being basic elements of passion in the reconstruction of our bodies, ever prone to yield to invented, but not false emotion. It is not false if I write you:

'Look, the keen-bladed knife of your silence is eager to turn round and round within my belly . . . Cover my eyes with your fingers so that I cannot see that I am losing you, nor see myself losing you, and thus will not lose myself.'

Then there is hate, another principal element of love. A love whose object will never be, in and of itself, the principal cause, but merely the motive, the point of departure, and never the sole objective, or even the fulcrum: the Other.

And if in my heart of hearts I do not believe in love as a totally genuine feeling apart from my imperative need to invent it (in which case it is real but you are not), I nonetheless refuse to deny it, since it truly does exist in and of itself: a vice, an urgency, a precipice, whereas you are scarcely more than a motivation, a beginning, a garment in which I envelop you, a garment woven of my much greater pleasure at feeling myself moved by passion than in loving you, a cloak for involving you in my much greater pleasure in saying that I love you than in really loving you.

It is not false, then, if I write you:

'I know that I have lost you and am foundering, that I am also losing myself because I am completely powerless to make you love me.'

And so I suffer, apparently because I love you, but in reality because I am losing the motive that will sustain my passion, which most likely I am more fond of than I am of you.

I cannot cure myself of my frantic ravings, nor rid myself of my anxious desire to see you. But in this particular instance, certainly, it is desire and not love that is the cause of this other feeling or the food for an emotion that can scarcely be mistaken for love or regarded as anything but the mere corporeal exercise that it is in reality.

I do not reject love as an exercise. Nor do I reject suffering as the exercise of love and love itself as the exercise of passion, whatever its true nature may be.

What, then, do I give in exchange for what you give me?

– My love. Or more precisely: my love for you.

Hence never will any one of the three of us, each of us a woman, give herself without harming herself and another. A hidden ramification that we shall carry with us into the vortex of knowing ourselves, of discovering ourselves, on the journey through ourselves that we are deliberately setting out on as we seek ourselves or surrender ourselves.

Through the systematic dissection of the little we have left? or of the great deal that we possess?

2.3.71

Third Letter I

Ponder the fact, my sisters, as our flesh today is warmed by this gentle sun shining down on everyone and bringing in flocks of tourists, that this literary novelty of ours is going to sell well. That I assure you, o six little feet of us three cunning travellers. Think about what I told you – it's like the sun: it's for us and for others. Think about the contract proposed, the shattered cloister walls we would disclose, the three of us exposed to public view, like girl-children placed in the convent turnbox, once born in secret of our threefold womb. Girls cast out at a tender age from the house of their parents, their dowries sold off at auction to the highest bidder in the country. Isn't that how it is going to be, isn't that how it already is? What is going to become of us and of Mariana after starting off like this: a lament for the absence of something, for something missing, regret that Mariana or others are no longer part of our lives – or wanting to know the reasons behind our sense of loss?

Whether it be Beja or Lisbon, whitewashed walls or paving stones, there is always a cloister awaiting whoever proudly defies custom and tradition:

a nun does not copulate

a woman who has borne children and earned a diploma
    writes but does not overcome obstacles
    (and certainly not in a sisterhood of three)
through Literature
LITERATURE in capital letters
hands cannot be joined in a circle
– and yet, readers, you have bought
    Mariana and us
    Mariana who long ago
    mounted the chevalier
    and put him to good use to dismount
    her/others' reasons for being banished to the cloister.

And what about us, whose words go out into the world unsigned, the paths between us untraceable—merely a trio of hands, an anonymous chorus? Oh how many problems I foresee, sisters: the three of us will be considered a single case, though we have no way of knowing if it will become a cause, and for that very reason we give each other our hands, and hold them out to others, hands joined in a circle, warmly clasped and firmly wielding the pen. Writing: a whirling of paper skirts, a vortex, an overturning of what? But nonetheless a promise to anyone who leafs through these pages: the theme is a passing one, a rite of passage, the impassioned exercise and experience of passion; and the tone is compassion, a sharing with passion.

3.3.71

Teresa

of roses you teresa and a voice of glass
quick dragonfly shattering and never
with light artfulness exhausting exhausted words
aftertaste of tart tender sorrel, a whistling (you of Silves)
placid furrow gravely traced over some
whitewashed wall, a quiet poise
an easy turn of phrase at the tip of your tongue
swaying hips glad ship and petal
soft flesh cradling blazing axle, uncorrupt
stamen in light
a single thread of a metal all your own teresa

6.3.71

Isabel

Listen Isabel stones are so old
we do not deserve to be in touch
with smooth basalt or rainbow quartz.
You spring from what sustains them until they turn to sand.
Not of granite, I say, or not granite alone
but of all stone, even of sand, you bear
the sign and majesty.

Listen of sand I speak and of risk
mineral redoubt, crystal of white rock, learn
that sound is made of metal and air as well
and drops of air are grindstones for the music of words.

You keep perfect order in the form of your flesh
and controlled gesture
the order of stone imposed and chiselled
transparent or veiled colour
sapphire   pebble   hill   rose   dawn
only abrasive words wear you down.

Listen

how the barren waters have worn away your bearing
the name of Isabel surrounds a high coral island
and contains it.

Rather you were azalea
the name a flower of stone, set apart.
Not from some inert mass do I think you came
nor would I return you there.
You place yourself in peril where support is narrow
and with each separate act the groove cuts deeper
with you the tax of time is spent, its cunning eye, flint, finds you void
carving through your polished surface and roseate crest
shielded spoils pact darkness
the illuminated rock fades.

Listen isabel as dim and old
as stone light are the few who live
and give forth signals
consent to what is moulded for beauty
human flesh soft and sublime.

6.3.71

Fátima

Fated you were to the gesture and
the word
the barren body that inhabits you
the woman you did not tame, who saps you
maina[1] possesses you
placid, hidden

Scant is the measure
you take to evade yourself
and never sated in your own terror
you break
in her the risk
of what persists in you as luminous metal
in which you encase yourself

So the sun's bronze
is no longer in you
but rather in her the sound, the wrought silver
the light that recalls your form and in the sunset
buries its blade to the hilt

Having tempered the sharp edge
of your rage
so female you and determined in your fever
bending over
you observe through your skin the urgency of the vortex
where you suspend your fingers

How abandoned you are
by yourself, fátima
and well loved

You come avenged by time
and you have withstood her
your well-formed breasts
have nourished her
hips swaying you tensed your thighs
to skirt the bed where you lost her

In thirst fátima you drink up fortitude
you have made your words
so fruitful or painful
that you are your own food and sustenance
in the immense solitude
into which you slip

You were maina
the woman who maintains you
curse of a poisoned land
intact, suspicious, softspoken
supple waist
knees of sunrise

If you are amending a wrong fátima
in secret
like someone embroidering a cloth behind her back
you put down the garment sewn
by hands that maina refused
only to be shackled
The loathing you knew and tasted
you transformed into the fruit of the landscape
in the street you designed
and chose
to create a future in your house.

How abandoned you are
by yourself fátima
and well loved

Famished you will give yourself
I know you are contrary
yet you allow without objection
someone to possess your body
as though you were but prey, and as the price
you must yield to arms and bow your head

The sin of muteness
is not yours
only maina, inheritor of other voices
never makes peace

Ill will you reveal
briefly
perhaps a wound fátima or dull blade
as summer slowly runs along your nerves
and your arms never hold back the sea
in the brief crests of happiness
that you absently add to your dress

Fated you were then
to light
to parched shores
and spare gestures so faithful to maina
that seem arid but not effortless

You stand off from yourself
and the distance is right
as if it were clothing fátima made to your measure
from water

Malevolent then maina inhabits you
or you habit yourself fátima
in words

11.3.71

Isabel

I do not know
if you are listening
if you are lost

you with face or mast
set against the wind

age-old stained glass
which for so long
has been your shield against defeat

You carry the lines of correction
in your face
and the clear rigour emerges
while you dissemble isabel
spinning off
in your voice the days of your disguise

Absorbed porcelain caressed
composed hips that break at a touch
abandoned skin because
a sudden near-by dread
is unleashed
and then dies away

Possessed not
you avoid the roughness
of the alien hand
that wants you and leaps at you

You a burning stone
the colour of raspberries
stone carved of fortitude and calm

since cruelly you recognize
isabel the death of words

and not even by chance
are you captured by them

I do not know
if what you say
        is fragile
        is fruitful
        is anything
you say:
I desire and do not gather the fruit
may you be the whole sea your body encloses

12.3.71

Isabel

You enclose yourself, isabel
in the temporal transparency of stone
hair swirling, volatile
in yourself
an errant one

Spare of body you
beg for words, biting them
like fruits of hunger
that burn you

And so, isabel, you hold
in yourself
the curve of the sea as passage

(a woman not used up
in keeping house)

imposed confinement
which you refuse
in our letters which bear no message

13.3.71

Senhora

Lady, what makes you so pinched
So correct
So suspect?
Who chooses the docile life
Soon knows what she rejects.

Go and bring me one hair
Of a dragon in love
For if you speak to me of love
I want to see it made and proved.
When you return I shall give you shelter
I shall seat you by my side.

Lady, what makes you so subject
So lacking
So yearning?
Who spins, embroiders and sweeps
Fades swiftly as the rose
Has neither science nor prose
And knows not the name she carries.

Go and steal the Seven Sisters
From a wicked, wrathful god
For if you say you know
I shall want proof, indwelling.
When you return I shall suspect you
Of not being on my side.

Lady, what makes you lie there so famous
So absent
So poignant?

Who chooses, severs and rejects.
Who severs, goes and reaps nothing.
Who goes, acts and loves nothing.
Who acts, speaks but feels nothing.
Your eyes are submissive.

My breast is granite.
Who spins, embroiders and sweeps,
Who waits, stays behind and fails to choose,
Who keeps silence, so quiet in bed,
Is myself, lying here feeling
Your circle of flight
Your head in my womb.

13.3.71

First Letter II

'You won,' I say. But then that means that I'm the winner and you the loser, because you were so certain of victory that you neglected to keep close watch on me, and now I'm examining you.

Coldly.

What other way do I have of examining things, of examining others with all my passion – that passion fed by the simple pleasure or pain that it gives me to feel it? – So I seek you out, I use you, I write to you; but words are not links in a chain, or bridges, or bonds to loosen in the solitude of parlours.

They wanted the three of us to sit in parlours, patiently embroidering our days with the many silences, the many soft words and gestures that custom dictates. But whether it be here or in Beja, we have refused to be cloistered, we are quietly or brazenly stripping ourselves of our habits all of a sudden and riding life bareback, as though we were males – they say.

And so men immediately want to grab us by the waist, pin us to white bed sheets if necessary, tie us down with children. Hands reach out for our flesh to retake possession of it, forcing us to be wombs for the master, because our refusal to bow to men's wishes is harmful and our menses will be the stigma that they will seize upon as an excuse we women resort to, and hence an excuse for them to make us submit to their will and stifle the gesture whereby we strip ourselves naked or deny our bodies to them for our own advantage, in obedience to the vow we have sworn to ourselves.

And we have also won the right to choose vengeance, since vengeance is part of love and love is a right long since granted us in practice: practising love with our thighs, our long legs that expertly fulfil the exercise expected of them.

And we thus come round again to the theme of exercise, as though we were again speaking of passion and as though vengeance were one of the forms of love's justice. So that the exercise of justice might devolve upon the three of us, a right granted to us by love alone, pehaps as a means of defence or as a way of opening our eyes.

Like Maina, we will hold sacred 'from this cruel distance, the right of each and all, including oneself, to behave foolishly'.

One day we will have had our fill. I ask: will it be because our voracious hungers have at last been appeased? We shall go about unveiled, even though we know that this will expose us to threats, to bald slander whose flames are fed by the firewood of custom and wrath.

What will be left of us after this adventure?

They will try to break our spirits with the bridle and a tight rein. But from the place where our mother slept there has not come down to us even the ravelled fringe of this fear; we are stitching ourselves other garments for our happiness and abandon. For abandon is another supposed habit, or a right traditionally granted us, a distaff for spinning the threads of our pleasure.

And that is what is making it possible to put together a mosaic, a stained-glass panel. Letter by letter, or via the volatile written word. An act of surrender, to ourselves first, and then to Them: to whoever cares to read us, even in a fit of rage. And never has love been such a fiction, and hence absolutely true:

'this pleasure that I embrace if I embrace you and your fingers slowly glide across my arms, my thighs, my breasts. – What giddiness I allow to overcome me, willingly lingering in its spell. With what hoarse cries I struggle and grow bigger, swell in size, expand, lose my senses and become sufficient unto myself; or else not sufficient unto myself and therefore obliged to invent you, reinvent you, create you, and destroy you so as to sustain myself.

'Be on your guard, then, against this: the danger of our loving each other or spurning each other. You, the man and master who mounts me and rides me, or attempts to, and I who seem to you to enter into this game with you, to consent to it, though in fact I am refusing to, journeying as I am through other labyrinths, through torrid climes, certainly, but following my own paths.

'Because all that really matters to you is possessing me: me, your domain, your colony, your shade-tree programmed to appease your senses. You want me to be cloistered within you as well: you yourself my convent, my sole ambition, and in the end my one and only wasteland.'

'You've won,' I say, and you think: 'I've won,' but you've been beaten. Slowly tracing dizzying circles found a centre of nothingness, letter by letter, I enlarge you. Trying to catch a glimpse of each and every imprisonment of the three of us, of its motivation as one of the workings of passion, or as passion in and of itself. And that is the point we have now arrived at: this reaching out of hands, this surrendering ourselves to each other, this independence of ours.

We are seeking ourselves, we are seeking to understand you men and your reasons for acting as you do. Who knows how senseless a desire this is, who knows whether our motive is self-indulgence, spitefulness, avidity:

'It is by way of my body that I allow passion to take possession of me: the body itself being this passion or its object, its root, its motivation, its indolence. – How not to remember your slender hips and never tell you of my passion for them? And so I love parts of you, and hence you yourself, and parts of me because of my joy at possessing them, at taking my pleasure by way of them.'

And like Sister Mariana, perhaps we will even go as far as to say: 'What would become of me if I did not feel such hatred and such love . . .' Yet it is not for the sake of pain that we go on, sisters, but for the sake of pleasure; we go on neither out of nostalgia nor out of faith. Since we have broken out of the cloister, we have broken out once and for all.

What would become of us without all the love we feel – if only because of the sheer displeasure the loss of it would cause us.

14.3.71

Second Letter II

I shall meanwhile tell you the story of the Mother of the Animals, the myth of a North American Indian tribe – and what nostalgic, relentless passions these Indians have invented on their reservations, as they die inch by inch, despite their ownership of oil wells on some of them, and their costumes adopted by hippies, and their recent last-ditch fight on Alcatraz. – The Mother of the Animals was a woman abandoned by her tribe, who decided to undertake an arduous journey to some other place just as she was about to give birth to a child, and continued to wander forever in the forests, spattered with blood and hideous-looking, the Mother of the Animals, who protects them against hunters; and whenever a hunter catches sight of her, he is so terrified he has an erection, and the Mother of the Animal then rapes him, thereby assuring him of unfailing success on his future hunting expeditions.

And I still vaguely remember the story of the man who came across a seed underneath the tusk of a wild boar; when he planted the seed it grew into a coconut palm. The man had received a wound in his hand, and his blood fell on the flower, whereupon a girl sprang forth from the bloody flower. She then went off to dance in the public square, where the townsmen killed her and buried her there where she had danced; the goddess who protected these people then withdrew somewhere behind the stars, and refused to help them any longer.

I scarcely remember these stories; I have forgotten the names and the details, though I remember, doubtless, what interests me about them: I wonder whether the Mother of the Animals is avenging herself by protecting the animals, by raping the hunters, or by granting them unfailing success when they go hunting; and I wonder who destroyed the girl who danced – whether it was the men who killed her, or the other one who maintained he had engendered her by shedding his blood on a flower. And seeing that the ruling passion of the Mother of the Animals is to wander forever down through the ages, I wonder, finally, whether her exercise of protecting the animals is nostalgia for the world or vengeance against men in the form of raping hunters; whether it is vengeance against the world or nostalgia for men that causes her to grant them success in any sort of hunting expeditions they may undertake. And since the passion of the girl was dancing, I wonder who or what she was dancing against. Needless to say, my exercise is that of vengeance; may any man who is wounded not seek refuge but shed his blood in the world. Because the object of passion is simply a pretext, a pretext, in or through that object, for defining ourselves and discovering the meaning of our dialogue by whatever means we have left.

Let's see: what we have left is the world; and our theme is passion.

Mariana wants to leave her convent, she wants to divide herself; the chevalier appears on the scene, and Mariana asks him for a lift: 'Take me somewhere else, take me inside myself.' Mariana mounts the cavalier. But farther on, the cavalier says: 'This is where I am leaving you.' And Mariana acquiesces. And there she stays, making her inventory, her circumnavigation, ever so artfully: 'Consider, my love, how far your madness took us.' Mariana is artful, and hence limits herself; her journey is over, her adventure is ended, and she must now return. What means of transportation will she choose for the return trip? The chevalier again, travelling down the same road in the opposite direction now, and Mariana keeps pretending that she is distracting herself, simply writing embittered letters: you really didn't take me anywhere, you ungrateful cavalier, you fled to France and here I am cooped up in this convent. Mariana returns to the convent, which this time does not take in a young girl sent straight there from her parents' house, but a nun abandoned after her journey with her cavalier. This was her object, her pretext, and passion her pretext also, her strength of will to forsake what she still had left, her passage to another status; her exercise was that hostile grief of hers, that tone which varies from that of lucid perception – I love my passion more than I love you – and translucid self-deception – the chevalier was mad, I am obliged to break with him because his madness was a trick he played on me. Mariana does not acknowledge her own madness, much less her marginal status – her exercise was a nostalgic one, but we know very well how cunning and crafty timid nostalgia is. Might not the moral of the story be: if a nun and the convent are at odds with each other, either the nun or the convent must change. Did the nun change? and how can the nun change without changing the convent? What sort of respectability is left for a convent wherein a nun writes love letters that are proof that the convent does not keep its inmates strictly cloistered since French cavaliers can freely enter and leave it?

Mariana – Maina, Maria – it will be only by sheer coincidence that the cause will be discovered after its effect, and a third woman thereupon enter the combination, one without a name. For in this exercise shared by the three of us I see the need to discover which of the letters of our names are the same and which are different. Mariana is a disguise of Maina, and might not Maina's exercise be a son of the cavalier yelling at the top of his lungs in the convent, giving off a sour, bitter smell in the convent, or Maina raising pigs in the silence of her cell, and then letting them loose to grunt and trample all over the convent? Maria is the root of Mariana, and Maria's exercise will be contamination through suspicion, a quiet, stealthy work of under-mining, until all the bread and all the oranges are strongly suspected of being poisoned. Maina and Maria would not want to abandon what they still had left; they would do their best, rather, to make it increase and multiply. Phantoms are not certain proof of anything, doubtless; and that is why we are here where we are, once again.

16.3.71

Third Letter II

What certainty are we trying to arrive at, what greater self-effacement, what plaintive trio ensemble playing concerts for a three-stringed instrument, what launching of a new boat are we engaged in that makes us head in the direction of the inflation of metaphor? What sort of metaphor is Mariana for us if we come close to killing ourselves in order to leave her out?

Fear has begun to overtake us – and excitement. A theme that makes our hearts pound, knocked down to the highest bidder under the auctioneer's hammer: and has another sort of excitement also remained? Once we had defined our object clearly without mincing words, and set aside the theme of the galloping rider as unimportant, we mounted ideas like Amazons. But genuine feeling is also being born, the sacred pact: we are telling each other about our experiences with men and our childhoods, the landscapes we have seen, the stops along the way; we are composing hymns of praise to each other and saying *what* each of us will do and *how* we will (or will not) carry on the original project – closely following Mariana and the letters.

I for my part find myself in that mood of pre-expulsion which I know that only words set down one by one can relieve, and I don't know who to blame for this serious tension, this depression, this great dull pain which is only slightly lessened by writing about it, and hence I'm lying when I say that writing resolves things. To *resolve* is neither to deal blows nor to receive them. The mind invents lies as it writes. And so I feel that writing to you (to each of you, to myself) is always a lesser good.

Who obliged me to abandon the solemn laughter with which I said *yes* to the journey with you, to having lunch with you regularly, to accompanying you on rambling walks along a (predestined?) path with no destination, though it always led us from the offices of the *Capital* where one of us was working as a columnist to the Trece restaurant and back – amid the frightening roar of traffic and trucks bearing down upon us?

And yet, my sisters, the god who watches over the innocence of the bedchamber and the bassinet knows that it was gravely, timidly, with a sense of gratitude and self-recognition – that is to say, without any sort of sly smile – that I read in Oporto the letters of a possible Mariana, when I was all by myself and hoping to learn to love the city with another (and hence, through this discipline of waiting for someone with whom to help create it, of learning truly to love it?). But I did not say as much, I did not tell you as much, in the beginning, perhaps believing at that point that my talent and my age might prove more useful than what might have appeared to be sheer ingenuousness on my part.

What is it, then, that is freeing me from my lonely freedom, that is gradually revealing to me what one of us thinks of thinking, of the 'exercise of passion' as a search for effectiveness and a meaning for our lives, while another of us prattles, recounts her experiences, talks seeming nonsense, and all three of us think and talk together, each of our paths already crossing and crisscrossing as we try our best to fall into step with each other?

We have now laughed together and talked together and written and shared repasts together, red snapper (O Alexander O'Neil, O frivolousness of your poem on that creature of the deep), plain ordinary chicken, firm-textured squid. And a few evenings together. You, my one sister, say 'That's not very much; up to now we've done nothing but exchange little notes': and you, my other sister, say 'How marvellous, how marvellous,' as you say of everything that's new, of everything that protects you without constraining you, 'you who are made of glass'. Remaining on your guard, you calmly go along with all of this, saying less and less as time goes by, thinking everything over carefully, and deciding, hesitantly but with your usual good sense: 'Letters from Sister Mariana? Why letters from Sister Mariana?' When you come right down to it, they're like the whining of a pitiful housemaid who is secretly happy at being abandoned, the wailing of a mere slavey who's been 'forsaken'.

'*The Green Years* on canvas.' But that's not it at all. And you, my other sister, say 'How dreadful!' and skilfully weave a garment made of a soft fabric of spoken words, a habit for both the other two, and I answer you, and you, my other sister, answer as well, so that we may take the habit together. Taking as our vestments an alba – or an alb – to celebrate what is dawning.

And you of glass and new flesh give your space to the night and your past, you gossip about your entrée into the world of letters, you chat of your minuets that never bring you closer to people (even in that world of letters, that world where *words* and giving one's word mean nothing, that world where people are objects marked by your scornful dismissal of them), you talk about your age, because you are at once the oldest and the newest of us – you will lie about love so seriously and so beautifully that any man who desires you can only thank you for the favours you have granted him and gallop off into the sunrise, towards the quintessentially real, for with your day-to-day inconstancy, you will offer him the reality of illusion: the desire of the desire of desire – a real need for the superfluous – the convulsive, precarious, precarious excitement of beauty. Perhaps it is for this reason that the man who is living with you is the only one to have visited us thus far, to have visited the trio without fear, since as far as you yourself (or Mariana) are concerned, you believe only in that which you find believable – you define yourself by the feelings of desire you arouse and you hesitate on this threshold of our circle, wondering whether to seduce us with your song, entice us with your siren's voice, or bear with us (and through us) the pain of discovering what has been missing in our lives.

And you, proud 'falcon's claws driven into our flesh' (I quote what we all quote, having apparently failed to learn, from either Mariana or Maina, from myths and rites, the proper road to follow – why do you encircle me with your grasp of stone? So be it, even though at the same time it is not so). You who think it better to think well and say exactly what you think, you who calm one of us and deeply distress the other, you, the manor house and the private preserve, what are you trying to achieve through this work (and this love invested in this passionate exercise) – are you trying to prove that Mariana never was, that her

convent and the Chevalier de Chamilly were no more than a pretext allowing her to become our sister by writing, to meet us here
today in a house of women 'of learning and talent at writing and
respected names', who *are* without defining themselves *by way
of* or *in behalf of* any desire and forever against all desire? If you
hold the exercise of passion to be more important than the tragic
commercial trafficking of its intimacies, if you tell us without
mincing words that its object is always simply an object, and
approve of Mariana if she is writing within the walls of her convent, but disapprove of Mariana if she is gasping with passion
within the embrace of her lover, then stand before us and tell all
of us (I can already foresee your answer): where do you find rest
from yourself, where do you discover peace outside of yourself,
you who are never beside yourself, you who never lose control
of yourself, you who are – what *are* you like? Out of whom, if
not your own mother within you (am I right?), are you creating
yourself?

And don't you two others call me a stone or a knife edge (even
though that too is true), for I am already whining like Mariana.
Don't think of me as the sort who thinks without feeling. You,
my one sister: don't keep merely dancing your desire. And you,
my other sister: don't keep weeping as you ponder what is lost
forever. Between clearheadedness and convulsive emotions, the
cousin of the male foreigner will have no other place to lay her
head save this uncertain womb (a virgin one? a compassionate
one? Could Mariana have given birth to a child?) – her own
letters, her past, her blighted life and blinding love, her vale of
tears, her nun's veil, her rent heart, her rent habit: a fact or a
fiction set down in writing?

Those who draw closer to us or spy on us can already hear, between this exercise of ours and the pattern that each of us is
tracing in her life, the surging tides of love that are swelling
between us, tides not of nostalgia or of vengeance, but rather,
like those between mothers and daughters of one and the same
house, or what is even more scandalous, like those between
women workers confronted with the same resistant material,
competent workers, competing and drowning our cares and setting our boots down at the edge of the bed, living the disciplined

life of the barracks or the convent, withdrawn from the world, guarding against the corruption of hierarchies and strict rules, instituting the law of a new sister (brother) hood – do outsiders realize the danger?

'It seems to me that I am doing the greatest harm in the world to the feelings in my heart, by trying to reveal them to you by writing them down. . . .'

We have already decided that this is to be a serious undertaking. What I shall do with you will be serious, even though that very fact will make me feel like laughing. Or, as today, not laughing one bit.

16.3.71

Here We Are

Here we are in combat
exposed
with no victory all these days

our groins
steadfast
in our resumed stride

A review of houses and causes
the stirring of things
that were sleeping

Each day the choice:
insane agitation
or meek appeasement heavier
than what wakes and will not be conquered

than what we shred
and shape
letter by letter to its exact profile

We are female
faithful to our image
clothed in thirsty opposition
women seeking no advantage
but certain of the men we mount

And never prey
shall we be

nor object
given

nor the compliant scent
of dead leaves

stained glass, we say
stone
trod upon

coming to ourselves
by water
or wind

Distant breeze dividing itself
this we use to serve
as maintenance

of ancient moorings
where we are secured

separate from the others
and so close

17.3.71

First Letter III

'This is not a reply to a written letter, indirectly addressed to me. A letter written to two people at once, and thus seemingly ambiguous, expressing two contradictory emotions: unhappiness at loving me, or an even greater unhappiness at never having loved me – if such a thing is possible.

'If such a thing is possible, I say, for in reality you are more the object of your passion for me than I am, since despite your complaints that you are suffering terribly, you are benefiting much more from your passion than I am (you are enriching yourself, becoming more human, gathering new strength from it, you maintain), and that is why you love me. My only benefit is the attention you pay me, the use I have made of it to fight against my loneliness, the escape you force upon me each day.

'Éscape: rejecting you because you make demands upon me. Escape even when I accept you, or merely appear to accept you, since I reject love as surrender to another, or as condescension.'

That is why, my sister, there was written to you the sort of letter that one is always so reluctant to write to the person directly concerned, to the person to whom or about whom the letter speaks and wounds to the quick, but to whom it also brings a message. When all is said and done, to the person who blames himself for (our) not being 'a little Chinese shadow held in one's hand', but rather, a sun so intense 'that it blinds yet also sheds a dazzling light'.

And again the three of us find ourselves together here, as on so many other occasions and at so many other times of decision: refusing to be shadows, a sedative, the warrior's repose. It is we who are warriors – women whose bodies are intact and whose hands are sure.

We leave a touch of laughter on things, returning from places we have never been before. And thus each of us bares herself to the others, telling each other of our experiences with a man perhaps, though our talk is not always of men but of ourselves as well, our empty space, our suffocating lucidity, the dizzying vortex of everything we touch, our constant discovery of the fuzzy contours, the precise outlines, the hardness of forms.

You call yourself fluid, me glass, and our third sister a falcon (or must, or a mast). You call me desire: my body in search of the pleasure and the passion that deceives me: sudden, urgent, immediate desire, mounting astride passion as though to possess it completely, in a long act of love without sperm, with only my own juice.

Is it possible to be a woman without being a fruit?

And so you call me a rose even though I still decorate no parlour, in this peaceful secret place that I say nothing about, that I am in the habit of saying nothing about – save to you two. And that is how, or why, we feel close to each other. And though we may still hesitate (almost always it is you who do so, you the stone-woman with your quiet transparency), it is merely out of force of habit – the habit of being mistrustful in the company of others. A habit imposed upon us by custom and tradition, wild fears: habits of the uterus and the convent. Habits part truth and part lies, meant to cast us in the proper mould.

Suddenly Mariana strips herself naked for hands that hurt her, arouse her, send her into a delirium as she seeks her own self. I don't know if she was artful in her letters, as you claim, or cleverly making a great show of her grief and thus freeing herself of blame, justifying herself, still taking possession of the cheva-lier, using him as food for her passion, as sustenance and support for her freedom.

For it is through passion that the nun escapes the cloister.

And the chevalier was nothing but a pretext, a motivation. A man who thought he was doing the mounting and instead was mounted.

Will love ever find any other way save this: love that uses or is used? Love that devours or is devoured; that pretends to be devoured only to devour in its turn?

'Do not devour me or seek to tame me by weeping and whining. I am now beginning to forget you and no longer desire you. I am far away now and the victor; I am now selling you or trading you for the calm peace in which I find myself.

'"Spurn me," I write you, but you refuse to, living on hidden dates and memories that have to do only with yourself, doubtless masturbating yourself with them, which may or may not be enough for you, meanwhile meekly accusing me and subtly pretending to be grief-stricken, telling me that you love me even amid your torment (of which I am a partial cause, and hence a passion, thus using your torment as a means to force me to cease being cold to you), blaming me for your dejection, your despair, which you weave about me like a web.'

But the three of us will weave even more webs if necessary – cunning spiders spinning out of our own selves our art, our advantage, our freedom, or our order.

In the end, what work are we seeking, what paths are we tracing over a deliberately chosen plot of ground, what cruelty are we resorting to, and who knows what else?

Not only do we talk of ourselves, not only do we speak of the men who are living with us, to whom we open the door leading to the trio; men who are our accomplices, though timid ones, and for that very reason mere accessories in an adventure that they do not understand, but which they enter into because they are close to us and in the end feel an urgent need of us.

Nor is Mariana our only nun today. Another one has entered our story, lingering in our memory with her fear: her naked body torn apart on the bed, her eyes hidden beneath her fingers:

I find myself in a strange room, gazing into mirrors and looking at myself in them, pale, impassive, at the image that I share with her, never having recognized it before this moment. Rigid, divided between the pleasure that has been experienced, anger, panic, the fear of beginning everything anew. Who knows if I am beginning it all anew, if that is why she is looking at me. – Yet I am here only to take her from her house to the convent. I wish to teach her a strange way of exercising her passion, a corporeal exercise; a passion that is dead, but will perhaps be rekindled by my presence.

A hope of vice. Yet another disappointment. Yet another dizzying bewilderment.

I pick up the habit that has fallen on to the floor next to the bed. I know who stripped her of it, and I am here as though defending the man.

A messenger for the male, I become an expert horseman and wait.

– All you would have to do would be to make her go back to the cloister, after escaping to visit cities and ending up being visited by a man, neither a chevalier nor a Frenchman, but simply a man, who by his own accounting is virile and good in bed, knowing everything there is to know about orgasms.

I touch her on the bare shoulder, with no particular feeling of compassion. My role and my gesture do not scandalize the world: the world has always dismissed women. I am simply obeying the law whereby might makes right: a woman ridding herself of the image of the woman created by men.

And even today I remember, I tell you about it, and you look at me.

– And so another nun concerns us now, along with Mariana. Why not invent letters of hers since we're inventing a new image of ourselves by carefully reconstructing our lives, remaking ourselves by building our own house?

Thus repeated, passion becomes our possession again. A plot of earth already cleared, being ridden of weeds by our own hands: dissecting its motives, its causes, its reasons. Recognizing them by their symptoms: fever, pain, the thick blood of silence.

'Never beg me to be your mistress, your prey, and never beg to be yourself a prey exposed to my weapons; they are held firmly in my hand, aimed steadily at you. Expect no pity from them: they are impassive, cold, obsessively pointed towards anyone who seeks to take me, entering into my lonely domain, my solitary strand. – I vomited on it, unaware of my exhaustion, my prison walls. Savouring my nausea as it mingled with the sun, the sea, the rough grains of salt in my mouth.'

Let no one ask me, tempt me, force me to return to others' cloisters.

19.3.71

Peace

Mariana takes her pleasure with her body.

The habit she has taken off, lying on the chair, slips to the floor, where the stockings that she has hurriedly removed now seem thicker and whiter.

Her legs, soft and thin, lying stretched out on the bed at first, slowly rise, half-open, hesitant; but now her knees come up and her heels dig into the sheets; now her haunches arch with a moan that soon will become continuous, and then break off, absorbed by the silence of the cell, drunk in by the mouth that awaits it.

Why should Mariana care what hands guide her – her own that slowly descend along her hips, or his that suddenly set her free . . .?

The walls of the cloister are breached then: he holds her fast by the breasts, tearing her nipples with his teeth.

Have the walls of the cloister been breached then?

Her tense pubis arches again: his swollen tongue. His burning-hot, rough tongue, wet with saliva, and the long, lingering, persistent, rhythmic sucking, slowly draining her of life.

Mariana is taking her pleasure with her body, self-taught, forgetting the reasons and the sorrowful complaints that lead her to the writing of letters and the forging of a self. 'I discovered that I loved him less than I loved my passion . . .': she is now immersing herself more and more deeply in her exercise. The exercise of bodily passion, the exercise of baring the roots of passion.

She keeps her eyes wide open, fixed on his face, staring at it intently as though mesmerized, inventing its outlines engraved upon her memory, or not certain whether she is inventing them as she falls upon his chest, her thighs writhing rhythmically, possessing him as though she were a male – she feels – and seeing his taut lips she buries herself deeper within him, she impales herself upon an enormous pleasure, on the outcry of one who flees or surrenders. Yielding herself entirely to that blinding conquest of the violent hardness of a penis: his fingers deeply buried in the slippery wetness of her vagina, his shoulders erect, his head leaning against the pillow, his arms tense, as though to hold down her narrow haunches moving compliantly in this common search for the vortex of the uterus.

'You know how dangerous you are: a woman swept up once again by the river that you seek to silence in your veins, you wicked creature. In the silk of your buttocks, in the scorching smell of your armpits. A plot of land, that I breathe in with great gasping gulps and form with your sperm, my seed; the mistress-wife you left behind is neither won nor lost; you see how I surrender myself and offer myself, guide myself and show you the fastest or the slowest ways to enhance our pleasure. Standing on my feet now, I take you again, I traverse you, I possess you; my already thick secretions, mingling with yours, flood my terribly sterile, sealed, sleeping womb.'

Mariana allows the fingers to withdraw from her vagina and search up higher so as to end the spasm that softly creeps up through her body. The mouth that sucks her, that traverses her is like a well in which she deliberately drowns herself, throwing herself into it in a mad frenzy.

Slowly my love, slowly reaching our orgasm, your tongue or mine tracing its outlines. Slowly I suddenly lose you, I forget you, as everything becomes a single great wave of vertigo.

And the watchful night devours the room where Mariana lies stretched out, her sweat soaking the bed, sticking to her smooth skin, her fingers lying forgotten on her benumbed, drowsing clitoris.

Peace has returned to her body, still lying stretched out as before, ready to burst into flame once more, should Mariana again wish to take her pleasure with her body.

21.3.71

Second Letter III

We are happy, though in a vague sort of way. I do not know who we are excluding, who we are killing. But I am experiencing the happiness, a happiness that has no definite shape and is not set in a stained-glass window, of having disturbed a myth, deflowered a law, killed a form of love in the hearts of those who claim they love us – out of necessity. If we were living lives that were clearly defined (or were ourselves defining our limits?) in terms of those who claim they love us, how could we then speak of the absurdity of death? I added that phrase about our defining our limits in parentheses, and I believe that this is how it is. Those who block our path are the ones who love us; but to a far greater degree, we define ourselves for those who love us by our limits of flesh and skin, since knowing and feeling each other's outlines, each other's contours and form is what makes us become palpable and comprehensible. I myself might go, for example, as far as the outer edge of blue, or even of indigo, but I am not the one who likes or knows anything about purple, the point where you begin, for instance. That is also how anniversary presents and love gifts are exchanged, with years becoming things and persons becoming things. For vengeance is one of the uses of love and love is given us by custom and wont, for us to use.

We are also well aware, however, that our one true limit is time, and that until the day we die we will always be far from having defined ourselves. The idea of dealing with persons as though they were divisible wholes is absurd, and if everyone tells us that death is absurd, how can anyone take pleasure in locking us up inside an endless present, in fixing our final, definitive portrait? That is why we divorced ourselves from you males, and refused your support.

First mountains were scaled, and only now are there hesitant expeditions to the bottom of the sea, and it is my belief that we know much more about the moon than about these ocean depths. Men have always been involved with and have always dreamed of what is extroverted form, in what rises up straight and tall, in what rends space. And so they know nothing of abysses and depths, they know nothing about us women. They say to you: 'You're fluid,' and fail to recognize the solid rock that sustains the weight of this ocean; and that is why it is necessary to come to know women through 'their learning, their talent for writing, and their respected names'. We are defending ourselves against traditional uses and customs, and so we are refusing the support of those who use us.

But we too do not yet know what we are. We are happy, but in a vague sort of way. We also do not yet know what to invent; how to abandon that definition of ourselves in terms of our limits, how to invent a love that will recognize all the abysses. Each of us is sure of each of the others, that is true. Each one of us knows how to count the ways of loving and of safeguarding love, and on that score we understand each other. I said: 'What is most important is the exercise of love itself, what we have left is vengeance on the world, till a new day dawns,' and you other two answer: 'What is most important is waiting for someone, waiting to exercise our passion, and hence learning truly to love the City and refusing your aid in our cause, you male rulers of citadels.' And we have been telling each other about our men and what we have done in the past, we have been composing little lyric poems in honour of each other and little notes, as we have already said. Yet all three of us are deeply aware that we are now going beyond that; we know for certain that we are leaping, hand in hand, towards depths that we have not yet created, and are still not certain we will be able to create.

I do not know who it is we have excluded, who it is we have killed. But we are sure of one thing at least: the leap has begun, with the smell of must, the voice of stone, the cutting edge of glass. We have set up the sacrificial altar, laid out the cup, the wine; we have looked at each other out of the corners of our eyes and asked: 'Who is it we are sacrificing, who is it we are vanquishing, who is it we are using?' But we have already killed, already excluded; we have sucked our victims' blood, cleverly beaten him at his own game, and stripped him of his arms. And not just as an adventure, the goal of which we will be obliged to decide on later; so let us keep ourselves aloof from this feeling of being trapped in a nightmare, from the shudder of someone who awakens in terror after fighting in the dark in legitimate self-defence and says 'What's to be done with these corpses now?' There are those who die out of good intentions and those who die out of necessity. I have already spoken of the seriousness of our undertaking, a fight for life, which in our time and our place is not considered legitimate, even in self-defence.

23.3.71

Message Invented by Mariana Alcoforado

Lady of Myself, to you I am
a body you have fashioned
and I compensate by trading
nakedness for clothing

image of my lament
a great show of weeping

letters written because I feel
I shall lose myself, become unhinged
if I do not blame you or kill you

I dedicate my suffering
to my own rightful pain

For a reason unknown

My lord, I no longer remember
your end
or your beginning

23.3.71

Third Letter III

'What will become of me, and what do you expect me to do? I find myself at a far remove from everything that I had anticipated.'[2]

'... I caught a lot of fish in that river and back then the water was clear you could even drink it, I didn't drink any, but I saw somebody who did and he didn't die from drinking it ...'
'... in order for the sea to be pure the rivers must first be pure'.

This letter from a man who thought himself fortunate to have emigrated to Canada came into my hands and I have brought it here to you. It is as though this entire exercise of ours were the culvert, the cove, the caul into which all the rivers must drain if the sea is to be cleansed for us women who are polluted by the flow of time and words, driven out of so many places, or left behind by men who emigrate, or turned by males into flowers: *Qui s'y frotte s'y pique.** That was my tragicomic theme, my fragile, familiar refrain for this year in which I changed my life so radically, without knowing what instinct of mine I was obeying (a provocative dance in a public square/putting myself up for public auction by publishing a book/auctioning myself off in private).

A man who knows the three of us (who is suspicious of us) said that our project might be the death of us. And another said: 'What monsters you three are!' And another made his peace with us by giving us a drawing of doves. And I find that we are merely repeating Agustina Beça Luís's story called 'The Mother of the River' (O, Agustina, you who are so alone and so independent, so much your own woman!). Let us hope that our hands will not be crippled or our bodies shattered as in Agustina's story – that those who love us for what we are and do will not divide themselves by dividing us. This is what is meant

* Gather thistles, expect prickles. (*Translator's note.*)

by poverty and chastity. Out of fear they even call us lesbians, because they are unable to lay their hands on our bodies (our six breasts of heroines out of a popular novel – our little parody on that best-seller *The Three Beasts of Novelia*), either to offer or to demand favours. The sex of a man is frail and fragile if he divides his mother from himself. Let all us women love one another as the three of us love each other for being orphans suffering the same deprivation: all of us needing someone who will bring us peace and a sense of adventure, smooth waters and active love, clean bread and unspoiled oranges and poor beans growing amid rock crevices, for 'on this earth created by God's hand, we women are all equal, and this gives us the courage to set out on our adventure together!'

24.3.71

Proposal from Me to the Trio

I know or am my all
a house and bread
my nourishment
clarity

I acknowledge no habit
of custom or grain
seed of water then
sown by a bird

I shall give you
land at your disposal
knowing well it is only for leaving
and nothing grows there that is not born

Journey into myself
I give you the magic
whereby I know no longer how to be masked

24.3.71

A Nun's Little Trinket in the Form of a Word Game[3]

mariana loves to be bad (in bed)
maria smells of sea-salt
as mariana is borne on the tide (of love)
who can settle the salt of her tongue?

dropping stitches in the net they weave
three leap through it, without asking leave
sheep straying from mariana's fold
while she loves quiet, they are bold
married marias, escaping the foretold

    isola bella (isolda?)
    teresa (leda?) with hands soft as down
    fátima with the sharp sap of holm-oak

they read others' writings (empty homes)
write themselves, eyes brimming with tears
whose sea-salt corrodes mariana's convent and its empty years
the waves of their love or hate for her
(born of) (borne by) the wind
lapping or lashing at its whitewashed walls

which of us bedevils beja
(puts a pox on the Pax Julia)
and sweats the royal salt
the law of Se(i)smarias
the pact of the people-king?[4]

mari(a)nating the stew, setting out in our beautiful pea-green
tureen, trading orisons for perorations, sail-less, veil-less, watchful queens.

mariana sent into the garden of olives
marias who are seasprites islands spritsails
in this airy puff of unconventional conventual
breath and breeze

24.3.71

Song of Mariana Alcoforado to Her Mother

Lady Mother I know I was
in your womb
engendered

taste of pleasure or silence
your entrails I wasted
tricked into entering

O fate of immense anguish
O my remembered labour

O the intense agony
O your delayed delivery

fear sadness and sustenance
your shoulder in my childhood

Endless pain of absence
like a cold stone set
in the ring on your finger

The daughter placed in the convent
is not wanted at home

Lady Mother you found yourself
without knowing
pregnant

saw your belly grow
and never felt
inhabited

27.3.71

Saddle and Cell

I maintain that in the order of the body
the emblem placed soft and high between the thighs
should not be raised against anything.

Dry burning stick, mast, or must spilled
the clefts it turns in always bleed
and the harm is not in this.

The male organ exposed can reach a flower's height
bulbs of life tender testicles (milky water coming)
and so humble that one hand can disable or sever them.

Strong only in that place
where he finds shelter   and reaches the roundness
that sustains his uncertain vertex.

To give sustenance is not to be devoured
and in the name of wholeness let not a woman's
mouth and its discourse become ravenous.

I maintain
that wedge and hollow are inscribed on everything
on trunk and rough bark the tender drop
on the roundness of the breast the sharp edge of loss
in some brief hour.

Thus coupled in collusion with you
I do not know   *per juris causa nostra*
if this new grape is acid
and so I impose (tablet or rose?):

To love someone with love
concave or exposed
good rider or house (womb) enclosed
is to hold in your hands, suspended, your other face.

27.3.71

Letter from Mariana Alcoforado to the Chevalier de Chamilly

Senhor:

Forgive me for writing you even though I know – my reason and my heart tell me so – how relieved you feel each time you leave my side.

I am no longer a *mar* – a sea – to you, or even Mar-iana ... Nor does my womanly ardour now remind you of that blinding-bright Alentejo[5] to which you compared my body as your fingers stroked it on exhausting afternoons ...

Why, my love, this silence you swear me to (I have already been trapped by the vow of silence: a gag has already been placed over my mouth), a silence that I anxiously devour? If I do not take my sustenance from you, what fate awaits me?

Forgive these frantic ravings; forgive my anxiety, which was not the reason behind my writing you this note, nor was it dictated by love; rather, it was motivated by my urgent need to beg you to come see me, to discuss a matter so pressing and so serious that I can wait no longer, for I am prey to worse and worse fears with each passing day, not knowing how to resolve a situation that I should not rightfully be obliged to resolve by myself.

I shall therefore expect you tonight. You may rest assured that I shall not vex you with wearisome floods of tears or warm embraces. I shall avoid, my love, I swear to you, supplications, irony, fond reminiscences.

As always, wait just outside the grille. Dona Brites will conduct you to my room, where I shall be waiting calmly, with the hope that you will yet be able to save me, for if not you will be condemning me to suffer my family's eternal wrath.

27.3.71

Letter from Mariana Alcoforado to Her Mother

Madam my Mother:

Since I can no longer bear seeing you engage in this sham martyrdom of grief and anxious concern for me, I am writing you immediately following your departure (I felt that today it was a most hasty one, and it was evident to me that you were indifferent: could you perhaps have thought the contrary?) to give you news of myself, your daughter, and apprise you of the reasons that have plunged me into such cruel and profound despair or fear.

I may perhaps speak to you of love, or perhaps of death; of the cloister (the one to which you had destined me ever since I was a child, where I would be clothed in a nun's fine garments, and live a peaceful life), of habits: the one I am wearing at present, as well as the one acquired by me and through me for another, even though such a great distance now lies between us. Since there is a vast sea between him and me, I believe it inevitable that I shall be forgotten; I am forgetting him, and he is forgetting me. You need no longer fear, inasmuch as nothing more can happen to me in this world save living all by myself and inventing an image of myself, lamenting my grievous fate (I have passed from the arms of a man into my own arms, perhaps through my fault alone, having proved myself a woman unable to trap him, or to spurn him in time), deceiving myself by way of letters, since I have far more knowledge of the ways of writing than the ways of passion, and all of my imaginings have been cast in a language that is not my mother tongue and far from maternal (and thus I reject you, I free myself from you a little – O vengeance, O peal of laughter ...), a language that has turned bittersweet ever since I first heard it from his mouth and put it to my own uses.

Allow me to say to you, Madam my Mother: nothing of what is yours is of any concern to me, either your thoughts or your customs. Customs that despite everything I continue to bow to, by force of law and out of cowardice, accepting this state in which you placed me, with my father's entire agreement, because I was not born a male and because I was a hindrance to my brother and stood in the way of my sister, who needed a dowry so as to get herself a man who would marry her even though she was ugly. I have thus cost you nothing save a confinement to childbed and furious fits of rage when you discovered that I was loved and my body possessed against your orders, your command, and your will; and even despite your threats.

But you may set your mind at rest: I now find myself abandoned, and this, I know, makes you happy, though in truth it enrages you as well, since you are unable to forgive me for enjoying in life what you have never enjoyed in life. And now I find you supposedly distressed about my health and concerned about my apathy ... and find myself with no other recourse save to accept these concerns of yours, pretending not to see in them your secret happiness at discovering that I have been spurned and hence savouring the vengeance you feel is now yours for my having dared to refuse what my parents had so generously given me by sending me to this convent ... I am being punished for having surrendered myself; for having become the mistress of a man for the sake of pleasure; a surrender of myself that goes by the name of love, *and it is love that has been my ruin*, Dona Brites says.

Nonetheless ... I gave myself for pleasure's sake and proved myself the victor, to all appearances defying the world and myself by this act of rebellion, my motive for so doing being either courage, ingenuousness, or the great temptation to make my escape, the one temptation that has ever come my way.

My truce; peace. The limit of myself, Madam my Mother.

You were never a woman and I shall never be one ...

I am hiding very little from you, and yet you do not understand me at all. By writing this letter I know that I shall merely rekindle your wrath, your haughty pride, and your sense of power over me. You may well have me put to death: who will defend me? The law? The law that gives parents the right to

61

stifle freedom, that gives males primacy and the woman infinitely less than nothing, while appearing to give her everything?

Mind you, Madam, I have no illusions. This convent will be my tomb, my fierce guardian in death as it never was in those months when I was given shelter and at the same time permission to speak to others. For true guardianship is alien to its nature. And I am distant from myself. Allow me to remain aloof from myself, a stranger to myself, that is all I ask: let me spin out the thin threads of my remaining days, hour by hour, on the distaff of memory. You arranged to see me and endeavoured to discover my motives, though you were already certain what they were, speaking harshly to me at first, and then with a certain gentleness craftily seeking to draw out of me what I am in the end unable to conceal about myself. I prefer harshness, Madam my Mother, being more accustomed to such treatment at your hands.

What harm did I do you by being born?

It is as though I had been forced inside your vitals, as though you perhaps gave birth to me out of guilt ... and to your vast annoyance, certainly.

I should like you to tell my brother that I would be most grateful if he would not come here again to summon me to the parlour to speak with him; he will thus spare me the pain of resolving not to see him, or to be more precise, to hear him. His fits of rage leave me in a deplorable state of nerves; hence I pray him not to make his sister even more unhappy.

If only I could have believed that he had visited me out of friendship ... but it is merely his name that he is defending, invoking principles of honour that at times convince me, and at other times terrify me.

I informed him that the Chevalier de Chamilly will never return to our country, and as I have no intention of ever writing to him again, I no longer have any need of my brother's permission to send him letters, as has been the case heretofore; and so it is that everyone commands me, uses me, and abuses me ...

I kiss your hand, Madam my Mother, as a token of my great respect

Your devoted daughter

Mariana

28.3.71

Letter Found Between the Pages of One of Mariana Alcoforado's Missals

Senhora:

Keep the respect that you owe yourself.

Love is better served by silence and dignity than by complaints and lies. Remember that I am only too well acquainted, out of experience, with your excesses, your sudden fits of rage, and your caprices. It will be best for both of us if I depart, turning a deaf ear to your tricks and stratagems and refusing to believe you capable of them, for they ill become you, being suited neither to your condition nor to the state in which you find yourself.

And if you invoke love and passion, what proofs of passion did you ever give me, save that for yourself, fanning its devouring flames to serve your own aims and purposes?

Senhora, be on your guard against yourself, for everything about you is poison; protect yourself from yourself as I protect myself from you and ride away, overcome with astonishment at encountering so much malice and hatred and selfishness in a single woman.

It will be far better for you to accept the world that has been forced upon you and mould yourself to it, inasmuch as there is no possible escape for you.

I felt great pity for the life you led, Mariana, and great indignation at your imprisonment behind those bars that so cruelly arrest the flow of your life's blood and your laughter. On meeting you and becoming enamoured of you, I came to realize, however, that it is best that you be kept a prisoner, confined within those walls, secluded from the world.

You were a virgin when I first took you, yet I had never known a woman who had reached such depraved heights of sensuality, mad ecstasy, frenetic desire. You had me in your power, as you knew full well – suffering from your fever, which set my body on fire. I took you in my arms as you fell into a swoon, as I fainted in your womb, my precipice and my end, my absurd beginning and my death, a great abyss yawning wider and wider and deeper and deeper each time I sank down and down into it beneath the gaze of your imperturbable, unclouded eyes . . . for never once, Senhora, did I see your eyes cloud over . . .

I found myself lost because I loved you, and unloved because I scrutinized you, quite against my will, and on coming to my senses I found myself obliged to leave you, for had I not done so it would have been the death of one or the other of us.

What contempt you allow to overcome you! And by so doing you demean yourself, to the point of resorting to sly tricks and cheap pretences that you must surely have learned from your maidservant.

Do not trouble yourself further: you will never see me again. I am fleeing you and willingly confess that I am doing so without the least shame or remorse, since I am well aware of how you used me for your own ends without ever wholly surrendering yourself to me.

How is it possible to lose you, to refuse to see you, to possess you, to love you . . .

Let me go, Mariana, I beg you. Are you still not tired of tormenting me as you have?

What am I guilty of?

I am being used as your means of avenging the cruel injustice your mother is wrathfully inflicting upon you, by forcing you to sacrifice your life in that convent . . .

If you are obliged to live in God's house, take comfort in Him, giving yourself over to pious devotions rather than surrendering yourself to the worship of hatred.

Dry those tears that I know to be tears of rage and not of love; do not stoop to lies that are so clumsy and artless that they are unworthy of your intelligence, which is vast, and, indeed, excessive in a woman.

But if your words were perchance sincere and your fears genuine, set your mind at rest: you are so pregnant with your own self, Mariana, that your womb will never engender any other life save your own, forever and always.

Respectfully yours

Noël

28.3.71

Ballad by Mariana Alcoforado in the Manner of a Lament

They take me for taken
within me I trade them
my breast and my convent
for nothing

in absence I walk
so absent I walk

They take me for nun
conforming, conformed
I inhabit the habit
by habit

in absence I walk
so absent I walk

By law I'm a prisoner
so well placed in donation
I continue to keep myself free

in absence I walk
so absent I walk

They said I would die
if I loved for myself
and they threaten me still with my sin

in absence I walk
so absent I walk

Now all I have left
are the days I have lost
and the cloister I have not destroyed

in absence I walk
so absent I walk

28.3.71

The Bloodstained Nun

A phantom that haunted the Castle of Lindenberg, making it uninhabitable . . . It was a nun wearing a veil and a bloodstained habit. In one of her hands she carried a spade, in the other a lighted candle . . . A Spanish nun, she had left the convent to live with the lord of the castle. As unfaithful to her lover as she had been to her God, she betrayed him, but was in turn betrayed by her partner, whom she wished to marry. Her body was left unburied, and her soul, deprived of a final resting place, wandered about for nearly a century. She begged for a little plot of land for her body and a few prayers for her soul . . . once both things had been promised her, she disappeared.[6]

– Mother Abbess, here I am sent from the house of my parents.

– There was no bread for us at the table of men.
  Our useless body was pledged to the Lord
  In the house of the Lord we shall eat.
  In the house of the Lord we shall sleep.

– Mother Abbess, and what shall we be with no body
  and no cavalier?

– Our passion is the Lord, our exercise
  Paradise, our object the world
  We shall be nuns in a convent.

Elisabeth de Hoven

A nun in the convent of Hoven, in the twelfth century. One day she found the devil in her cell. Recognizing him by his horns, she went straight to him and gave him a resounding slap that sent him flying through the air . . . On another occasion, she thought that a man had succeeded in entering the convent, but when she later became convinced that she had been face to face with the devil, Sister Elisabeth exclaimed: 'My goodness! Had I realized it at the time, I would have boxed his ears soundly!'[7]

– Mother Abbess, here I am sent from the house of my parents.

– There was no bread for us at the table of men.
   Our fertile body was husbanded to the cavalier
   In the house of the Cavalier we shall eat.
   In the house of the Cavalier we shall sleep.

– Mother Abbess, and what shall we be with no body
   And with no cavalier?

– A prime orchard, a mount
   For his empty battles, cheap labour.
   Our passion is the world, our exercise
   Its children, our object the cavalier.
   We shall be given in marriage.

Ralde (Maria de la)

A pretty sorceress imprisoned at the age of eighteen. She had begun to practise her art at the age of ten and was taken to a Witches' Sabbat for the first time by a sorcerer named Marissans. After the death of the latter, the devil himself took her to the Assembly, where, according to Maria's testimony, he assumed the form of a tree ... but also appeared at times in the form of an ordinary man, sometimes red, sometimes black. Maria never entered into carnal embrace with the devil, but witnessed how this was done. She added that she liked the Sabbat very much because 'it seemed just like a wedding'. The witches heard music so sweet that it was as though they were in heaven ... and the devil convinced them that the fire that burns eternally was not real, but artificial.[8]

– Mother Abbess, here I am sent from the house of my parents.

– There was no bread for us at the table of men.
   The work of our bodies we hired out to the lords.
   With the money of the lords we shall eat.
   In the dung that remains we shall sleep

– Mother Abbess, and what shall we be with no body
  And with no cavalier?

– Barren earth, a mount
  For his empty battles, cheap labour,
  Where you shall hire out your body.
  They will say: 'Your strength – why not?'
  And where you hire out your strength, they will say:
  'Your body – why not?' Our passion is bread, our
  Exercise the world, our object
  The lords of working women and whores.

Maillat (*Louise*)

A demoniacal young woman born in 1598. Having lost the use
of her members, she was taken to the Church of the Holy Re-
deemer to be exorcized. It was proven that she was possessed by
five demons, called wolf, cat, dog, poppet, and griffin. Two
demons flew out of her nose in the form of balls the size of a fist,
one of them as bright-red as fire and the other, the cat, completely black. The other demons left her body in a less violent
manner. Once expelled from her, the demons circled round the
fire and then disappeared. It was discovered that Françoise
Secrétaire had caused the young girl to swallow the demons by
concealing them in a crust of bread the colour of dung.[9]

Mariagrane (*Marie*)

A sorceress who said she had many times seen the devil coupling
with a great number of women, and that it was his habit to take
pretty women from the front and ugly ones from behind.[10]

– Mother Abbess, here I am sent from the house of my parents.

– There was no bread for us at the table of men.
  If our strong body fills with passion for the cavalier
  The bread of the devil we shall eat.
  In the house of the devil we shall awake.

– Mother Superior, and what shall we be with a body
  And with a cavalier?

– Earth of yourself, a mount
  For its empty battles, a working woman's hands
  Lost, when you yield up your body.
  They will say: 'Your body, our distance.' Our
  Passion will be the cavalier, our exercise
  The body, our object the world.
  We shall be mounted as cavaliers.

Gabrielle d'Estrées

Mistress of Henry IV; died in 1599. It is common knowledge
that she did her best to get the King to marry her. She was with
child for the fourth time, and was living in the house of Zamet,
a renowned financier . . . While strolling in the garden, she had
a serious heart attack. She spent a bad night, and on the following day was overcome with such terrible convulsions that she
turned completely black and her mouth twisted about so violently that it ended up at the nape of her neck. She breathed her
last amid great torment, hideously disfigured . . . A number of
persons attributed this charitable act to the devil. They said that
the devil had strangled her to keep her from causing further
scandal and disturbances.[11]

– And what shall we do, Mother Abbess, what shall we do?

– There was no bread for us at the table of men.
  If all of our bodies were meant to be married, the value
  Of money would fall, the demand would be balanced
  With the convents, the boredom of brothels would be
  Embellished for use. With neither lords nor cavaliers,
  Neither brothels nor convents. The men
  Divide themselves into men
  And lords. But of women all men
  Are lords. In the houses
  Of lords and men
  And cavaliers we give them their meaning, for in opposition
  They define themselves. We give them their foundation
  And thickness; outside these houses we shall roam. No house
  Is ours. No one is our brother or sister. For sisterhood
  Only the convent. In solidarity
  With no one, married and sold from ourselves
  There was no bread for us at the table of men.

Cecilia

Around the middle of the sixteenth century, a woman named Cecilia attracted attention in Lisbon. She possessed the art of projecting her voice in such a way that at times it seemed to come forth from her elbow, at other times from her feet, or even from a place it would not be proper to mention. She had converse with an invisible being . . . who answered all her questions. The woman was reputed to be a sorceress, and possessed by the devil; by special dispensation, however, rather than being burned at the stake, she was merely banished forever to the island of S. Tomé, where she died in peace.[12]

– And what shall we do, Mother Abbess, what shall we do?

– I will tell you what we shall do with a body
   And with a cavalier. Our passion will be the body
   Our exercise the world, and our object
   The cavalier. Our strong body to the cavalier
   We shall give at night, but the body
   Of the cavalier we shall take. The exchange
   Will be broken at dawn. We shall say:
   'Cavalier, I want my body back so that I
   May take up my day.' They will call you
   An Amazon. But do not roam the world
   As far as hell. In the convent you shall love
   The cavalier. You shall bear witness to this
   And demand justice. In the house of the cavalier-husband
   You shall love the cavalier-lover. You shall bear witness to this
   And demand justice.
   And you will be given a convent. In the brothel you shall say:
   'I have faith in the Lord,' and you shall love a cavalier.
   The foundations of the convent
   Will tremble. Let the cavalier run
   From convent to brothel, and from there
   To his house, without ever finding you:
   You escaped to yourself in your passion.

Brinvilliers (*Marie Marguerite de*)

A young and pretty woman who, from 1666 to 1672, poisoned, without malice, and often with complete indifference, kinfolk, friends, and servants. She even went to hospitals and there administered poison to the sick. All her crimes must be attributed to a hideous madness or to the most terrible sort of depravity, but not to the devil, as is frequently the case. It is true that Brinvilliers began her criminal career at the age of seven and that superstitious folk suspected that a fearsome devil had possessed her ... Twenty-four hours after she was burned at the stake, in 1676, people were searching for her bones and regarded them as relics, claiming that she was a saint ... for the poisonings continued after her death.[13]

> – You escaped to yourself in your passion. In solidarity
> With no one, married and sold from ourselves
> There was no bread for us at the table of men.
> And what shall we do, Mother Abbess, what shall we do?
> No one is our brother or sister. For sisterhood
> Only the convent. Let the cavalier roam
> As far as your madness. Do not whip your body
> In his, as refuge from his dread. Let him fall
> With no house. There you shall come
> From your passion.

> – And what shall we do, what shall we do?

Deshoulières

Madame Deshoulières decided to spend a few months on an estate four leagues distant from Paris, and was invited to choose the finest chamber in the château, with the exception of one that was visited every night by a phantom. Madame Deshoulières had long wanted to see a phantom, and despite all the objections that were raised, she installed herself in the haunted chamber. When night fell, she went to bed, picked up a book, as was her habit, read for some time, and having finished it, put out the light and fell asleep. Suddenly she was awakened by a noise at the door, which would not shut properly. Someone opened the door, and entered the chamber with a heavy tread ... Stretching out her hands, Madame Deshoulières seized two furry ears, and patiently held on to them until the following morning ... when it was discovered that the supposed phantom was a large dog who found the chamber more comfortable to sleep in than the stables.[14]

> – In the world abandoned where shall we roam?
> Passion shall be the sole object and exercise.

Do not call me sister till another world comes.
Reject the possibilities of a new convent. In the rubble
We shall find brothers. Those who lost nothing
And were crushed by nothing, since they had no
Houses. But let us still keep our guard, for these brothers
Will say: 'You made the citizens
Now the City is ours.'
Three times will our brothels betray us:
In bread, in body, and in the City. Do not arm me as cavalier
Of your anguish. We would take up again in the rubble
Old phantoms. We shall find our way back to the root
Of our anguish, women alone, till we say:
'Our sons are sons are people and not
Phalluses of our machos.' We shall call the children
Children, the women women, and the men
Men. To replace the demiurge
Of Cyclopean works,
We shall call a poet to govern
The City.

30.3.71

First Letter IV

How is it that love is possible?
How is it that love is not possible?
what matters more:
the history of a love?
or a love in history?
        in a story?

30.3.71

Second Letter IV

I may perhaps speak to you of love, or perhaps of death.

Of death today because I fear it, of love because I refuse it. However, I can say in all truthfulness that in reality the love I refuse is the sort I use for my own ends, with a man whom I have chosen to join in combat with, in long tourneys of exquisite pain and expert pleasure, the kind of love we women never totally embrace but nonetheless assent to.

I put up a good fight – he's not a man only when his fly is open. I create this distance between us that I suffer from but accept, I dissolve it in my flesh and in nights that later turn into sleepless ones, nights filled with terror; my body now lying stretched out on the warm sheets, now tense, bent over, my knees close to my mouth as though I were a foetus, or as though I were running away in headlong escape.

Can this be my way of trying to return to my beginning?

In the end, what other beginning do we have? Here we are, dressed in women's clothes, loneliness thrust into our sides, and yet laughter still is ours, just as we also still have left great expanses full of clear insights, of empty spaces into which we sink our fingernails, so that as a result they gradually become as sharp and piercing as claws.

And so we are pitiless now. And we no longer speak in gentle voices: your lilac-coloured dress will never soften your face, my one sister, and the blue shadow you put on your eyelids will never soften your eyes, my other sister.

From Mariana we have drawn our theme, from ourselves the motive, the must, the metrics of our days. Thus we are now inventing Mariana's gestures, letters from her, her abortion. She is becoming the mother that the three of us had or never did have and are now giving to her. We accuse her, refusing to rehabilitate her, to forgive her for her weakness, her cowardliness, making a stone of her in order to cast it at others and at ourselves.

We accuse ourselves, though at the same time we are aware of our weight of rock, our sturdiness of plants, our strength. Of the power with which 'we take the leap together' – as one of you put it – and of the nourishment that we always manage to extract from someone, enveloping ourselves in it as though it were a garment, the more easily to recognize the taste of it, and donning the world as well, the more easily to recognize the fraudulent ways in which it has always barred women's access to everything.

We grant access to ourselves only to the man who approaches us gently, or comes to us in such burning fury that we hold out our hands to him, though continuing to keep our distance. And we grant him this access to us only if he is not afraid of consorting with us; for doing so is very dangerous, and he is running a great risk, since he may find himself deeply involved despite himself.

Who, then, have we killed and destroyed?

'And who have we excluded?' – you add, denying that you feel the slightest remorse and calming our outbursts of rage, stubbornly refusing to accept the reasons we offer to explain and justify them. Whoever loves us uses us, and we use whoever we appear to have joined hands with. For we love love and enjoy making love with others. We will build *our* love with words, houses to shelter us and time to reflect. – Each of us her spontaneous self when alone, apparently fragile and delicate, but firm and exacting, a mantle, a plot of earth when we are together, arousing fear in any man who thinks he 'knows' us and listens to us. There has already been one man who has tried to intimidate us by predicting: 'One of you is going to die . . .'; 'already we are refusing to accept letters sent us, letters that I tear up; already you, the fluid one, the sea, maina, look at me suspiciously, and I hear my body being praised by someone who has never possessed it or even seen it, having merely read about it in a book suspected of being a self-portrait and a confession, when in reality it was a cry of rage, a womb refused to another, but accepted by myself:

'I turn away from the mirror, stretching my arms out towards the bed and laying my nightgown down on it. I turn around and languidly allow nakedness to touch me with its adolescent softness of small firm breasts and thin haunches down which fingers glide, lose themselves, find themselves again, on the taut, smooth skin of my belly, then gently descend into the vertigo of my pubis. And my long, smooth legs can scarcely bear the weight of what I see; my tense wrists can barely guide what I am holding, slowly introducing your penis inside me: my great distance and my accepted death, my total reconstruction of life. The exercise of you: your hard flanks, your untamed thinness atop mine.

'O spasm! O all-encompassing sun! O immense burning lands as far as the eye can see, my Alentejo – orgasm, amid the total drought of my days here in this city where long ago towering convents were built. O my tender, tender, tender violent one.'

I refuse any man who creates a false image of me.

But because I do not know whether you understand me, whether you believe me, I draw back, silencing the song of the trio.

Am I the only one?

The three of us fallen silent, lost in thought, following different paths, the atmosphere tense.

And I confess that it was my fault that a man brandished a spiteful dagger, deliberately seeking to strike a blow that missed its target ... Am I perhaps straying away from the subject?

Because I am writing to you today to speak to you of love:

'I was so bedazzled by your attentions that I would be ungrateful if I did not love you with the same madness to which my passion led me once you had given me proofs of your mad passion for me.'

Once more, through love, with love as our point of departure, we find ourselves face to face with passion: a feeling that we recognize is useful to us because it is so enriching, yet at the same time destructive because it gives others power over us; a feeling to which we can never quite surrender ourselves, as we must confess if we wish to be sincere – (that also being the reason, perhaps, why they have called us monsters). – And here we are, face to face with its proofs.,

Proofs of passion: that is to say, facts proving its weakness.

'So here are the proofs,' we say, but on presenting them, we are merely attesting to the weakness of passion, if such proofs are its only form of expression. – Proofs, guarantees, testimonials.

Ordinarily, it is the woman who gives proofs, and the man who receives them. It is for this reason, among countless others, that we were born male or female.

For even when Mariana maintained that she had received proofs of love from her lover, it was her own proofs that she was boasting of, not his, thus enhancing their value, offering them to her French cavalier as testimony of her blind love, her mad passion, with the aim of receiving the same from him in return.

If a woman refuses to love the man who loves her (having been conditioned since the day she was born to lead her life hoping and waiting and most assuredly not fighting for the right to be strong-willed and express her wrath freely, since once these rights were secured, they would be considered as weapons being used against the man) such a woman will be accused of being ungrateful. Hence we three will be accused of being ungrateful; we will be regarded as peculiar creatures, and the courageous battles we wage will be dismissed as mere literary skirmishes, though their roots lie much deeper, the fruit of vines that have intertwined, grown, and been toughened as we have trained ourselves to be more conscious of ourselves as women, as something more than vineyards for men.

We are deflowering myths, and we have allowed ourselves to be deflowered. But let men not take us to be willing victims. Let them take possession of me if they can. Or you, if you can. Let Mariana take possession of herself by writing of herself within her cloister, thus acquiring her measure of freedom and self-realization by way of her writing; a woman who writes and boasts of being a woman even though she is a nun, flouting the law, order, uses and customs, the habit that she wears.

'I may perhaps speak to you of love, or perhaps of death' – she supposedly informed her mother in a letter written in feigned hauteur and indifference. I used her words in order to write to you (to us) today, just as I was about to refuse to do so.

Yes, there is a threat: 'before our very eyes' Irene Forsyte left her house, abandoning her husband, with passion as her pretext – as my sister, absent-mindedly knitting something or other out of green yarn, listened to us attentively.

1.4.71

Lament of Mariana Alcoforado for Dona Brites

What terror, Dona Brites, what tenderness.

Everyone has always had such a biased or distorted view of my entire life ... But never have I felt as lost, as trapped by others, as eager to deceive everyone in every way within my power. And to put the question bluntly: of what interest are others except to use them?

My poor soft breasts, my slender body to be stripped bare day after day, bared to you, Dona Brites, who were never a mother, and if I have confused your image with my mother's or mistaken you for her, I have thereby been led to worse and worse deceptions. I have been distracted and distant from myself for years now. But how can one bear to grow older if there is nothing left to cling to?

I know by heart each and every footstep of mine that has been chiselled or will be one day chiselled in these flagstones. I have turned into stone to engender stone, and when I run my fingers, my tongue, over these walls, what I taste and feel is roughness, a cold emptiness.

Cattle, Dona Brites, tamed since we were suckling calves, don't you too feel that? So who is of any use to us? Or rather: who is it that uses us?

O my beloved land! O Portugal! O such great expanses! Can it be possible that I am really trapped here, gasping for air?

I stretch my bare arms outside my cell: how cold the bars are, and how high the window is ... I stretch them far out, pale and thin; a thinness that is my self-defiance, that allows the sun's rays to touch me as I weep. I weep, Dona Brites, as you well know. How many times you have wrenched me away: stiff, rigid, naked, my arms uplifted, stretched outside the window, and my face raw from rubbing it, in tears, against the rough wall, and from the deep scratches of my fingernails. You always bent over me then: your eyes the colour of hazelnuts, of honey, my wrists held fast in your firm grip, my cry of pain stifled, against my will, by the silk of your lips. Seeking again and again to quench our insatiable thirst, and never succeeding.

You are not a friend, Dona Brites, you even hate me (when suddenly, and so often, I withdraw, lose myself, go far, far away). No, Dona Brites, I have not found a friend in you, nor yet a mother, for barrenness will be your brand, our stigma, our white nightdress, our ultimate end.

We took the veil, and surrendered our bodies to tyranny; who will take pity on us, if it is men's usual habit to draw satisfaction from a wife and children?

I would be so happy to die that I doubt that death can ever overtake me soon enough, even when fever spurts from my vitals and I lie panting and exhausted, bathed in the blood flowing from my private parts. A useless sign of myself, the mark of sin, of evil: were it a sign of pleasure, of carnal satisfaction . . . all this would be so welcome!

But what hope awaits us? What hope is there, Dona Brites, when life is one long torture? There is nothing to protect me from the many blows: a woman does not take up a sword or a shield, or mount a horse. Were I a man I would proudly go off to fight in the war against Spain, like my brother. They say that French troops are coming (have they already arrived?) to aid our land, which is in such great need of help, or so we are told by those who are well-informed. What further harm will this change bring us? And what does all this have to do with me, sitting here counting the hours, the dawns, as if I were weaving them, or telling them like the beads of my rosary, in total disbelief.

In disbelief, do you hear, in disbelief. Only my burning passion raises my spirits, and my sudden accesses of hatred under cover of night, although I have already spoken of them in secret. Yesterday I was summoned by the Mother Superior, and confessed them without shame. She ordered me to discipline my feelings. And my unhappiness? 'If that be the will of thy esteemed Father and Mother.'

What do my feelings matter?

Mas viver entre lágrimas, que importa?
Se vida que entre ausência permanece
É só viva ao pesar, ao gosto morta.[*15]

(Do you remember when I read you these verses, and how we both embroidered upon them? We gave each other long, lingering kisses as though to counterpoint the music of the words.)

'Reverend Mother,' I said, 'this convent need have no fear of my excesses, it is only I who suffer from them, I gather them up within myself and they come forth from me through every part of my body, every one of my deserted places. Of what interest to others is this yearning of mine for the world, this dizzying pull of the earth, this will of mine to drink the sea (to drain it, Reverend Mother, to the very last drop), this mad, forgotten craving to touch all things that wander in order to grasp them firmly in my hand. My life will ebb away little by little, Reverend Mother, if I do not express my longings, if I neither fulfil them nor take my vengeance for them. I keep them hidden, but I still have them, I confide to you in secret that I have them and keep them hidden, torn to bits, yet still whole, as I cry out in pain, tearing the pillowcase and biting it, as I bite my arms. Reverend Mother, I like to imagine myself a man, for a woman's only role is to give birth and to remain stillborn herself. And yet I am a woman and feel myself to be feminine. Who cares why I moan and why I lie, why I wish to be all alone and completely forgotten, even more forgotten than I am today, if such a thing is possible. What use is my life to me if you forbid me to use it, or even to tell of it? I have been obedient ever since I was a little girl, cast into the proper mould by lacework embroidery, linen, customs in the house of my father and mother. Therefore you need not fear my excesses, for I have cloistered them, Reverend Mother, as I have been cloistered, looking upon myself as a creature of habit since it is a habit that I wear.'

I wear these garments that I hate, Dona Brites. Since even the garments I wear have been forced upon me . . . How many times

---

* What does living in tears matter? What is its measure?
  If life goes on even when it is ended
  Alive only to pain and dead to pleasure.

have you yourself very nearly forced me bodily into donning them yet another day?

'For your own good, Mariana, you know it is for your own good ... what will happen to you if you refuse to go to chapel ...'

But do you have any way of knowing what my own good is?

'Mariana ... Mariana ... Mariana ...'

What terror, Dona Brites, what burning thirst. What blind depths we sink into together, locked in each other's arms. Our legs give way to fatigue, and then to pleasure. What wild pleasure taken against my will; what sudden tenderness surging up and up into my breast.

How relentlessly I seek to lose myself. And in the end how relentlessly I hold on to myself.

3.4.71

First Letter V

Because today I wish to speak of cruelty.

(Of my own alone?)

Sisters, I wish to speak to you of cruelty; of that which I use, day after day, even against myself, sometimes as a punishment, sometimes as warmth. A calm, daily cruelty wherein I strip myself naked, and thereby lay myself bare; wherein I clothe myself, and thereby go on: my indifference becomes my armour.

All our rigour towards men will be no less than they deserve, and it is necessary to tell them so.

They will no longer take us as warriors once took over castles won in battle – to inhabit them, extending their dominion over them not only through laws and the sword, but by the vineyards they planted: their strength, their wealth.

The woman: the man's wealth, his image and likeness, his plot of earth, his inherited estate.

Men will accuse the trio of secret things; we shall frighten them by refusing to be their prey. But they shall be chained falcons, alighting on our gauntlets, on our covered, protected hands:

* Harder, more cruel, more unyielding
  Are you, Lisi, than comet, rock, or wall
  More unyielding, more cruel, more hard
  Than what the sky sees, the sea encircles, the earth feels
    rising tall.

Alighting on your hands, you, my one sister, who refuse to accept the difference between man and woman, our caste, our hardness, yet agree to use that hardness like a weapon; wielding it like a sharp knife blade, accompanied by a friendly smile and gentle words and gestures if necessary, in order to make sure it will strike home, you cut off men's testicles.

Alighting on my hands, I who hear you, hold myself aloof, grow tense, begin to feel sad, and suddenly fall silent, withdrawing out of habit, I who of the three of you am most separated from the male, and hence reject him violently, bitterly (and fearfully?), after having had him (loved him?), after having nourished (loved?) myself through him, after having coldly used him (loved him?) for my own ends.

(Am I not speaking to you today of cruelty?)

There is a man living with me who fights tooth and nail with me and satisfies me in bed, and my vice (I am in love) is the breath of life to me, to the point that I desire even the pain it brings me, but despite this, I never allow him to lead me, to distract me, to destroy me.

Alighting on your hands, you my other sister, you who never disguise your true feelings, who have openly declared war, who have taken a firm stand. You who stoutly maintain that you are against sly, artful tricks as the only possible way of conquering a world for ourselves. You who are must, just as you are a mast.

In what way are we mothers?
  The three of us: mothers of men and not of a river, mothers neither of stone nor of women. We have responsibilities and we realize this: the responsibility of not raising our sons to be either expert horsemen or panderers, in this staid country that has made a name for itself in history: thanks to its sailors and seafarers.[16]

How to tell a woman in this day and age: make a bridge, as once upon a time she was told: make me a son?

Yes, we will give men sons, but they will be conceived in pleasure and be the fruit of *our* loins too; and at the same time they will never be our way of asserting ourselves or our only work in the world: we shall refuse to allow them to be the bridges of our longings or our dissension.

I repeat: I keep my distance from everything that makes demands on me, traps me, or simply lays claim to my attention, my laughter, my availability. What does my being available, my being *disponible* mean: being at someone else's disposal or my own?

(Why do you keep suddenly appearing, my love, every time I try to keep my distance? Why this peril, this risk, this thread I continue to follow, only to find you on the other side, as we fight with each other and desire each other?)

What are we refusing?

Why our chiming laughter at Mariana, why our rhymes on her name and ours? What are we refusing?

What are we acquiring from Mariana? Her concern?

I my concern? You your concern?

Our passion?

If I have sided with her, it is because I am inventing her, not because I am veiling her in false colours. Can that be why I defend her? Am I perhaps defending myself? I avoid myself, I am in love, I drive her to suicide, I kill her, I masturbate her.

I want to tell you about that man who said to me during a long afternoon together: 'I can only possess you if you are clothed – in a nun's habit, if possible,' he added in a low voice, turning his eyes away. 'I would like to lift up your habit and roll it up around your legs, which would then appear to be virgin, shamelessly bared to your haunches, to your defenceless belly, across which I would lingering glide my tongue. I can only possess you if you are clothed – clothed like that,' he added, in an even lower voice. 'That is how I want to take you, to rape you: as a defenceless woman, as an object. At least let me possess you in a church!'

And so here we have another exercise of passion: Mariana now became my sister in her role as a supposed object, with both of us asserting ourselves, though in different ways: I asserting myself by refusing, and she asserting herself by accepting. The submission of the woman, then; domination of her through passion-desire, which nonetheless bears a certain relationship to possession, to rape, even if only simulated rape.

– Men are fragile creatures nonetheless – with their nostalgias, their fears, their entreaties, their feigned gentleness. Men are fragile creatures in this country of identical nostalgias and fears and depressions. A fragility they attempt in so many ways to disguise: fighting bulls in public plazas, for example, or competing in automobile races and wrestling matches. O my Portugal of males concealing their impotence, copulators, stallions at stud, such bad lovers, in such a tearing hurry in bed, their attention entirely devoted to demonstrating their virility.

Harder, more cruel, more unyielding. – And therefore men will call us lesbians: only our bodies resemble those of their spouses, not our will or our disgust. We need men, but not that sort of man.

(My love, love, my desire, my table and thirst all through these long years. My abyss that I have flung myself into; the violent, violent abyss that I have myself become; a naked body where I abandon myself; my narrow, narrow haunches in their vice.)

My Achilles heel?

5.4.71

Third Letter IV

The moment came in which our seed germinated, our spiral of intertwined words grew broader, and the part of each of us that remains outside is beginning to become smaller and smaller, since everything is being brought to the meetings between the three of us and talked over together; and I am now going to put before you what I am writing elsewhere, perhaps all of myself, if that is possible for me, though it will be better if it does not prove possible, since the written word is far from being the only way to rebel and wage a revolution; perhaps, then, almost all of myself in my present life-situation, and if I repeat here what I have been writing elsewhere it will only be because words are so inadequate and so stiff and formal when set down on paper, for when I say 'I am going to put before you', what I want most is for whatever talent I have at writing to take on a new meaning when I am using words for you in my exercise for you, when I am using them for our common exercise. But this is a subject to be left till the end, so I shall abandon it for the moment.

Inevitably, we proceed from love to history and politics, and the myths that underlie contemporary political and historical conditions, and one of you asks: 'Is it a pact with the devil that you're suggesting?' And this is not simply a chance question – we pass judgment on ourselves from outside, but it is our deepest fears that link us to what we reject – nor is it by chance that the devil is a black man or a yellow one, or takes on female form, in the dictionary of witchcraft; the devil is the fallen angel, cast out from heaven for having threatened the order established from on high. Hence we arrive at the myths surrounding contemporary historical and political conditions, because it is not yet possible for us to speak of love; because in the relationship between one man and one woman, in which the partners each believe themselves to be alone, the man enjoying a man's pleasure and the woman a woman's, what society makes and demands of each of them intrudes on this relationship; because it is not only marriage that is a relation *à deux*, for this relation is in fact the political basis of the pattern of repression; because if a woman and a man make love with each other in privacy, each enjoying their separate pleasures, this is immediately considered as an attack on society, which unites a man and a woman only the better to dominate them, and Abelard is castrated, and Tristan is forever separated from Isolde, and all the myths of love describe this relation as something forbidden and unfulfilled, and all love stories are stories of suicides; because we must trace our way back along the river-course of domination, unravel its historical circumstances and analyse them in order to destroy its roots. I realize, therefore, that it is not enough merely to consider the relations of production from the point of view of the fact that socially woman is a producer of children and a seller of her labour to man-the-boss. This is a precise and very necessary interpretation of the reality of the situation, but it is not a complete one. Such an interpretation is necessary in order to arrive at the real crux of the question, and also necessary, perhaps, if we are to trace this situation back to its earliest beginnings in history, which so often people have attempted to conceal from us by repeating the age-old refrain about the constant improvement of the lot of women over the years. But at the same time such an interpretation must be broadened to include all the systems of cultural crystallization that have come to sustain, to reinforce, to justify, and to extend this domination of women (and the domination of others as well), since bringing about a change in today's economic and political system, which is founded on this domination, would not necessarily bring about the destruction of all the cultural crystallizations whereby the woman is made out to be an imbecile in the eyes of the law, a socially irresponsible creature, a castrated man, the wicked flesh, the sinner, Eve tempted by the serpent, a body without a soul, the virgin-mother, a witch, the devoted, self-sacrificing mother, the vampire that feeds on the man's blood, the good fairy of the household, a stupid human being who is ashamed of her sexual desires, a whore and at the same time an angel, etc., etc. And I use the present tense because she still is called all these things, because these images have never been attacked at their very roots, although the logical and practical consequences of some of them may have been vaguely questioned, insofar as they no longer suit men's needs or purposes, but the tone of this questioning of them is simply that of a mild and complacent 'Well now, let's not exaggerate, let's not go too far in either direction'. And I wonder, as I have already said, whether the *guerrillera* who battles side by side with her brothers in this effort to renew her blood, insofar as she is a *guerrillera* and not a mere producer of children, is a *guerrillera* who has no anguished concerns about the future. And I also wonder whether she is fighting side by side with her real brothers, or whether these brothers may not still bear within themselves the root of treason, both in the dialogue of the present struggle and in the future City. I ask myself what the precise meaning is of the freedom or the survival for which she is fighting, whether she will continue to be a second sex, in the shadow of Man's culture, of the Male with a capital M, forced to provide men with maintenance services, to be the ultimate receptacle for the male's frustrations, since for the man eroticism itself, with its illusory banner of untrammelled sexual freedom, is an act of aggression against the the woman. And all this is my answer to those who say the problem of the woman is a petty-bourgeois one, nourished by bourgeois sap, forgetting that the bourgeoisie as a class sunk its roots in soil already watered by the sweat of women; and my answer to you, my sister, when you say 'no battle flag must be hoisted on the flagpole gently planted high up between our thighs'. Playing with words and clever conceits is a pleasant enough pastime – in fact it is our refuge as bourgeois women – but it will be hard when we begin playing with other people's lives. If economics and politics have proven resistant – after all the old forms of capitalism, colonialism, and socialism, we now are seeing all sorts of neo and revisionist forms of them, and as long as there are no machines for producing children it will be the woman who will produce them, and the problem will not be merely one of who is going to be the overseer or the boss, but also that of building a society on the basis of the meaning of work and of the person who performs it – if economics and politics have proven resistant, everything that underlies them is even more so. To return to the long list of the scattered crystallized facets of the woman, only when we are able to line them up along axes, along vectors, will we be able to see the extension and the depths of what oppresses all of us alike, men as well as women. Laying out in a line, for example: the body of the woman, where the hard sex organ of the man is sucked dry during his brief participation in the procreation of his child – a child who represents wealth, a labour supply, immortality through another – the body of the woman, with its blood and cycles, tearing itself apart to bring forth another body, that of the child, the mystery of life and death, the scandal of a body too close to nature which the man attempts to dominate, eternally fearful of its vengeance, male fear of the female body, the body of perdition, fear of castration inside it, *homo erectus*, *homo faber*, but for all that a man whose sons only a woman can bear him, woman marginalized by becoming the repository of what man rejects in his pragmatic choices, feminine intuition (woman is cunning and crafty according to popular tradition, and Freud rightly considered her much more attentive than the man to the meaning of lapses of memory and intentions never carried through), the eternal feminine, magic, a witch, demoniacal, possessed, a temptress, a bloodsucker (ah, woman! it's to buy you that I've worked since time immemorial, and laid down laws, and still you escape me), a body that is self-possessed, man's plot of earth, flesh of his flesh, Adam's rib, man making himself the mother of the woman to reorganize her very creation out of chaos, woman the power of temptation and the accomplice of disorder, a power and a scandal, the guilty conscience of man, his marginal critic, his negative image ... Our fears, our dictatorships, and the demiurgic portraits of our leaders reach far back into the past. In this whole long line that I have traced only very sketchily, our politics, our ethics, our loves as couples are steeped in such myths. Our loves as couples, to which men come to us, after this long gallop down the years, in their present social image, still destroyers, who like their forebears turn everything around them into a great wasteland, forever asserting themselves by being *against* something or someone, sitting tall in the saddle not because of their own inner strength but because they are attacking someone else, forever blind and forever alone in the soliloquy they deliver in our presence, a substitute for the dialogue with us that is impossible. 'My shadow of nothingness' the man calls us in his emptiness, 'my root of everything' he calls us in his fear, and because of this lack he feels, because of his fear, what is being prepared is a new invasion: 'I insert myself in you, like a graft, I the worn-out stump, sucking out your sap.' Will there ever come a time for love, when two people love each other without either of them seeking to use or exploit the other, seeking only pleasure, the pleasure of giving and receiving?

Our loves, to which we women too come rigid and stiff, not flesh of human flesh, but instead made of stone perhaps, caught up in that same mad gallop that our mother made us part of, our mother become man's plot of earth, Adam's superfluous rib; our mother who possessed nothing, who was hoping for a boy-child through whom her ego might even the score and take its vengeance, and who on seeing the girl-child that she had given birth to felt only grief and guilt for having brought into the world a creature like unto herself, with rights worth less than nothing, guilt at this girl-child's being her vengeance and her curse, with her access to becoming another now denied her, having merely created a child in her own image and likeness. From our earliest days as suckling babes in diapers we have had no mother; no one ever told us we were wanted and needed for our unique presence. And for this reason too our interchanges with each other – and all friendship between women – has a uterine air about it, the air of a slow, bloody, cruel, incomplete exchange, of an original situation being repeated all over again. There is that, certainly, but also something else that enters the picture, at any rate in our most secret terrors and those of others: the ambiguity and the confusion that society sows in relations between women, who meet together only to entertain themselves and babble endlessly about what worries them and oppresses them and never about what they are constructing, who meet in a group so that only one sentinel will be needed; society sows confusion and fears which cause women to abstain from friendships with each other, and at the same time it sustains such friendships once they are formed. Two men do not kiss each other, but two women may; hence they have some small compensation for what is denied them in other domains, but let them only lightly and innocently touch each other's lips, and perhaps also exchange confidences if they so choose, but let there be no further consequences, since in the eyes of society woman is an asexual creature.

And in this turning of love back in the direction of history and politics, I see our interchange as the fundamental journey to the lower depths that we must take together, for we must root out what terrifies us (and why not 'a pact with the devil', if it is a deconsecrated, demystified one, if we are aware of 'the devil that we hold in the palm of our hand'?), just as we must combat all the frightening, monstrous, confusing charges that others will levy against us. (Let us never forget that a black extremist is now respectable, but that a feminist is slandered; she is some-one raising the frightening spectre of what has never before been put into words, a trouble-maker, a ridiculous creature, even for the self-righteous knights of the liberation movement as a whole). This, perhaps, is the first path we must take in order to dismantle our historical and political situation.

6.4.71

Letter from the Chevalier de Chamilly to Dona Mariana Alcoforado, a Nun in the Convent at Beja

Chamilly, Good Friday of the Year of Grace 1671

Madame,

Marianne âme amère mère
  my sister, your letters that I have cast forth into the world, filth and suffering discarded for the filth and suffering of others to feed on, are now lying on the bedside tables of ladies and gentlemen who have made the pleasures of love their raison d'être. Her Majesty the Queen is enjoying them in secret, everyone finds you charming, Marianne, you have attained your goal, you are now bound within the pages of a book that gives promise of being world-renowned and been crowned a clever, talented woman, a woman of the world. There is hence no further reason for you to use me as a pretext for your grief-stricken outpourings, to make me the pretended cause of your suffering.

  Monsieur Pascal is dead: 'He who seeks to know to the fullest the vanity of man has only to consider the causes and the effects of love. Its cause is un je ne sais quoi (Corneille), and its effects are terrifying. This je ne sais quoi, a thing so small and insignificant that one cannot even recognize it, shakes the whole earth to its foundations, princes, armies, the entire world.'

  But its workings and its effects have been quite different for you and for me. While the love that you have described, that you have decried, has brought you praise on every hand, my life for seven years has been shaken to its foundations by your aloofness.

  Yet I loved you truly. It was only my first acquaintance with you that came about through vanity. I had the means at my disposal, the words that come easily to the lips, the jaded, blasé heart, the hands and body untroubled by the absence of love that are so well suited to libertine love affairs. And yet, my beloved, to whom I shall never speak of the divine service to which you restored me, to whom I shall never again fall into the habit of writing, I shall

93

leave you a legacy, written in your own language, revealing what you were to me and how you betrayed me, perhaps unwittingly, simply because you were a woman. Hour after hour, your shining eyes, mirrors of calm water, your pure voice singing worldly love songs or piping childish ditties that were such an incongruous contrast with your cell and habit: and I talked with you; perhaps because of the white plaster of your walls, the comfort of your crucifix on them, I spoke with you openly, divested of my military decorations and my duties, telling you how distant you seemed, at the same time praising your gentle grace, and telling you of the slit that opened in my blind eyes as I galloped in the bright sunlight to meet you, as though there were nothing of myself that did not have its proper place and substance in you, as though the barren plains of your country were my own arid wasteland, my silence, and myself a desert until I gave myself to you, admittedly to take my pleasure with you and prove how skilful I was at giving you pleasure, but nonetheless, Senhora, I gave myself to you. '*I approve only of those who moan as they seek,*' *you said. I moaned, for I thought that I had found what I was seeking, I moaned at your knees, for my moans were the only things that came naturally to me without my searching for effect.* Do you understand that though I am aggrieved, I bear no grievance towards you, Senhora? No, you could not possibly have ever understood me, since all your attention was devoted to making flattering remarks about my courtly manners and my graceful body, to counting the hairs of my head and the anxious hours spent at your side, since your only concern was my concern for you, and never the far greater harm that befell me because of you. '*It's that little nun of Beja,*' the Seigneur de Magny said to me derisively, and my comrades at arms as well, and the stable boy saddled my mount with a sly smile, until it was discovered that I was neglecting my duties as an officer and a gentleman, growing hollow-eyed at finding that everything now meant less than nothing to me, and even when I crossed the threshold of your cell it all still meant nothing, for your body and your gaze and your vain chatter and laughter and the pleasure you found with me and your passionate but anxious words were of far less concern to me than what was happening to me on your account. All I wanted was some other sort of words from your lips, an avowal that you too were feeling stripped of your self-esteem and humbled at seeing my own lack of respect for myself, or that you were touched by it and recognized it for what it was. And it was then that I said to you: 'Let us take off together, let us go far away.' And this distance that lay before us was so vast that I had no idea where our travels might take us, where I might find a place to be joined in such close embrace with you that the horror of not being with you would fade away. And there you were, as always. at once so humble and so cunning, loving me out of passion but no more than that, and you said to me: 'How, Milord, how could we possibly do that? Where would we go?' with a complacent, patient smile, since you were quite satisfied with my company and my suffering, and I found myself unable to protect you from this tender, ambitious dream of your wanting me and me alone.

Day by day my self was dying in your arms, and my not liking myself because of your love of me, such as I appeared to be in your eyes, was making you the death of me. My lady of you, or perhaps merely a tender, chaste young girl, able to express in artful words only your grief at my absence from you, this being the one subject best befitting your talents, without your ever providing balm for the horror I was suffering – having forever lost my place among my peers, my pleasure at sitting a horse smartly, at wearing my uniform proudly, at leading my troops well, at feeling at home in lace-trimmed frock coats and parade dress, loyally defending with good gunpowder my honour, my King, and my possessions. You, Mariana, on whose account I committed every sin save that against the spirit, you my draught of my own nothingness to the dregs, you who took refuge in the firmness of my flesh without my ever being able to share my terror with you – since I filled your days with pleasure, but never dared speak to you of anything save what befitted your situation and made it easier to bear, thus lessening your guilt at your own misdeeds, knowing yourself to be innocent of mine.

My lady of my sorrows, hence: sleepless nights, your bare walls and Our Lord hung on them, scourged and stripped to the flesh, and you with your white body lying there naked, bathed in moonlight, and I face to face with your love, satiated with you, the shadow of the bars of your cell falling across my shirt, my cold semen spilled out on to the ground, half naked and a stranger, Senhora, watching over you as you slept and struck dumb by my nothingness.

For little by little you abandoned your habits of prayer, your words murmured in the morning to faces of plaster, to simulated bleeding wounds, to the frozen image of your childlike loneliness – I became your god and your offering, your saviour in silk undergarments, whereas I for my part, terror-stricken by my tenderness, suffering from the terrible absence of me in you, experienced the absence of God in all things as I ran my hands over your body.

Oh, how I longed for you to be another Chimène [17] for me, helping me to sit tall in the saddle, leading me to a battlefield where a combat was being waged in which neither my heart nor my body had any further desire to participate. Why did you not keep your promise to love me beyond death, since what was in its death throes as I lay by your side was the meaning of my life, and it was in order to ward off this total destruction that I endeavoured to hollow out a shelter in your vitals, riding your supple body too gently, with too gentle a fury, thereby discovering within it only your absence as we took our pleasure, your compliance but not an ounce of compassion, nothing save the tomb of my presence. You were empty, Mariana. As dry and bare of soil, and at the same time as burning-hot as the torrid plains that I once crossed, raising dust as I rode to meet you, wastelands where your countrymen laboured, outlined in black against the setting sun, dripping with sweat and lives slowly leaking away, where your people raised their eyes as I passed in the morning, eyes as dark as yours *and full of the same sardonic, shameless joy, for I was their saviour, the right hand of the King of France, come in his service to further his interests by ensuring your freedom from Spain. Can you Portuguese know love or freedom only against another, only against your neighbour? And you, Mariana, you who are so gentle, so self-absorbed, so gracious and hospitable – are you incapable of being moved by suffering, by the horror of human love save in the absence of your beloved? Are you able to measure the degree of your arid, avid eagerness only through memory and the written word? Have you forgotten that I came to you like a beggar, as desperately poor and empty-handed as the* mendigos *that came to eat the soup ladled out to them by the indifferent hands of your well-born sisters? Whose sisters, Mariana?* – for you were never a sister to me, nor to any other person deprived of his heritage, save yourself, for I praised your beauty, your deep, dark eyes, your rounded breasts, the gentle curve of your ankles, your graceful feet, as they praised your kindness of heart, but in the end the only thing any of us discovered in you were mocking laughter and frivolous concerns, for you never noticed the despair in our eyes, and you have turned your belated tears into an elegantly polished tale of blighted courtly love.

I take my leave of you, Senhora. For some time I have neither sought nor awaited news of you. My last attempt to return to the state in which I found myself before meeting you were the campaigns I waged in the Lowlands in the service of His Majesty my King.

I spared myself no effort, yet was spared from death. And my life henceforth will be spent solely in searching here on my estates for a place for a wisdom that my heart will not gainsay, for feelings that my wisdom may accept as genuine. My becoming cloistered and shut up behind walls was your doing, Senhora, and I pray you to pardon me for my being unable to pardon you for having lost my youth. This letter will remain among my papers, so that one day, in your old age, or in the youth of someone of your blood, it may justify me, not for having abandoned you, for I never left you, Senhora, but for feeling so aggrieved at your aloofness, since I have served as the pretext and the object of writings and feelings that should never have existed, being more the product of illusion, Senhora, than of the rigorous and austere discipline that might have been born of our love. Yet I blame you for nothing, Mariana, and may time bring clear proof of the truth of this, for the sake of future generations. Nor would I choose another companion for this most bitter search, which would not be so bitter were I sharing it with you. For I am very much aware, through your letters and your art, that the talent that you have given proof of in composing them is the talent that has always been yours alone: that of finding happiness in every possible way of freeing yourself of all constraints. You are not a serious woman, Mariana, and I, who discovered in your company how serious a person I was, would have much to gain from the acceptance of life and its ultimate end, were this acceptance conjoined with your lighthearted gift for considering only what is well-polished and full of grace as being of ultimate significance or importance. Hence I have taken you as my spouse, or the memory of you, and may what never came to fruition in us come to pass in another place or in other times.

Adieu en Dieu,

Antoine de Chamilly [18]

6.4.71

Dawn Song

Como se não houvera
bosque mais secreto . . .*

Maria slowly pulls the sheet down: the heat of the room has gently drenched her hair with sweat, and it is clinging to her temples, her neck, her shoulders on the pillow; she turns over, aware of the silence of the house, of the huge garden. The terrible silence of the bower:

'The bower with its lingering shadows, its gently rounded hummocks, its greenery drenched with water; dunes. Its dunes of sleeping sparrows. Its uterine torpor, its almost monstrous vortex, into which she would willingly plunge, wrapping it about her, stripped completely bare of herself.'

'But what bower, Maria, what madness, what flight of fancy is this?' he says as he caresses her, as he kisses her free breasts beneath her clothing, unwilling or unable to notice the emptiness of her eyes, the tenseness of her lips, the limp indifference of her arms. To gaze into her increasing fear, growing worse and worse with each passing day, possessive, all-engulfing, radical, within her green, veiled pupils; an ashen green that has lost all transparency.

One morning when Ana lolled in her lap for a longer time than usual, she said in a low voice, as though it were a secret between the two of them:

'Come, daughter, let's go to the bower.'

Then she laughed softly, ran her hands over her face, and went over and leaned her head against the warm panes of the window

* As though there were
  no more secret bower . . .

overlooking the huge garden with its dahlias, its chrysanthemums, its mad profusion of yellow marigolds, as far as the eye could see.

– What bower, Maria? What bower, what path do you mean? The front gate is over there, and beyond there are houses, and people, Maria; but what bower is it you keep imagining, what kingdom, what bower, my love; what river, what mad thing?

Maria slowly pulls the white linen sheet down; the afternoon heat clings to her skin, to the sleep she has only half awakened from, to her drowsing body that her pink nightdress reveals more clearly than as though she were nude.

Maria gets out of bed, sliding her long legs to the floor, raises her arms and strips naked, in a daze, feeling just a bit dizzy or nauseous as she becomes aware of herself . . . On her feet now, she stands there waiting for a brief moment before walking around the bed, parting the white, loose-woven lace curtains; as in the bed sheets, a soft fragrance lingers in the curtains; the curtains, like the house, a thin transparency outlining her nakedness, defining her haunches. Her long, pale, tense legs sag slightly, but then straighten to bear the weight of her body; her burning, dry, languid thighs; her waist arching away from her fingers, from all the violence.

Her feet soft now on the burning-hot flagstones of the terrace, there in the sunlight. Her footfalls soft and light. Her movement fragile as glass, her gestures cautious, watchful.

The shadow projected by her body is broad; its outline stirs, grows larger, looms taller and taller and flowers in its own shadow. As Maria now descends once again, she passes beyond the danger of the others and continues to descend, into the bower that she knows so well, though she has never really gone there before. Tender leaves brushing her lips, her breasts pressing against the earth where time passes the night, her body given shelter, given asylum in the grass, mingling with the acrid taste of the river. Maria closes her eyes and knows that she is sleeping, so safe, so peaceful, so forgetful of everything, so disarmed, her knees raised, touching her mouth, as her own daughter had once nestled within her body.

Dear Mother:

I am sending you Ana who can't stay here any longer. Take care of her, and help her forget what happened here and what she saw here.

Maria has apparently gone insane (the doctors tell us there is little hope of curing her), and Francisco refuses to accept the truth, spending all his time in her room, day after day, silently watching her as though trying to awaken her to life.

I'm concerned about him, but don't let it worry you over much because I know my brother and I'm making it my responsibility to persuade him to put Maria in a clinic.

Don't talk to Ana about her mother. It would be better for her if she began to forget her, and never remember the way she's always been.

You know I always predicted that nothing good would come of this marriage. But now that I'm here, everything will be taken care of, and soon be the same as it was before.

I hope to bring Francisco back with me to live with you. I promise you I will. Meanwhile I'll write you how things are going.

A loving kiss to you from

Your devoted daughter
Mariana

9.4.71

Alba

As cool as the pale wet leaves
of lily of the valley
She lay beside me in the dawn.

EZRA POUND

Alba

As though there were no
more secret bower,

As though the wellsprings
were none but fire,

As though your body
were life entire,

Desire wavers
between sword and flower.*

EUGÉNIO DE ANDRADE

*Como se não houvera
 bosque mais secreto

 Como se as nascentes
 fossem só ardor

 Como se o teu corpo
 fora a vida toda,

 O desejo hesita
 em ser espada ou flor

Beja and Verona in the Same Dawn

– Come back to the brimming bell jar where round geraniums sing
come to the yellow night made for you in the well of my arms

– I go because you say nothing of what you are making of me
I go because you took me from my gentle side

– Come back to the hidden places where promises are kept

come back to the rigour of laughter
that I made silent in you
bravely I kept you
freely I painted you
at my great cost

– I go by burning candle to the grove where the pines are new
suspension of possessions
in place of the outcries
never given before

– A house in the clearing dances in your secret

– Come and count me the hours hidden deep in old names

– My sword surrendered now sleeps by your side

– Pale green rose   lord of the first awakening

– My married wife   I know not who I am

– You lie in my heart

– Sleep in stillness
my smooth water
where I am faced with myself

Conversation Between the Chevalier de Chamilly and Mariana Alcoforado in the Manner of a Song of Regret

– By your breasts
  my lady
  I remember you

– Possessed by your mouth
  with the fear
  for their loss

– By your belly
  my lady
  I remember you

– Your milk overflowing
  blazing
  burning in me

– By your thighs
  my lady
  I remember you

– At having been
  had by you
  wretched, complaining

– By your arts
  my lady
  I remember you

– Robbed by you
  through them
  and their hold over me

– By your moan
  my lady
  I remember you

– Less a cry for your
  pleasure
  than a moan for myself

– By your orgasm
  my lady
  I remember you

– Your body
  the field
  my body the song

– By your tongue
  my lady
  I remember you

– In your mouth my sap
  in your member
  the awe

9.4.71

Second Letter V

[In the guise of an inventory and as a guide to what is going to be.]

Suddenly it happened. The encounter became a family, passion a work of love. Torment and fear turned into rules and pacts. The theme changed from fire to a piece to be forged, to an object to be situated. Encirclement, a circle, a parabola. An open parabola.

Once hesitant sisters, each of us adorning ourselves in our own feathers, one of you in lyrical, emotional outpourings and eroticism, the other of you in 'analytical distance', and I in ironic detachment, each of us the prisoner of her pretended strength, in the heat of what was happening, we found ourselves touched by, revealed in the common childhood that we *made it our task* to discover, sharing our grievances with each other, and in so doing gaining the courage to accuse and suspect each other, going on from accusing our mothers to accusing each other to our faces, and discovering that we could tolerate this – and that is how we made each of ourselves the mother and the daughter of each of the others, and sisters determined to talk about precisely why we were orphans and suffering and destitute. A new family.

All this linked in a chain, each of us intermingling and trying on forms of the others, as though attempting to possess each other, and succeeding in so doing, each of us impregnating first one and then the other of the two in turn. The one of us who never used to analyse things now does so very well, the one of us who had never written poems began to write them, the one of us who had never bothered to use eye make-up now does so. The one who almost never wept, who never got upset, now does. But always the three of us together, openly discussing what was happening. Passion threatening to become the same thing in another form (that is the nature of passion): that is how the pact was sealed (in our zeal to be ourselves), the rule we set ourselves for our work together. The time of discipline began. Each of us the pupil of whichever one of us could best teach what each of us needed to learn. In Mariana's fire, which we sometimes called 'the fire of fires', at times the soft glow of an ancient brazier, in the interplay of the world within and the world without, our will is being forged, and we are determined to pursue the method, to investigate the object best suited to each of us. You, from within Mariana's skin, seek to acquaint me with her griefs and her tragic situation – let her come and go and her story enter History spontaneously. You, my other sister, being forced into more limiting confines, against your will for all I know, are narrowing your focus – your point of departure the vast theme of women and their origin, you have turned to dealing with women as cloistered creatures and as witches, in verse now, however, and in the form of the questioning of the Mother, drawing in the vast myths and the broad questions closer to yourself and hiding your eyes from the sharp vigilance and entreaty of the most intense and most malleable of the three of us, just as you also take refuge in me from the emotion (in us) which is most exposed in her. And I vacillating with all the firmness within my power between the two of you, ambiguous and ambivalent, using you to help me, taking advantage of the contrast so as to make (it) (myself) complete.

And the chevalier: 'Of course,' you say, 'he had to exist,' the cavalier now my responsibility, having settled down on his estate, years after Beja, listening, following his straight and narrow path, reading Pascal and reading of the latter's passing, without having passed that way himself, without Mariana there with him and without her having written. Do you think, miladies, my mothers and my daughters, that I write of the cavalier because I care more about him than I do about you?

I say to you, rather, that you wanted me to tell you about him, because we all like to ride and because of the sly way we all have of leaving the door ajar for the cavalier who will come to our rescue, even though he still lies sleeping in our hearts – as Sophie, the sorely tried little heroine was rescued from her perils by her Paul, who was rescuing himself as well. (We've all read the Comtesse de Ségur's endless tales of Sophie's misfortunes – how much we've read!) And if you, my one sister, say that 'there was no bread for us at men's tables', isn't that good enough reason for me to tell you that there was no salt for me in the house of women who served sweet, sticky custards known as 'nun's bellies'? (try to say that poetically, you who are the bluestocking among us); and if you, my other sister say 'I am going crazy looking for data on the legal status of the woman in the seventeenth century,' isn't that good enough reason for me to ponder the case of a Frenchman (of parts) who came to these parts, serving in the French post-Restoration Army sent to our country to further the sinister aims of Cardinal Richelieu (and paid for out of the latter's secret funds), to try to imagine what the state of mind and soul of this chevalier stationed in Beja were? (and try to say that analytically, simonedebeauvoiresquely, you the poet(ess). It may well be true that because I am the one who since childhood has lived in military barracks among army troops, I have taken particular notice of their mannerisms, their gestures, their way of confronting danger and going down to defeat and have thus perhaps come to resemble them. But isn't it out of chivalry that you, my sister, went about weeping outside (behind) doors and isn't it out of chivalry that you never complain? Isn't it as a charitable gesture towards cavaliers who are not really cavaliers that the two of you let go of the hands of any man who climbs down from his horse before your very eyes and trudges along like a clumsy foot soldier? Riding along side by side, the many amorous sons of some king of ours (oh my deliberately imprecise precision!) will die. Isn't it in search of a story, of a History with a better ending, isn't it towards a worthy end that we guide the theme of Mariana and her partner and the theme guides us?

> *Amazone, chère Amazone,*
> *vous qui n'avez pas de sein droit*
> *vous nous en racontez des bonnes*
> *mais vos chemins sont trop étroits!* *

* Amazon, my beloved,
  with your right breast removed
  you tell fine tales
  but to no avail
  for your paths are too narrow.

Sad tropics,[19] the heat of the body, a sad anthropology, that of the convents and barracks in us. But this is not the house of pairs. Poor, poor couples who are only two! Three is the end of virginity,[20] the beginning of the true history of equal partners. Each one of us a third link – the door to the City, to the street, to others – so many people, Judith as well as Holofernes, her illegitimate superior, deserve their hell, for the queen of the deck of cards (we all read, if we can read) said to Alice: 'Off with their heads.' Something that made Alice increase enormously in size from volume to volume.

I have also pondered everything about our lives that was a *substitute frantic preoccupation* as we found ourselves confronting paths, deep crevasses whose names we perhaps do not even know – our loves we clung to so stubbornly, our own spaces (your space at the newspaper marked by you, the walls there hung with posters, to which you returned; my room of my own, my own space that I occupy, my space step by step; our sons, all of whom we describe as little tyrants; our writing; we are ceasing, we have ceased to torment ourselves in petty little ways). And I have also pondered how we have deliberately put an end to everything that served to allow us to forget or to compensate for what we had never had in *the* 'family of our childhood' – the frivolous but serious games of dolls wrapped up like mummies yet lulled into going on with the mummery – as though in this, in this work and time of 'familiness' lay our only possibility of stability and access to our very roots, to the (marrow) bone of our pasts.

9.4.71

First Letter VI

We have arrived at the halfway point of ourselves.

Perspicacity? Insecurity? An ambiguity deliberately fostered, out of necessity.

The mutual surrender of ourselves that we consented to: then our refusal, the sudden coldness of our relations with others, our reserve, our hauteur.

They are already calling us a commune of women or suffragettes, with an icy laugh, out of a feeling of insecurity at seeing us together: an uncrossable barrier, the group of the three of us still not fighting *against* anything, but *for* something, never dressed in such a way as to suggest that we are prepared to give ourselves totally, though one of us has already allowed her hair to be stroked by fingers whose caress she had previously rejected, and her house is full of artificial flowers to put up on the walls and place on the pieces of furniture she describes one by one, planning where they are to go; allowing her house to appear to be lived in, occupied by someone or given to someone to whom yesterday she denied herself; her house that she lives in all alone, beleaguered . . . a Mariana whom we do not forgive for having been what she was, but in the end having taken on so many of her attributes that we have become her equal, in our easy consent, our baseness, our 'let things take their course', it being much easier to slip outside in the rain, and leave you lying there stretched out full-length on the carpet like some strange creature in pain, an animal that hunts prey but nonetheless is tame, alongside the man caressing your shoulders beneath the thin wool of your sweater which is no doubt impregnated with the smell of smoke: the smoke that wafts all through the bare room, an odour sharp enough to penetrate our skin, the smoke of a fire that stubbornly refuses to flame up on the hearth, as in your laughter, in your words as you try to rediscover some path for your body to follow, as you entreat (as you order about) the man (the one there with you at the moment) as though you were in bed, as though you had him beneath you and might give yourself to (possess) him (yourself) if we did not happen to be with you. – I accuse you of that. – A Mariana you have so indolently given flesh to and gratified by way of your own body, thereby restoring speech to her, adorning yourself, as she did, with everything you felt as though your feelings were garments that would slip easily over your head, till finally they hindered your every step. – The court, the world, your sustenance, your memory, your face.

A trail:

You of roses – maina as a young girl – roses you bought in paper of as many colours as you are within yourself – a woman whom I see trapped by the myth of the male, and hence grown pale, become the wound that you have suffered, the colour of your eyes dulled, their sparkle gone, and I am enraged that you are not as strong as – stronger than – I am (am not), stronger than I would like to be, never giving yourself to a man-as-a-male but only to man-as-the-master, mistakenly expecting from him tenderness, tolerance, sympathy: the flag of males recaptured over and over in nightly fornication (that is what we are good for in their eyes), under cover of sheets, bedcovers, our nightdresses lifted up, with our loins thus exposed and the air of quiet composure of someone fulfilling a duty, one handed down from, inherited from our mothers and grandmothers, our pleasure (not very great, naturally) a feigned pleasure, a good imitation, in order to give males continual reassurance of their vigorous virility, to enhance their aura of self-satisfaction: men good in bed and good at their work, excellent heads of families and bosses of women with pay-cheques coming in regularly at the end of each month so as to have food on the table and a car.

Our freedom: you my other sister, who have a job and a salary, live alone and nonetheless allow yourself to be trapped, keeping your place in our story, but letting yourself be used . . . a Mariana disliked, disdained, disinherited.

What injuries did they do us which are not brought into the open here, pointed out, discussed with each other? What punishment, what myth, what habit, what sister-fears?

My hurts so deeply concealed
There is no need for you to fear
If you are here revealed
Should one secret still remain
It lies on some sere, distant plain.

What handicap are we creating for ourselves by holing up in a garrison with reduced troop strength, by persisting in hiding and seeing men only in secret? – Have times changed, even though we are still living in the same era, and are we making a public show of our freedom despite the fact that we know that we are prisoners? Are we allowing ourselves to exist? Despite our declaring that we are free to lose ourselves, aren't we in the end still doing so as a function of love, of passion, knowing that we are being deceived, that we are being used – in order to sabotage all this machinery that we have been caught up in for so many long years?

Centuries.

'I am bare naked – or almost; and I know that in the position that I have chosen, a driver of a car coming out of the curve right over there is obliged to immediately plunge his eyes between my legs, to the very depths of my intimacy.'[21]

Intimacies that we use to triumph over traditional mores, thereby arousing men's wrath and their desire, trading intimacy for other advantages, because 'When men desire a woman, they are always docile . . .'[22]

And through docility, even though it is a minor weapon, they manage to touch us, to manipulate us even, to deceive us; we recognize the game that they are playing, we enter into it out of stupidity and out of habit, but also out of slyness. For slyness, up until very recently, was our only recourse, our only defence.

And at times we feel a little like exiles; a woman feels like that when she does not live up to the image of her required by the times, when she does not interpret it, and hence searches for paths, for other 'countries' where life for her will be different from that in her own country, in the homeland given her by her mother's womb.

What mother are we fleeing? What mother fled from us? We are fleeing whomever we can, we always end up saying, just as we are fleeing anything that plays a part in passion-as-love:

> '. . . once you were life to me,
> but now you are only hurt to me;'

passion-as-hurt; love-as-surrender; harm we do ourselves, our fear, our terror, our anguish? Mariana-Maria-Maina and my silent woman, intensely silent, my very own self, though not only myself. We assert our power over men so baldly, so proudly, that even they believe in it and allow us to lead them, despite themselves. They allow us to lead them into this sort of crime, this violation of the law. But not only today; let us remember that Mariana too violated laws. She was born in a decadent era, however, in the age of the Spain of the Philips, when Portugal had been castrated of its virility – of its independence and a king of the purest Portuguese stock, of our Portuguese blood – an age when scaling convent walls was an adventure that amounted to very little, at least when it was not known, seen, and avenged by the nun's family.

But today we are accused of other crimes. Also crimes of passion-as-outrage-to-honour, avenged by our husbands, by the law, if it can be proven that we were taken in adultery. Our life, then, delivered into men's hands, but still we women are prepared to make mistakes that are regarded as deserving the death penalty.

What difference is there, then, between Mariana's time and ours?:

'There was the crime of passion, typically Latin, and very Spanish, its apogee and literary glorification having occurred during those reigns that we are now studying. Killing the beloved woman because of her real or supposed infidelity, which was rarely a proven fact, was a form of vengeance and almost always a monstrous manifestation of desire. Many times the pretext for the murder was obviously invented out of the whole cloth, and there was something barbarous about this crime, a supreme ecstasy. The murder of women by their lovers was an everyday occurrence, then, in those times . . .'[23]

10.4.71

114

Letter from a Woman Named Maria Ana, from the Town of Carvalhal, Parish of Oliveira de Fráguas, Circumscription of Albergaria-a-Velha, District of Aveiro, to Her Husband, Named António, for Twelve Years an Emigrant, Residing in the Town of Kitimat, on the East Coast of Canada, Opposite the Queen Charlotte Islands, Close to the Alaskan Border

Carvalhal, Good Friday, the day of the Passion of Our Lord of the year 1971. My beloved and never forgotten António I am taking advantage of our cousin Luisa's visit to me today to send you this letter that she's kindly offered to write for me to tell you how much I miss hearing from you. Listen António you haven't been back to see us for two years now and this only makes things worse even though you're very good about sending money – our Jorge cashes your money orders in Aveiro every month and may Our Lord repay you for working so hard and your children and I are very grateful to you because others there where you are do nicely but only send home as little as they can. The land we already have is more than enough and I've bought still more. Amélia's husband helps till it when he isn't drunk but the only thing that will grow on it is brambles and briars because the waters of the Caima are filthy and as you saw when you were here it made all the fish die not to mention the beans, so all the money I've spent on land has gone to waste, and the paper factory is still the only place where there's work for anybody who stays around here till he's called up for military service and as you already know once our Júlio's finished his he's going to sign up for a job in France, I wish you'd write him and try to talk him out of it I'd rather see him go there where you are to work even though it's farther away and you've written how cold it is there but it's a cleaner life than up there in France where all I hear about is men running around with indecent women and the filthy houses they have there and how much trouble it is to send money back here. There are dead fish floating down the Caima and you can't even wash clothes in it because of the stench and even animals don't drink out of it. Everybody around here keeps asking about you and so did the new parish priest who came to give me his blessing and I don't complain because the helping hand you give me makes me hold my tongue and I'm only telling you this because it's Luisa who's writing this letter for me but even though you've spared me the many hardships and miseries that so many people around here are suffering and even send me enough to help them out and this makes me more respected, still and all it's as though I were wearing widow's weeds because I'll be thirty-eight this year and I bore you three children before you went away and raised them and now they're all grown up and in all these years that you've been away I've never done anything to tarnish your reputation and when I shed so many tears last time you left again you gave me your word you'd send for me to join you there in that faraway place because I'm not the sort of woman who's afraid of the cold or hard work but then you wrote me a letter telling me to wait till you'd set aside enough to make your children rich and could come back here with more money than anybody else around. But listen António what good does it do me for you to come back here and lord it over everybody and for us to be able to spend money like water and be filthy rich, as filthy as the water in the river, of no use to anybody, seeing as how Jorge is already a skilled workman and they're going to send him to a special school and Júlio has gone off to fight in a war, heaven only knows how much all this upsets me since you're not here and I also worry about how cold you must be when you're outdoors sawing wood because I know you're not the sort to bundle up the way you ought to and I hope the woollen sweater I sent you is the right size because it's been so long since I've seen you that I don't remember your measurements any more so I fitted it on Júlio, and you'll see how big and tall your son has grown. And our Cândida is now a teacher in the school run by the nuns in Aveiro who want her to become a novice and lately she's been shedding the tears that I know so well are a woman's lot in life, on account of Mourinhas's son, who's also in the army in Africa and never writes to her, the way you never write to me, and she's living there in Aveiro with her godmother, with nice clothes and a trousseau she's bought with the money you've sent. And since this letter is being written for me by Luisa who's as dear to me as though she were my sister I'll tell you that I'm as careful about my appearance and as calm and collecte as I can be when you're so far away, so certain people still pay me compliments and get ideas in their heads, because I still know how to make myself attractive even though I'm worn out and dying of loneliness, because a woman without a man is like barren earth and a bake oven that there's no use lighting. I'm embroidering things and making the house look nice for your return even though I don't have any idea whether you really will come back since all you ever talk about in your letters is how hard you're working and how much money you're making, and the only memory that's any comfort to me is how grief-stricken you looked when you left me and how reassuring it was when you came home two years ago this March and we suddenly looked years younger, like sweethearts again and even today people talk about it I don't know if they respect us or despise me for all the things I have, all I know is that the only way I got them was by having you so far away and heaven only knows whether you'll leave me for good I don't want you to come back and see how grey my hair has got and how I've aged and how I look and act like a rich widow because of you. Goodbye, António, may God bless you and keep you, today is the day of His terrible suffering on the Cross don't forget to wear something on your head so it doesn't get wet in those huge forests you told me about and keep yourself bundled up and don't drink any more than you have to so as to keep warm in those snowdrifts. Luisa sends you her best regards, and your children ask for your blessing, and many kisses from your wife who will remember you in her heart and soul forever and has made an Easter pudding with six eggs because I never know when you may be coming home and because last time you surprised us and came for Easter, and I kiss you with all my heart.

From your wife, who is yours till death do us part

Maria Ana

10.4.71

Poem Written in Portuguese by the Seigneur de Chamilly in the Year of Grace 1670

upon reading from the notebook found sewn in the clothing of Blaise Pascal after his death

> 'God of Abraham, God of Isaac, God of Jacob,
>   not of philosophers and scholars.'

(god, god,)
What hands didst thou leave to bind again the arc to its meaning?
What tongues didst thou grant for the perfect pronouncing of thy true
    name?
if thou dost reproach the servants of thy temple for being imperfect
if all architecture constrains thee and is unworthy
if flesh and bones of man always debase thee?

We know thou art present in oats and rye as surely
as thou art well served in the thin host.

Who could dare profane thy servants
if all are badly served in being told the time of agony is brief
when its single moment confirms its endlessness?

Who enquires after promised love
more than in the text where no face is?

To whom dost thou promise the grave or expose the living rose
if the scandal is unlawful since the kingdom is unknown
and one single condemned criminal is enough?

10.4.71

Intimacy

The house, the ark, the bed; the coverlet, Mariana, woven in vain, the fringe turned a yellow colour, slowly slipping down, touching the floor, suspended on the wood, lightly brushing its surface, then silently ceasing to move as the wood touches it, rather than the stone corroded by time, the floor of your cell, eaten away by your naked feet, those feet of yours, Mariana, that are so small that they seem disproportionate to your height, as measured by the length of your naked body over which he slithers as he mounts you, inhabits you, gently bites your soft nipples, sometimes as pale as mother of pearl, sometimes as deep a chestnut colour as though they had stolen the tawny glint of your smooth golden hair or the curly fur of your pubis that scarcely seems a part of yourself.

He knows precisely how to bite your mouth, your breasts; how to slip his tongue gently into the half-open crevice whose lips his fingers part, exposing it completely. The tumescent fruit is erect and enfevered, juicy, heavy-scented, in your burning uterus.

He knows precisely how to sip your mouth in little swallows; his teeth rousing the cry you give, Mariana, the unrestrained, prolonged cry that you allow to escape from your lips: your orgasm, your spasm, your moan. Your fingernails scraping your skin, the coverlet, the linen sheet you find yourself on: the floor, the stone, and again the coverlet, the one that your wet-nurse embroidered, in red lace openwork on a soft green background, on which you faint now, Mariana, on which you transport yourself beyond the cell where the cold lies in hard layers, one atop the other, in the dark.

Your back tense, your knees drawn up, your thighs opening in that slow movement that voracity prompts, provokes:

'Slowly,' you beg, 'slowly, you are stripping me of myself so quickly ... thrust yourself in farther, up higher, more slowly, take your pleasure more slowly, spurt more slowly, more slowly still, there where I am selling myself.'

The bed, the house, the table, the climax, and superimposed on all of this, the coverlet, where your body surrenders, loses itself, rekindles itself, struggles, bursts into flame, forgetting the convent but still caught in its bitter web, never freed of it, forced into it because your body is defenceless, hesitant, offered.

The coverlet displayed by hands that are going to use it, the bed welcoming a penis and testicles is not a nun's bed, Mariana, and even if they stripped you of all your earrings, silk garments, and necklaces, your body still has not fallen asleep.

Delicate and fragile the cloth of the coverlet, the wet-nurse's flow of milk and we women if even we are still like Mariana – arms, shoulders that lull us to sleep . . .

. . . and sweet sperm with the sourness of grass . . .

And now the coverlet reappears and Mariana allows herself to lie on it, forgets the reasons that lay hold of her, overpower her, destroy her life which is not only burning heat, the sea, the shore of the vagina.

And thus Mariana asserts herself, kills herself, thus she yields herself, surrenders herself, doubts herself. Thus the woman-Mariana-Maria silences herself: a fenced-in preserve, herself the prey, the low stand of trees, the weapon she uses to affirm herself, to steady herself. Her breasts flattened on the red lace of the coverlet that she now remembers once again, that reminds her of her voracity, though in recollection it is now no more than acquiescence.

From the pewter of her armpits, from the stone of that cell where she loses herself, an Amazon emerges with thighs spread for the mount that she is for herself, her own friend and enemy, her own song of exultation and exhaustion:

> . . . *a nenhuma parte vou*
> *que lá não ache fadiga*
> *que aquesto só me ficou*
> *de minha amiga, ou emiga . . .* *

* There is nowhere that I go
  that I can escape my weariness
  for that is all that I have left
  of her my friend, or her my foe . . .

BERNARDIM RIBEIRO

Your old coverlet or mine, even though an imitation one, lilac lace not hung up, the white fringe on the floor, on the wood, ragged and torn, a flag that you display, that you show because it is pretty, but also because it is an affirmation of the freedom you have learned, which hurts you and protects you.

Its soft old cloth a fabric of dim days, woven of milk and wine and or the habits of hers.

That your mother snatched you out of. And expelled you, you who were conceived in her menses, from inside her:

You are tired of being inside her.

12.4.71

Poem Sent to Sister Mariana Alcoforado by the Chevalier de Chamilly on the Day of His Departure

Lady you give yourself
neither to God
nor to tenderness

taking care not to care
in guarding your body
and thirstiness

You are so much in pawn
to the cloth and the damage
in adventure and pleasure
that love never blinds you
and desire for me now never lights up
your countenance

Lady now if I lose you
and your mouth's bitter aftertaste
be it I who in freedom
shall distance myself leaving you
all the fury of wanting me
near you

14.4.71

Monologue for Myself Inspired by Mariana, Followed by a Short Letter

Listen, Mariana, to the silence with its stones set in place one by one to build a convent.

– What mother ever helped you, what hand ever touched you on the shoulder, what dagger dealt you the final blow?

Mariana the fair-haired one, thus contradicting your lineage (is that how you would have liked to look?), with soft skin, or Mariana the *morena*, the dark-haired one, as your name suggests: the sea and the earth – your torrid, arid Alentejo, your inner beach, where you stretch out full-length, your thighs, haunches, vagina lazing and indolent.

You the fair-haired one protected and exposed.

Exposed despite the bars where you stood watching and waiting. Waiting and exposed. You who were so precise. You whose existence today is doubtful.

You saw too much or else nothing touched you because you were rejected; you who were too intense, you who wanted yourself to be rejected, and rejected yourself. You never knew or understood anything about yourself. – What did you do? What schemes did you contrive? What did you forget? What did you take to be certain truth? Surely there were days when you forgot yourself, and they were warm food for you.

I have been too possessive of you and destroyed you; I refuse you, I hesitate, I re-create you out of myself and make of you a seductive temptress.

What can be said of a woman who has been taken, who has been received by men, under cover of a nun's veil?

In your cell, in secret, you learned to enjoy embraces, learned to know the sweat of bodies, the sweetness of tongues, the erect hardness of a man visiting your womb. How many men, Mariana, thus freed you from the convent? Some left you, others were deceived by you. But after all, what other way could you have had to assert yourself?

My complaint about you, my continual accusation. I know you to be hypocritical, crafty, querulous, but I also know you to be a document, a testimonial through your very presence in the world of these days.

You were pleased to feel yourself slowly dying, unloved: O vice, O pleasure, O long torture at finding yourself alone and discovering yourself only through men.

– Listen, mother, my belly is smooth and my legs open to life. You denied me life, you castrated me, you made a prey of me.

How can a woman exist without a father, without a uterus, without sustenance?

I will tell you, Mariana: by hunting for your own prey to sustain you.

Listen to how quiet everything is becoming, and around you clearings are opening up and fires are flickering to cast light on the innermost shadows of the convent with its stones set in place by silence.

You are the fruit, Mariana, the product, the prolonged moan of a symptom so often lost sight of, so often re-encountered, so often recurring all through the course of a pitiful story of powerlessness.

Would you ever have left a name for yourself if your letters had not made their way to France? Today there are many who do not believe you ever lived the life you supposedly did, who maintain you never wrote the letters attributed to you: you are merely a stained-glass window, a forgotten myth.

Listen, my sister: the body. Now only the body leads us to others and to words.

There is no one better than you or me, Mariana, no one better than thirst, the spasm of ecstatic pleasure: O silk, O soft, soft skin, O fear and yet more fear, with nothing kept secret and no artful tricks.

By all rights you ought to have confessed that you hated him. 'What kind of cavalier are you if you leave me without a mount, what kind of cavalier, what kind of lover, what kind of son, what kind of father, what anything?' All rights of possession belong to males, Mariana, even today. My testimonial to you, my trash, my dawn. Pale dawn and a dawn-song as you lay sleeping with the daylight already gently touching your hair and your legs flung out like that, just as your hands left them: spread apart, torpid, languorous, in a position so obviously one of freedom and vice.

A soft moan that escapes you takes possession of me, impregnates me, transcends me and kills me: my writing.

14.4.71

Letter from a Woman Named Mariana, Born in Beja, to a Woman Named Maria, the Nursemaid of Her Daughter Ana

Senhora Maria:

I hope this letter finds you in good health along with all your family and every one else you care for, because as I write you I'm still managing there are some days when I'm better, thanks be to God, though some days I am worse, for here in the city it's not the same as back home because back there where we all know each other we respect each other and still exchange friendly greetings because as the priest says we're all God's children but you wouldn't think so here in the city. Senhora Maria enclosed is the money we agreed I'd pay you every month for bringing up my Ana I miss her so much but my mind is more at ease with her there in the nice fresh air and those nice clean surroundings because what with the unhappy life I'm leading it would be more of a sin to have her with me than to leave her with you Senhora Maria because I know you're neat and tidy and even though you're a woman of few words and given to brusque gestures I know you're good-hearted and capable of tears because I saw them when I left my little girl there with you and she clung to my neck and begged me not to leave her.

Don't forget about the milk and we'll see if she puts on weight and her colour improves, because she was so frail when she was born that I don't know how she managed to survive.

Even if my life here is the death of me I'll get money to you for doctors if you think it necessary Senhora Maria. Just yesterday a man that's a doctor his speech and manners are very distinguished said to me: don't be so sad my girl you're much better off without your daughter especially since you're in such poor health. But Senhora Maria you know how happy it made me to be with my Ana the poor little thing but how could I raise her when I had no money and wasn't good for anything my mother has always thrown that in my face and now she has nothing but scorn for me it's killing me and I no longer have it in me to hold my head high.

It would have been much better to have gone off as a companion for Senhora Dona Mariana but the convent scared me and besides she was so old and ill-tempered always shouting at people and beating anyone who came within reach of her cane and her nun's habits so long they dragged on the floor. In the end even this unhappy life I'm leading is better Senhora Maria seeing that we must be unhappy in this life because that's the will of Our Lord and He knows what He's doing and my cross to bear was bringing a little girl into the world because a man is raised in a different way without any rules to obey and destined for a happy life but a woman is always unhappy, the way I am.

Senhora Maria this is all for today with my best wishes to you and yours and love kisses to my poor little Ana.

Thank you.

Good-bye

Yours sincerely

Mariana

17.4.71

The Mother

The rain falls with a metallic, piercing, painful sound.

Through the huge window panes, I look out at the street hemmed in by gleaming, transparent glass panes, down which the rain slowly, gently trickles, thus counterpointing the harsh, staccato, acrid noise it makes as it beats against all those smooth, flat panes, as far as the eye can see, their rigid, hostile skins all alike.

I don't even know if I feel afraid, though I do know that I am lost.

I drag my son along by the hand, and his warm, soft palm reassures me, calms me. We slowly walk through that empty city, neither of us saying a word, our footfalls as silent as though we were gliding along; stealthy fellow conspirators?

'Dear mother,' I think, 'you know I'm not familiar with this city at all. Did I write you to come meet me? To remind you I was coming, to call your attention to me?'

The streets stretch out one after the other ahead of us, with glassed-in passageways or arcades. My son stares into the distance as though looking for a way out, but it is here that we are going to have to live for the rest of our lives.

Oh, how the fever mounts, it climbs up and up through my body, in its anguished haste, its flame licking my hair, curling up into a ball in my belly, expelling itself through my womb.

I feel myself staggering and let go of my son, so as to lean against one of the many plate-glass windows of the city, but then my shoulder becomes soaking wet, for it is no longer glass so much as a way into the world of water, even though still only glass.

Dear Mother:

Tomorrow afternoon I'll be there with you.

Please come to meet me, because I'm not familiar with the city at all and I'm afraid I'll get lost. I'm so stupid . . . you yourself say so . . .

I'm still very tired but perhaps more resigned to life, to its rules, its knives, its prejudices.

A big kiss, because I miss you very much.

Your daughter and friend

Maria

The mother suddenly realizes that her son has moved away and then she sees him: he is gambolling in the rain, soaked to the skin, outside the shelter of the glass-enclosed passageway. And she is suddenly overcome with anger, a strange anger that takes complete possession of her, envelops her completely, churns up her insides, drives her outside too, calling in a soundless voice.

Dizzy and bewildered, she runs, fighting the rain, almost blind. 'He'll get sick,' she thinks, 'he'll get sick.' And when she manages to catch hold of his rain-drenched sweater, she pulls him towards her, forcing him to follow her through the streets roofed over with glass (or through houses, arcades, alleyways?). There inside, she perceives that her anger has not left her; on the contrary, its overwhelming, uncontrollable, terrifying vortex grows and grows, to an enormous size, driving her mad, taking possession of all her senses; implacable, inescapable.

And seizing her son by the shoulders, she violently beats his head against one of the enormous plate-glass windows; two, three times, until she sees, to her horror, a trickle of blood run down his face.

A thick, thick, sticky, slow-flowing wet criminal cord ...

Mother:

You know very well that I never want to come home again. I am tired of your help and the prison you are thus trying to shut me up inside.

I'm the one who is going to raise my son and not you, and not in the same way that you brought me up, so I'm hoping to do so without any advice from you.

I beg you to leave me in peace.

Mariana

I watch the crimson, crimson blood dripping down my son's head and begin to scream at the top of my lungs, my hands next to my ears, my body bending forward. Then I wake up, and in the darkened room with my eyes wide open, I lie there the rest of the night, in terror.

18.4.71

*Letter from Mariana, Niece of Mariana
Alcoforado, Left Between the Pages of Her
Diary, for Publication after Her Death, as a
Reply to Monsieur Antoine de Chamilly*

My aunt had said that she would abandon you to the vengeance
of her kinfolk, if perchance you should ever return to this
country. She dreamed of a vengeance through force of arms,
since she wanted blood to be paid for with blood, and since she
knows no other more ultimate form of vengeance, having lived
such a sheltered life as a woman and a nun that she imagined
life such as men make it out to be, a thing of sudden appearances
out of nowhere, of clashes of wills and powers, of direct and
violent confrontations.

But you ironically chose to return to France and went into
seclusion, reading Pascal and turning your affairs of the heart
into a mystical retreat, inventing another role for yourself besides
that of a Marshal of France, a man who meditates and signs himself Antoine. I know not whether it was hope of approval or contrition that prompted you to go so far as to adopt this new and
less worldly name. The sincerity of your motive is of little concern to me. I remember my aunt as she was dying, dressed in her
nun's habit, there in her convent, a very old woman, her eyes already glassy when I went to see her that day, carrying in my
reticule your letter, arrived the evening before, borne by some
kinsman of yours – a compassionate man or one who also expres-
ses himself with the cold irony that characterizes the language of
you Frenchmen? You at that time were already dead, having
chosen that refuge as a way of making your words irremediable,
with no answer possible, having thus kept them to yourself until
your destiny and that of my aunt were implacably sealed. And I
remember her saying to me that day, clasping my hand tightly
in hers: 'You know, Mariana, the worst is not having lived here;
it is having died here, in this burrow, in this silence, like an animal driven to its lair; as long as one is still alive, one always thinks
that something will happen, but now, Mariana, there is nothing

left.' And then I spoke of the letter in my reticule, in the name of what truth or what false compassion I know not: 'He says he never forgot you, Aunt Mariana, and died remembering you,' and my aunt's eyes turned more glassy, more opaque, and she said: 'But why, Mariana, why?', all the absurdity of her life and her death taking possession of her body, which until just a few moments before one would have said was too frail to accept with such clear-sightedness this terrible inner affront, and I thought: 'What a terrible death I have had a hand in preparing for her,' and then I read her your letter, omitting not a single word, and my aunt died with a smile on her lips, saying, '. . . woman of the world, Mariana, because Her Majesty the Queen is enjoying them in secret, woman of the world, Mariana, at least my hatred had a meaning, but I had hoped for vengeance through the force of arms of males, ah, Mariana, only my hatred had a meaning, woman of the world, Mariana, only you can avenge me, Her Majesty the Queen is enjoying them in secret, Monsieur le Marquis de Chamilly is boring himself to death with grandeur, and I am dying, without a secret place to hide and without grandeur.'

I return, then, to your letter, Monsieur Antoine de Chamilly, my heart bent on avenging my aunt. To you, who are already dead, to that other person invented by you in your country gentleman's retreat, possessed of a castle and arms, to all those others of your lineage, of your estate, of your invention, to those who said: 'It's that little nun of Beja,' to all those who will come along, for century after century, to defend your admirable reasons or your pious acts of contrition – to all of you I, Mariana the niece of Mariana, am writing this in answer – and you ought not to find it surprising that it is I who am penning this reply, since it was you and your kind who killed in her either the desire or the duty to answer all of you.

My reply to you, then, in her name:

All these men, cavaliers like yourself, made you enjoy settling down to riding in the saddle, to wearing a uniform, to commanding your troops well, to serving with all your heart and soul and good powder your honour, your King, your possessions, your place among your own kind,

Why should I now provide you with a meaning for your life? Does your sword seem useless to you and your powder scanty? What other possessions are you seeking? Think, rather, of blood and of the service of your sword and your powder, cavalier, and you will have a better solution for your anguish at being nothing. If your place among your own kind seems so confining, why call those peers of yours who so constrain you your comrades, and why come to me, without lifting anchor from that quiet harbour of yours, to seek diversion on the high seas? Only because I have no place among your kind? I was more honest, cavalier, when I distractedly gave alms to beggars, with my hands of a well-born sister, without making use of their misery to pity myself for not being what I had the power but not the will to be.

I love you and give you love and pleasure, but that is the limit of the bargain agreed upon, since that is how you wished it to be, you race of cavaliers. Do not come seeking comradeship from me, support and meaning for your life and your death, for I whose assigned place in the world was this convent cell have no comradeship to give you. You ought to have thought of this sooner, of what you are losing and of what you want, before making your way to me, if you wanted a true meeting and not simply diversion. But you want everything, and yet you want to lose nothing.

When I say to you 'How, Milord, how could we possibly do that, where would we go?' I sink my vengeance deep in your heart, cavalier, come to support with the arms you bear the independence of a people foreign to you, against another people, equally foreign to you, merely by order of your King, and daring to say to us: 'Can you Portuguese know love or freedom only against another, only against your neighbour?' But that is what our freedom and our loves are like, Senhor cavalier – you who are so certain that your arms are those of a rich and cultured and civilized country. And that is what our freedom and our loves will be like so long as our independence depends on the orders of your kings and the conniving honour of cavaliers. And to me, Senhor cavalier, you who have fought so many battles and rendered such service unto your King, to me, one sister among all those imprisoned in cells, the one thing you offer me is my own escape on the rump of your horse towards some vague, far-distant place, towards some possible outer edge of a fixed hierarchy where everyone is assigned his proper place according to name, fortune, sex, or estate, for some hiding place, some new cell, where the two of us might take refuge from the heavy carapace of this hierarchy, which on the other hand you uphold so well with your fights for independence by order of your King.

And in this, our refuge for two, you would keep your place among your own kind, even though perhaps proscribed for a very short time, doubtless receiving hurt letters, gently chiding you for your madness as a male, and since you are regarded as a true and just man, urging you to come to your senses, until finally you would give up, return to your rightful place, and be received as a prodigal son. Only I am forever proscribed, for only a woman's honour is unredeemable, not because it is her dishonour, for a woman in and of herself counts for very little, but because it is written in the law that her dishonour is that of males who ought to have kept her their possession and were unable to, thus contributing to a threat to sacred private property, a stain to male honour that can be washed away only with the blood of the rebellious woman.

Only I am proscribed and threatened with death, wholly defenceless; it is my life and my death that you toy with by making such a naïvely unconditional and forthright proposal to search for the absolute together.

Don't think of yourself as a mad and most singular man, cavalier, for it is the custom among males to find the horizon that will lead them to the absolute by playing with the lives of women.

In a love-adventure shared by a man and a woman, it is the woman who surrenders and risks her body and her soul, for a man does not become great with child and is already accustomed to the games of libertinage and love that tradition allows him to play.

What did you say to me, cavalier, when I told you that you had got me with child? What a bothersome woman, you thought, and said to me: 'Stop imagining things, Senhora, for you won't trap me that way.' The one thing that is real to you, Senhor, is that mystic escape you imagined you saw in the depths of my eyes and my flesh gleaming in the moonlight. My living flesh was imaginary, as was the direct consequence of our love within it; all the potions prepared by Dona Brites that I swallowed were imaginary, the cramps in my belly, and my cold sweats, and my excrement smelling of rot, and my fainting spells, and finally that ceaseless course of blood, welling up from my fear and my frailty and my nights of waiting and all these things so endlessly prolonged, cavalier, that it seemed to me as though my entire body was tearing apart and draining away; I swore that my blood would be paid for with yours. But none of this is real to you race of cavaliers, nothing of this is foreseen in your noble struggles, for blood shed during abortion is not blood shed for the King, it is always blood shed against all of you. O horror of not being me, you said; what an unthinking, complacent insult, Senhor. And I would not speak to you of this save that I wish to tell you how little you knew me. In this passion with a nun, Senhor cavalier, your dizzying ecstasy stems from your risking of my life, while your risk is merely that of my transgression of the laws and standards that are yours, Senhor cavalier, those of you and your peers. What were you searching for in my eyes, Senhor? The power of defying your world, that you feel is empty, or the vertigo of reducing me to nothing in your eyes, making me not only your possession but also a condemned criminal in the eyes of your laws? Not even that, Senhor. Because you denied my blood on you and the risk to my life. I was always nothing, nonexistent in your eyes, you looked at my graceful ankles and thought: 'my draught of nothingness, so dry and bare of soil'. My soil, Senhor, would be to help you to sit tall in the saddle, with an easy conscience, with peace of mind, because I would be the one to show you the way. My soil of myself, of my body and of my soul – that you did not want to see, impatiently abandoned by you, considered by you to be childish and futile, and when it was with child, Senhor, when it was bloody, you closed your eyes resentfully, because it was not an answer, but a new enigma in your petty life.

It is the custom among men to find their horizon that will lead them to the absolute by playing with the lives of women, but it is a game played without accepting the risk, Senhor, as children play with toads; when the creature dies it is not the doing of the child's hand, but what kills it is its fear and the affront done it.

If you lost your love for the saddle and a comfortable and assured place amid your equals on account of me, it was because of my total love for you, Senhor, despite the fact that my only concern was counting the hairs of your head and the hours you spent at my side, or perhaps because of this. But what do I find has happened to me because of you? I know full well that I never asked you to help me stand firm in my duties of devotion and in my place as a nun, I know well that there was nothing that I was afraid of losing. But it is also true that nothing about my situation ever made you tremble with fear for me; you merely trembled with excitement on proposing that escape to some vague, far-distant place, and now this mystic marriage, entered into by you alone; for such a marriage, Senhor, the convent and the Christ on my crucifix are quite enough for me. You may consequently consider yourself as nonexistent.

20.4.71

(*By Virtue of Long Imagining*)*

By virtue, I do not deny, of being at liberty
and faced with the distinct line of each object
attentive and intact
I behold with virtue and newness
its presence

By long imagining you superimposed
(finding you, moreover, from the beginning)
what I see is blurred
and I no longer can
love serenely my own being

No one was exposed to chains so much
and having gone so far said nothing, long
you knew of suffering which only seems to pass
when more is yet to be

My dwelling is within
a gentle circle of my own bars
and being unchained there I wear them down
holding my breath (virtue)
in the depths of still waters
open pools (here)
by long imagining your strong swimming there
what virtue will I find in the free fall I suspend above you?

(you circle of earth   wide solid embrace
                                               eyes of a bird of prey
restoring hand   I   perilous waters
                                               brutal mirror
dance of possession   dredger of peacefulness)

How can I with virtue imagine us
if having seen the whole in space and inmost depths
my eyes become as empty as our destinies?

20.4.71

* The title comes from a sonnet by the Portuguese poet Camões, 'The lover
transforms himself into the thing loved by virtue of long imagining.'

Silly Letter VI

my darlings
  because that is what you are, or if not exactly that, at least
  you are that while I persist in being joined with you

my darlings
  sisters, even when you are sulky and stubborn, you are the very
  best that could possibly be found in the way of guardian spirits
  to be familiar with in any mother tongue

my darlings
  today there was a sudden burst of sunshine and no one
  should be left out of its jubilee
    I for myself, at leisure, herewith open my heart to you

my darlings
  today Mariana went riding, dragging her arse on the ground
  but she cheered up with much laughing, today Senhor António
  (alias Noël, alias merry christmas) is off duty from barracks
  and bed and went for a tumble in the hay
    Little Mariana with her scraped bum and the marquis of
    nettles made truces and soup

my darlings
  different. kinds of peace. I declare you
  to be as good drinking company as young men
    I am a perfect bucket of affection
    cured today of all affliction

my darlings
  the death of difference, the soil of revolution,
  is good laughter flowering at hand

my darlings
  each one of you has her thing, at times it stings,
  other times it slumbers

my darlings
my contrasts, where I deposit my
trash and today this uproar

my darlings
grinding out curls and ribbons and cells and liberations
tender-tough little girls

my darlings
sisters and certainly fetching, whether serious or furious,
clever or silly

glory be to those who, however distracted or unwilling,
gave you their semen and held you to their breasts.

22.4.71

The Father

She was perverse:
she slept bare naked, her breasts free and soft, very white and all
exposed, with large, pink, distended nipples.

During the day she went about the house with her blouse
unbuttoned and sat about in such a way that her skirts kept
creeping halfway up her thighs, affording a glimpse of a dark,
downy patch between her legs, gently nestling in their half
shadow.

She was perverse:
she lolled about on sofas, her arms drawn back, stretched out
full-length, simply lying there, smooth and lithe, within reach,
running her sharp-pointed tongue over her already-wet lips.

She was perverse:
her hair a tawny blonde, her skin soft, her languid eyes a hard
blue.

She was perverse:
she put her arms around his neck, her breasts pressed against
his chest and her warm, silky breath grazing his mouth, crawling
round about him, as though torpid from saliva.

She was perverse:
she would forgetfully leave the door ajar as she undressed, dis-
closing her soft belly, her thin shoulders, slowly, in tiny little
motions, with secret sounds and pacts with childhood.

She was perverse:
her hair was uncombed and dishevelled from sleep when she
kissed him and greeted him in the morning, as though it were an
absent-minded habit she had long since fallen into.

She was perverse:
she slept bare naked, her breasts free and soft, very white and all exposed, with large, pink, distended nipples.

When he entered the bedroom the man hesitated, staring at her intently as she slept, but then he silently draws closer, and slowly comes to a halt at her bedside, hesitating once again. Then he stretches one of his hands out, runs it gently across the soft curve of her breast, over her warm thighs, his fingers tensing as they enter the silky hair of her pubis.

He bends over as she awakens, and roughly, brutally covers her mouth with his hand, holding her down with the weight of his body, now lying stretched out full-length on top of her.

She was perverse:
she had a frank, avaricious laugh, and a provocative way of looking at others; a wild, haunting scent as she opened little by little, like a fruit: obsessively, obsessively.

Lying there indifferently, Mariana feels him withdraw from inside her, dirtying the outside of her body with sperm as well. Then she sees him get up off the bed, hurriedly put his clothes back on, and leave the bedroom without looking at her, without having said a single word, even when he was raping her, even when he was taking her, as she lay there overcome by, submerged in, that torpor that she no longer has the least desire to emerge from, feeling more and more lost with each passing moment.

'You are going to have to leave this house,' he said to her in a toneless, monotonous voice. 'We can't all go on living together in the same house after what's happened. It was all your fault. You know that you were the one to blame for everything. I'm a man. I'm a man and you're provocative, perverse. You're perverse. A woman with no modesty, no shame. I never want to see you again, you make me sick, you disgust me, you make me feel ashamed. You knew very well, I know that you knew very well, what you were doing to me. I'm a man, my little whore.'

'Of course I'm a whore. You needn't have any worries on that score, Papa. I'm a whore.'

'You dirty whore!' her mother called after her as she headed for the front door, clinging to the wall so as not to fall. 'You dirty whore!'

23.4.71

Three Young Women Besides the Three of Us

(inês: the knife)[24]

Inêz young woman unripe and rotten
can all your given beauty or its memory
do more than ceremony or custom?

And by destroying Constanza
taking her place of radiance and honour
what do you seek but to be at peace?

sister's flesh	favourite mistress
guileless lamb	clothed serenely
fleshless fingers	hand covered with kisses
bastard mother	braid of myrrh and honey
weak smile	the weight of the moment
bread at court	quiet cut

merely a pretext of king against king
death nevertheless.

(ophelia: the water)

Having died with so much gentleness
and without a sound
simply drifting in (with) the wind of the waters
light and ordered and calm
as was promised
her breast a nest of seaweed
    (not caused by the harsh outburst from him
    or the hard action committed
    so alone and not curious, pure weightless slumber
    soft feather)

weight of a pearl her breast and her hours overflowing
with water
spilled without cause distant
distant she floats down the river white with green
foam at the shores of death
thin fixed smile on the surface of the play.

(joan: the fire)

A country has no reason for being
save the sound
of voices wanting it:

I swear that it is not from me
but from the mist it comes
and from the throat of the lily, its practice
(the king silent before the people, hero among heroes
    holy deaf man).

Spring hay armed in iron
only the young and strong could hear
the tolling of the land;
nor was it against anything,
soon   soon
the words restoring petal by petal
the usurped place to its right
needed nothing more.

That body of mine summoned and judged
served only the pure tongue free in flames.

25.4.71

Letter from Dona Joana de Vasconcelos to Mariana Alcoforado, a Nun in the Convent of Our Lady of the Immaculate Conception in Beja

My Dear Mariana:

Only today did I receive permission from your Mother Superior to write to you, without the knowledge of your parents and my husband, who despite the fact that he knows almost nothing about you falls into a rage at the mere mention of your name, doubtless because of the deep friendship he knows I feel for you, which makes him furious. Out of principle he hates everything that I love, continually scoffing at my feelings, their delicacy and sensitivity, and thus cruelly destroying them, with the greatest of pleasure and peals of mocking laughter.

But what has become of you, my Mariana? What is left of you, there in that cloister that you have been forced into entering? I shall always remember your outcries, your despair, your rage, your frenzied refusal to accept being put into a convent, your hatred; and then, in the face of the inevitable, your stubborn silence, your haughty acceptance of the facts, the scorn for everyone that showed in your eyes, the sarcastic smile on your lips, as though veiling your mouth with irony was a way of taking your revenge . . .

What a misfortune to be born a woman! Useless and helpless out of necessity, bred to be so, forced by law to be obedient to our lords and masters, who show no patience even for our suffering.

How many times I remember how we poured our hearts out to each other, how we rebelled against our lot! Oh life, thou cruel stepmother, how you have separated the two of us, who were such friends, who were so close to each other almost from the cradle! They forced the cloister upon you, and a husband upon me, a man whom I would have rejected had it been within my power or had my wishes been taken into consideration, but as we well know, my poor friend, our desires or wishes count for very little, whether they stem from our reason or from our hearts.

You doubtless thought that I had forgotten you, and hence had also forgotten the hours we spent together, the talks we had and the games we played together, our promises that they did not allow us to keep, since we have no power over our own lives or our own fate, being obliged to sacrifice our desires to those of our parents who rule us or those of our husbands who buy us, men who are always dressed in beautifully tailored garments, who are advanced in age, who have made a fortune and their way up in the world. – How revolting it is to be married, Mariana, what a martyrdom marriage is! – Do you know what it is like for us to be taken in our nakedness by hurried hands and soft mouths wet with spittle? Our bodies torn apart by a foreign member, burning hot, that bruises our souls even more than our bodies? A vengeful sword to hack our flesh to pieces, Mariana – do you know my sister, what it is like to remain silent, day after day, the loathing, the sorrow we bear dry-eyed, having no tears left to weep for ourselves, no longer able to feel even pity for ourselves?

The bars and the walls of that convent impede your footsteps, they have put you in irons, but without realizing it they have left you free to allow your imagination to wander, to live all alone with yourself, whereas each and every day I do violence to myself through others, through men, forcing myself to resort to behaviour and habits that I find most repellent, as you well know, for I am an object or an ornament only when obliged against my will to be one. I would have preferred it had my parents forced me to take the veil, like you, Mariana; I would far rather be a nun than a woman who hates her husband and is so vulnerable, so hungry, so thirsty for love. I am exposed to so many temptations, to so many desires hidden deep within me, and how long, how long will I succeed in living a blameless but unhappy life?

If only you could flee that convent and I this house where they keep me sheltered, where I am slowly killing myself, going mad . . .

They say that I am barren, can you imagine! I am told that I am barren, and my husband rebukes me for it as though he were accusing me of a sin, never once imagining what quiet, painful, yet total happiness it gives me to be so. How could I possibly conceive a son by such a man, whom my body rejects, even when it surrenders itself to him, tense with both desire and loathing . . .

Barren, dry, stripped of everything. What humiliation, what degradation! What a lingering death they condemn us to.

I see your sister almost every day, but I seldom exchange more than a few words with her. I know how joyously she accepted your being sacrificed for her benefit. She decks herself out in elegant finery and tries to be charming and does her best to make every man she meets fall in love with her, but poor thing, only her dowry will ever get her a husband – one who has had to be bought. Your mother, I am told, is now casting her glances (and smiles) in the direction of the Count of C., do you remember him? The one with the great green eyes, so shy, poor fellow, that he wasn't even able to answer back when we made joking remarks about him to his face, nor flirt back when we pretended to be flirting with him . . . How gay our lives were in those days, Mariana, without our ever imagining or thinking of what lay in store for us . . .

I shall do my very best, I promise you, to come to you there where you are, my sister, not to visit you, but rather to find out what it is like for you shut up there behind those walls. How it rained, Mariana, the day they took you prisoner and bore you off to the convent in your parents' carriage, keeping close watch on you all the way to make sure you did not escape.

What irony! Where could you have fled to that they would not have immediately caught you and taken you prisoner again? What would you have lived on, who would have helped you? Only some French cavalier, perhaps, captivated by your green eyes – a number of them are beginning to arrive, to invade our lands, in order to help us fight against Spain, or so I am told.

They are gallant, their manners quite different from those of the crude and vulgar men whom we are used to. Gallant and bold . . . Because of my husband's position, I am obliged to receive them socially, and there is one of them, the Chevalier de Chamilly, whom I wish you might meet. You cannot imagine how touched he was by the story of what has happened to you, which I recounted to him in detail. We spent hour after hour together talking of you, during which time he discoursed at length on certain subjects, and made certain remarks that surprised me, coming as they did from a man, and they have started me to thinking . . .

What else awaits us, despite the fact that you are already dead there in your cell and I am already dead here in my room? My heart tells me that our misfortunes have scarcely begun and that many more will come crashing down on our heads, that even worse unhappiness lies in store for us, however impossible that may appear to us today.

I may be of very little comfort to you in your many sorrows, Mariana, but I am on your side and I shall always fight for you if need be.

Many kisses from your hapless friend who sorely misses you

Joana

25.4.71

War

Above us grave and wide flies a wing
a given movement at hand, silken motion
that could swallow up all dignity
and pure liberty.

Since neither you nor I have ever lost
or gained stature
or any time except the time of questioning
a wing circles of a dense new bird (or cauldron smoke?)

so ancient
that I say I yield (it is early)
I know you not
and with my own palm outstretched and glad
I help you toward what you know not
and weave what I yield to you.

25.4.71

Extracts from the Diary of Dona Maria Ana, Born Around the Year 1800, a Direct Descendant of Dona Mariana, the Niece of Dona Mariana Alcoforado

Beginning with Mariana, the first of us, I belong to the seventh generation, a spontaneous, philosophically minded offshoot of this female line, which has as its point of departure the worldly deeds of a nun, then goes on from that point, gradually becoming aware of itself, of its necessity for being – and hence a lineage opposed to the forgetting and the diluting, the rapid absorption of a scandal within the peace of the family circle and the reigning social order.

If men create families and lineages in order to ensure that their names and property are passed along to their descendants, is it not logical for women to use their nameless, propertyless line of descent to perpetuate scandal, to pass along what is unacceptable?

Like religious orders, in essence. But these orders soon lose their original *raison d'être*. Because the spirit of rebellion is refractory to being institutionalized? But not for that reason alone; also because the spirit of contradiction gradually becomes a passive virtue, and all the imposed vows of self-deprivation – pain, poverty, obedience, chastity – little by little are transformed into a sort of self-satisfied, absolute, unquestioned virtue. It is my belief that in order to become comrades of those who hunger and thirst after justice it is not rules that must be established, not even rules to further justice. Religious orders chose the path that led by way of hunger and thirst, and followed it to the point of self-contradiction, to the point of establishing the reign of injustice. The Penitential Sisters of Saint Clare: a holocaust of women who for century after century have done penance, night and day, to make amends for the profanation of certain communion wafers. Were not the communion wafers intended to make amends for the profanation of persons?

But enough said about nuns, who are not a unique instance. What woman is not a nun, sacrificed, self-sacrificing, without a life of her own, sequestered from the world? What change has there been in the life of women through the centuries? In Aunt Mariana's time women did embroidery or spun or wove or cooked, obeyed their husband's will, became pregnant, had abortions, or carried their children to term, some of them stillborn, some born alive, cared for their offspring, and sometimes died in childbed, in their houses amid all their furniture, their over-stuffed chairs, their draperies at the windows. We are living in an age of civilization and enlightenment, men write scientific treatises and encyclopaedias, nations continually change and transform their political structure, the oppressed raise their voices, a king of France has been sent to the guillotine and his courtiers along with him, the United States of America has gained its independence . . . what else? What else is there in history that I find of interest to recount? What has changed in the life of women? They no longer weave, they no longer spin, perhaps, because industry and commerce have developed; yet women still do embroidery, cook, obey their husband's will, become pregnant, have abortions, or carry their children to term, some of them stillborn, some born alive, care for their offspring, and sometimes die in childbed, in their houses, where nothing has changed save the style of the furniture, of the overstuffed chairs, of the draperies at the windows.

Why do I call myself a spontaneous, philosophically minded offshoot of this female line? Out of contempt, out of rage, out of helplessness. What are all of us doing? Nothing. Mariana began it; did Mariana see her rights recognized? I doubt it. Mariana simply rent the veil of hypocrisy and decried it. Because men kept staring off into space, and saying to their well-born spouses; 'What is it we're thinking about, what is it we want? Nothing, nothing, our every thought is directed towards purity and lofty values. Nothing else exists save God's good grace'; and men went on with their wars, their fornication, their night-long drinking bouts, came home, and said to their well-born spouses: 'Don't ask any questions, Senhora, for this smell of blood, this stench of the other side of life is not for your chaste nostrils, all you need concern yourself with is your reputation and your children or your convent, all the rest is none of a woman's business.' And then Mariana came along, crying in the streets: 'Why did they invent love, and passion, if all they want is tender care and wives of blameless reputation? Why do cavaliers go about conquering women as though they were waging wars? What nostalgias do they suffer from at the sides of their virtuous spouses and their legitimate children? I shall show you the price of the order of chivalry, on what foundation its victories rest: on the torn womb of the woman, on the woman become booty seized between two military engagements.' No, in reality Mariana didn't cry any such thing; all she said was: 'Here I am, possessed by love.' A murmur was heard: 'How fine a thing the love of a woman is, but why bury it beneath all this respect and decorum? Wouldn't it be better to take advantage of it? Who is afraid of this woman who is so much at love's mercy?' The image of Mariana the niece then appeared, taking on gigantic proportions: she too a spontaneous offshoot; how did she come by all that intelligence? I identify myself with her; and aside from her knowledge and her gift for words, what was she save a mere woman, one who kept a diary and wrote a letter? As for the rest, she did embroidery and bore children; in terrible loneliness. Her diary is a rock; or rather, it is the only breach in her silence, the only possible place for her gift for words, but for that very reason a stone. What did she say? 'A woman's life is all like the act of giving birth; a solitary, painful, furtive act, hidden from the eyes of everyone in the name of modesty. Modesty is a nostalgia; it allows people to pretend that living beings who are too burdensome are already dead.' Mariana the niece, the one of the letter, who said straight out that the love of the cavalier was a fraud; a feigned nostalgia for the absolute, a remedy for the anguish of a hypocritical chevalier who prized his relative life so highly, his risk a calculated one and his transgression carefully planned so as to endanger only the life of another, and as a result, once he had thus exposed himself and taken this slight risk, he would come to feel that his life was more secure, that he had won a victory. Between Mariana the niece and me there have been four generations, decorative, absorbent ones, cultivating the delights of passion and of writing genteel love letters;

they did their best to dilute Mariana; one of them even attempted to turn conjugal intercourse into passionate love-making, and was quite astonished when her spouse said to her: 'Stop trying to be my mistress, Senhora, because I abandon my mistresses when their flesh begins to bore me; if you wish my respect and support for the rest of your days, try to be my wife.' Four generations that sought to replace the hypocrisy of decency and decorum with that of the hypocrisy of passion: 'All paths are closed to me, Senhor, and hence I love you, hence I serve you with passion.' I have no desire for love save that between equals; it is for that reason that I refused a husband, that I rejected men. I shall leave my diary to my niece. What can I be meanwhile? I define myself only by what I am not; I do not do embroidery, I do not bear children. I identify myself with Mariana the niece of Mariana: I am a woman whose words are solemn; a woman who keeps silent and keeps a diary, a woman who is advancing in years and living on her brother's charity. No one fears a woman who leaves herself exposed to love. But who will accept as knowledge deserving of being disseminated the words of a solemn woman, words that are even more solemn still?

From the beginning men were obliged to look upon themselves as demigods fallen from divine grace through the wiles of women; and then later they were obliged to invent a way to redeem themselves through the womb of a new mother, that saint, that creature capable of knowing God in her womb and incarnating therein the saviour-god whose life and exemplary deeds would one day cause him to be known – oh what subtle irony! – as the son of man. Because the man keeps building the world and digging his grave, and keeps calling to the woman, addressing her first as 'mother', so that she will point out to him what is good and what is evil, and represent both for him, and take upon herself the intolerable absurdity of the established order of things. And the man goes on building the world, with the welcoming and productive womb of the woman as its foundation, this time calling her 'my possession, my treasure'. And once having made woman the repository of good and evil and the unbearable absurdity of the established order of things, it is only right that she should now become the first victim, the guilty one, until finally the moment arrives when the man calls to the woman, addressing her simply as 'woman', and notices that the place at his side is empty.

The place at my side: empty, forever empty. A woman without a man, and with no power to change the world. And what if someone called me 'woman'? How could I hear him? Does the entire struggle become hopeless? Did my rule for myself become hunger and thirst? My life was hunger and it was thirst; but where could I have satisfied them? My rule is justice; hence I forbade myself injustice. Will a life that is merely a refusal have any meaning? Where are my comrades in the struggle? No, I shall not allow my bitterness at the outcome to gainsay me. I did my best and bared a great deal of myself; but on removing the veil of polite antagonism, petty antagonism made its appearance, and on removing that veil, fierce antagonism appeared. That is how men are: for them a woman's love is surrender, obedience, service, gratitude. When a bourgeois rebels against the King, or when a colonial rebels against the empire, it is merely a leader or a government that they attack. All the rest remains unchanged: their business, their property, their families, their places among friends and acquaintances, their pleasures. If woman rebels against man, nothing remains unchanged: for the woman, the leader, politics, business, property, her place, her (extremely perverse) pleasure exist only through the man. The warrior has his repose; the woman, on the other hand, has nothing to cling to for support and compensation for the battles she has fought. Will the day ever come when all this will change? Until such a time, the life of women like myself remains meaningless.

26.4.71

Reply of Mariana Alcoforado, a Nun in Beja, to Dona Joana de Vasconcelos

In the name of heaven, Joana! You were playing with your own life and came close to being my downfall as well!

It was only because she feels such great pity for me that the Mother Superior did not communicate the contents of your letter to my parents and your husband, and instead summoned me to warn me against you. Hence it appears to me that there is little chance of your being able to visit me, unless we can somehow secure her forgiveness.

Meanwhile, as you can see, I have tried to discover a way of writing to you without arousing anyone's suspicion that I am doing so: getting letters out of here is easy, but what will prove most difficult, it seems to me, will be getting them into your hands without your husband's finding out.

Dear Joana, how happy your words made me, yet at the same time they plunged me into the blackest despair: there again came vividly before my mind our hopes (unfounded hopes . . .), our shared concerns, our rebellions and secrets, our promises we meant with all our hearts though they later proved so impossible to keep. What is left of me, shut up here in this cloister, yearning for space, for sun (you know how much I love the sun . . .), hungering to wander across those arid, sere, parched fields that I can see from my cell at night, bathed in the acid light of the moon, inventing its imaginary images of cold, of days rubbed raw by heat and nerves.

Oh, how can you possibly wish, or even think you might prefer, to trade places with me if only you could . . . I would willingly marry any man my parents chose, any man to whom they sold me, however loathsome I found him, even though I know full well how infamous a thing that would be. I would do anything, Joana, to get myself out of this convent where I am suffocating to death and slowly going mad, day after day.

How I miss you, my sister . . . Do you remember?: I was instinct, you were intelligence, I was fire, the immediate, you careful reflection, perseverance. I came to think that you would win my parents over, that you would persuade my mother to take pity on my lot; but there is nothing and no one able to wring anything from that woman save coldness, deception, icy calculation; it is only towards my sister that she behaves somewhat differently, becoming almost tender, and forgetful of herself. Then she comes to visit me, the way her eyes stare at me terrifies me . . . Am I dreaming, Joana, when I feel my mother's hatred piercing my body through and through as she stares at me? But why does she hate me and punish me without ever taking pity on my innocence and suffering; why doesn't she tell me, at long last, what harm I did her by being born?

All these wounds reopened on reading your letter . . . in my happiness at receiving it I once again became vulnerable to the world that came to me within its pages. You give me news of that world, Joana, and my lips clung to the paper that bears not only your seal, but also your scent, your perfume, the sound of your voice that I remember so well.

So let my sister Maria marry and have children . . . poor creature, the only thing she will ever be used for is breeding children . . . so let her marry if that is why I am here in this cloister . . . but that poor Count de C. is going to suffer a great deal at the hands of Dona Maria Alcoforado! What with her fits of rage and sudden outbursts of anger she will make him an even more fearful man than he already is, since by nature he is timid and dull-witted. How you chided me when you saw me laugh in his face . . .

Your husband must be a very coarse and brutish man, Joana, not to admire and love in you, above all else, your intelligence and your delicacy of feeling. You must suffer intensely at his hands, you who cultivate beauty, sensibility, and subtlety as though they were living plants.

How unhappy both of us are, my dear friend – bound fast by laws so inhuman that they make a woman nothing but some man's property, his domain, his plot of earth where he spends a single night and sows his seed. Your barrenness is revenge, just retribution; it permits you to refuse to be used: to become the mother of a man or a woman fathered by a husband that you hate, to be merely a woman to breed sons on: male offspring continuing the family line, astride their mounts, in the name of the father . . . you have expressed your rebellion by way of your womb, you have refused this, Joana, and blessed be your name!

I spend many hours of the long afternoons of my dreary days kneeling in the chapel, my head between my hands . . . the other nuns presume that I am praying . . . but how mistaken they are! I dare not confess to them that I am weeping, that I am rebelling, that I would willingly abandon God for the world, that I am not seeking God but fleeing Him, withdrawing from Him, taking refuge in secret anxieties.

Can there be any more miserable future than that in which death is the only goal? You say you have a presentiment of even greater evils soon to descend upon our heads . . . mine is long since bowed, Joana, but you . . . you tell me Frenchmen are gallant and you appear to already be on friendly and intimate terms with one of them. Always keep in mind, however, how ignoble men are, and as for your Chevalier de Chamilly, who you say was so touched by my story, he may simply be attempting to forget his heartache for what he has left behind in his homeland; he is forgetting his homesickness with you, Joana!

Yesterday I was standing out on the balcony with several other nuns, watching those Frenchmen you tell me about: they were there beneath our windows, showing off for us, prancing about on their horses. There was one whose eyes appeared to be searching out one of us in particular . . . Don't laugh, will you promise, if I tell you that for a few moments I thought he might be your Chevalier de Chamilly? If indeed it was he, tell him that I am dead, shut up behind the walls of this convent, as punishment for some misdeed that I have unknowingly committed. I lost my life when I heard the portals of this tomb clang shut behind me: I undid my braids then, stripped off my garments, and exchanged them for this habit woven of such coarse cloth that it rubs my body raw.

What strict self-discipline I have been obliged to observe, what rage I have had to keep burning in my heart all this time in order to be able to go on living! But going on living for what, or for whom, I ask myself?

Farewell, my Joana

Your unhappy
Mariana

30.4.71

Medical-Psychiatric Report on the Mental State of Mariana A.

The Medico-Psychiatric Board of the hospital of —— has been requested to report on the mental state of Mariana A., who was brought to this hospital on the afternoon of 16 April, 19—, and admitted as a patient.

Mariana A. is twenty-five years of age; married; born in Beja; she has been residing in Lisbon for about three years. It is known that her father committed suicide; her mother, a very religious and puritanical woman, is now fifty years old. Three children were born of this marriage: two girls and a boy; the older daughter who is still unmarried, lives with the mother. The patient had also been living at home until approximately three years ago, or to be more precise, until 20 May, 19—, the date of her marriage to António C., who is at present doing his military service overseas. As the patient herself reports, her relations with her mother were very strained, since the latter was quite obviously much fonder of her other two children, especially the elder daughter, with whom she has always got on very well.

These facts, like those outlined below, are important, in that they would appear to shed light on the mental state of the patient, or the causes that led her to commit the act that brought her here. Mention should also be made of the fact that Mariana A., according to her family and to statements from doctors, has never shown any symptoms of insanity, or any tendency towards aberrant sexual behaviour. Since early childhood she has had a careful and rigid Catholic upbringing, and been educated by nuns in church schools, where she has always complied with the strict moral standards enforced in such institutions. On the afternoon of 16 April of this year, however, Mariana A. was brought to the emergency ward of this hospital, locked in copulation with a dog. The patient, who was in a state of hysteria, was accompanied by her parents-in-law, who made the following statement:

'We were resting after lunch, when suddenly we heard cries and sobs coming from our daughter-in-law's bedroom. When we finally managed to get the door open, at first we didn't understand what was going on, and thought that Mariana was being attacked by the animal, so we ran to help her, and then . . . well, we couldn't believe our eyes, because she'd always been so quiet, so well-behaved, you see, spending all her time cooped up there in the house, writing to her husband! We often used to tell her she ought to go out with us to get a breath of fresh air. . . . Naturally we never let her go out alone, or even with a girl friend of hers, and besides she's never managed to make any such friends in Lisbon – our son was very self-absorbed, and only liked to be around people he knew well. The way he treated his wife was rather peculiar, but she appeared to like that. She had been very withdrawn ever since our António went to Africa, she couldn't sleep at night and didn't eat enough. In fact, we were about to take her to a doctor.'

During her first few days in hospital, Mariana refused to make any statement whatsoever, and kept weeping and screaming whenever she was not under sedation. She then fell into a mutism on which the treatment administered apparently had no effect. At present, she will answer questions, but she still refuses to discuss what made her commit the act that caused her to be interned here. If she is pressed to do so, she appears not to hear, and her eyes stare off into space; she may remain in this state for hours at a time. Since the nurses informed us that Mariana A. often talked to herself aloud when she believed herself to be all alone in her room, it was decided that recordings of her monologues would be made. We transcribe below one of them which in our opinion was of the greatest interest:

'You never noticed, not ever. My mother said that the flesh is sinful it is lustful and that's the way it was even with you. You were always a prison; did it ever occur to you to listen to me? And now you have been away for all these many long years. Years and years. And what was I to do? What was I to do with all those days of all that time when the only light was your letters, where you told me everything about yourself in great detail. You boasted of your courage, your brave deeds under fire, and the battles you'd fought in, which have turned into an enjoyable pastime for you, something like a hunting party. Like in that photograph you sent me, where you're grinning from ear to ear – your father and mother had it framed and it's in the living room on top of the piano. The flesh is lustful it is sinful my mother used to say and I felt that way even when it was with you, when I came, though heaven only knows I tried to hold myself back. And then all these years that weigh so heavily in my belly all these thoughts these desires these ideas with your mother keeping a close eye on me and your father reading what I wrote to you and what you wrote to me. And you like a prison, all the time like a prison, and me screaming out my horror to you, screaming out all this loathing all this enormous fear.'

Summary:
1. Mariana A. is not insane.
2. There is no evidence in her case of any sexual disorder.
3. The act that brought her here is probably due solely to a serious nervous imbalance, the causes of which must be further investigated in order to attempt to cure the patient.

Hospital of ——, 30 December, 19—.

1.5.71

Letter from Dona Joana de Vasconcelos to the Chevalier de Chamilly, on the Eve of the Latter's Departure for France

My Friend

I am writing you this letter to beg you not to leave for France without first going to see Mariana . . .

Why do I deserve different treatment at your hands than that which you have accorded her: sudden flight or indifference or even contempt for her? Does her cruel fate no longer touch your heart, does her story no longer arouse your indignation, as it did when first I recounted it to you? — You are only too readily forgetting facts, feelings, causes; it has taken you only a short time to forget how to defend or lose these causes by your own hands, hands as bold as they are indifferent. Mariana was a toy in them, but I for my part refused to be your plaything, out of instinct, out of pride, and above all out of cowardice perhaps: though I gave myself to you, I preferred not to risk my love and my dignity, the only possessions I have that still remain intact, mine from birth, and mine alone, to dispose of as I please.

I was yours out of self-abandonment and pleasure, and perhaps also out of vengeance, out of weariness, out of defiance, yet I never demanded of you words or acts of surrender or promises that I knew full well you could not and would not keep.

What risk did I expose myself to by belonging to you?

What a much greater risk Mariana exposed herself to by being your mistress . . . a mistress who loved you, since I never truly loved you, but merely used you in my mad eagerness to forget, to escape from myself, to refuse to accept everything that is being forced upon me.

Hence how sweet the poison of perdition tasted on your lips, what thick glass your smell, your breath seemed, your breast and your dry belly as I ran my fingers over them and covered them with kisses . . . I became a woman with you, without the torments and the usual tender rituals of love; our transports were those of satisfied bodies, the sap in them giving them nourishing life-sustenance.

Was there any need, then, to sacrifice Mariana, already so pitifully sacrificed by others?

What acts of madness did you lead her to and what did you promise her? What schemes invented out of selfishness, what lies did you resort to in order to make her yours? A woman shut up by force in a convent doubtless offers very weak resistance to a gallant, intelligent man who pretends to be timid, deeply in love, and indignant at her fate, opening his arms to her in supposed refuge . . .

Through one of us you had the other – 'both of them weak,' you said to yourself – but you discovered that you were mistaken about me, and that intimidated you . . . How well I know you! And though I may have been duped in the beginning, it was merely because of the contrast between your behaviour and that of the crude and brutish men I had known previously, men descended from the very best families, of purest Portuguese stock, masters of their women, their lands, their offspring, and their horses.

From France you brought light, graciousness, wit, gallantry – but from your own nature: cowardice, coldness, cleverness, self-love.

Poor Mariana, who loved you. What am I saying? She loves you still and has been in the depths of despair ever since you abandoned her without forewarning or explanation, without so much as a single word of comfort and hope. It would have been far better for you to have killed her by telling her the truth; and less cowardly of you than simply taking to your heels as you are now doing.

How many sorrows and humiliations she has subjected herself to, and is subjecting herself to still, out of love for you! I had news of her yesterday: they tell me that she is dying little by little and takes leave of her senses for hours at a time, speaking of you openly, without prudence or shame, moaning loudly, kissing your letters, crying out to your body and shouting your name.

I shall do everything in my power to see that no harm befalls her and to smother a scandal which might well cost her her life should her kinsfolk discover that she is thus sullying the family's honour and the name she bears.

Very well then, go off to France, you have nothing more to do here, you have already done far too much, but do not leave without bidding Mariana good-bye! When you came yesterday to bid me farewell, I was unable to say anything to you, for my husband was listening attentively to every word we said, even though there is nothing left to hear now . . . I resolved, therefore, to write to you, hoping that you will heed my plea and grant what I ask of you . . .

Leave Mariana her self-respect, for by fleeing in this way, you are depriving her of it. Your memory rests in peace within me, with not so much as a single shadow darkening it: I asked you for nothing that you could give me, I never imagined you to be anything save what you really were . . .

Did my voice ever once quaver, or my hand tremble in yours? Take with you, then, this memory of my firmness and unyielding spirit that served me as the bedrock of my proud dignity.

Didn't my silences always tell you much more than my words?

Joana

2.5.71

Letter from Dona Joana de Vasconcelos to Mariana Alcoforado

My Dear Mariana:

You sent me word that you were beset with anxiety and asked me to communicate to you as soon as possible any news that I might have of your cousin José Maria, your guardian angel, as you used to call him in your heart of hearts – you say that you refuse to listen to your heart but that it refuses to obey you and makes you feel afraid for someone you will never forget. I know you love José Maria as though he were your own son, the fruit of your own womb.

What pain I saw in his eyes when he bade you good-bye, Mariana, and what an insane fit of rage I saw overcome him, his body racked with deep sobs, though the tears refused to come, when you disappeared, pale and dead silent, in the carriage that was taking you far away from all of us, into exile for the rest of your days. I tried in vain at that point to hold your cousin back, but he wrenched himself out of my arms, mounted his horse, and disappeared in the opposite direction, apparently galloping furiously all day long, since it was long after nightfall when he returned, his horse well-nigh dead from exhaustion, with José Maria fainted dead away in the saddle, his head dragging on the ground, till finally our uncle knocked him off with one blow and stretched him out on the ground.

Since that day, many long months passed without my seeing him, and with no other news of him save vague stories or strange rumours that I did not believe, but upon reading your letter and learning of your anxieties, I made sure that our paths would cross yesterday, at Mónica's house, where he has been a frequent visitor of late, and so today (my husband is in Lisbon and hence I am free) I have news of him for you, though unfortunately it is not good news: he is withdrawn from everything and everybody, silent and calm, a sad calm or a calm full of wisdom and clear-sightedness, whose beginning and end, I confess, are equal mysteries to me. I scarcely recognized him – it was as if I had never seen him before, though I have always known him to be a strange and unusual sort. My eyes never left José Maria all evening, I was so astonished: he is a grown man now and extremely handsome, but he was so heedless of what was going on round about him that it was as though he were not there. I contrived to remain alone with him for a time, and taking his hands in mine, I said to him in a whisper: 'Mariana has been asking about you,' whereupon your cousin turned deathly pale, although he appeared not to have even heard me, suddenly rose to his feet, and left the parlour. I followed him and saw him jump over the garden wall, like an acrobat, in one single, silent, agile leap, and disappear into the darkness of night . . .

How can I be of help to him, Mariana? I who cannot even help myself, nor you, my friend, my sister, my soul's companion for as long as I can remember.

I would have liked to set your mind at rest, but José Maria frightened me too badly for me to even pretend that I am not gravely concerned about him. I promise you, however, that I will seek him out again, even if good sense tells me I ought not to . . .

What danger am I exposing myself to by trying to save your cousin from himself? When I took his hands in mine and he immediately jerked them away, it was not you, Mariana, that I was thinking of; I was thinking only of him. Or of myself perhaps?

With fondest kisses

your

Joana

4.5.71

Letter from Sister Mariana Alcoforado, a Nun in Beja, to Her Younger Cousin Dom José Maria Pereira Alcoforado

My José Maria and My Beloved Guardian Angel,

I am sending you this letter in secret through Alfredo, who came to bring me news and the usual dire warnings from José Francisco, my brother and your cousin and godfather, to behave myself. Despite the seven years' difference in age between you and me, you are much more sensible than I am, and at this time when my powers of reason are so feeble and I am in such torment, I know of no one else in the family to whom I can turn save you, my childhood playmate and confidant. Thanks to the scandalized outcries that are the rule when they lay down the law to us in our houses, where your father is the eldest of the family and hence the ultimate lord and master, you must already know what is happening in the life of your Marianita. Yesterday I was told that you had not been allowed to see me when you came here to the convent, because of your tender years and the very early hour at which you appeared, just after matins. Hence I am thinking of you as I gaze at the bars of my cell with the same grave expression on my face that you always used to have as you watched me doing foolish things, only to undertake yourself, the very next moment, others that were much more serious, in order either to humiliate me by proving that you were stronger than I or in order to heap coals on your fire so that it would burn ever more brightly and cast its light ever farther. My little José, the only one of my blood, along with your hapless cousin who is setting down these words, whom everyone continually complained they did not understand – your exquisite talent for writing and drawing, your mad gallops in the dark of night at the age of fourteen, once the whole house had grown quiet, your friendly relations with servants and compassion for the disinherited of this earth, your elegant demeanour and gracious man-

166

ners and your biting wit. They allowed me to be your godmother and first let me rock you when you were still a babe in swaddling clothes, until the day came when my arms proved too frail to hold you – you were never a big, strong baby, but you soon were a very lively and impetuous one. Only you and my good Joana, so unhappily married, wept tears for me as I departed, the sound of the door of the house slamming shut behind me breaking my heart, Joana's hands clinging to yours, though not out of any great affection, for not even she was ever able to understand the brooding silences that came over you and your scornful disappearances whenever there were festive celebrations at our houses. Like a little angel of death, how many times you said to me: 'Run away, my Nita, I can't yet protect you – I am not allowed any say in family affairs yet – but run away, because if God won't help you, the devil will.' How I feared your innocent dark grey eyes, your face with the fine bones, the tears that I had never seen you shed before and that gleamed in your eyes that day, until I lost you from sight, with Joana waving to me, but not you. You could do nothing for me and your father made that very plain, for as I learned later from Joana, he locked you in your room afterwards and took a whip to you, since in his eyes you were guilty of encouraging your cousin's disrespect and irreverence. And she also told me that the house servants and your poor mother, who is so meek and timid and so unlike the one that unfortunately fell to my lot, heard the terrible insults and the blows dealt you by your father in his blinding rage, but heard no sound to indicate that you were in pain, no weeping, not a single word. But now everything is ended, my child of silver, and as you can see from this letter, I am no longer ashamed to speak of the loving caresses that I gave you as a child and that your solemn demeanour kept me from giving you as soon as the first trace of a beard appeared on your cheeks. They wanted me to be arid and barren, and only in you did I find a place for the caresses that I believe lie ready and waiting in every woman's heart and vitals for the children she will one day have. But I was unable to imagine you wielding a father's authority, for I could see you becoming more and more mistrustful of your own father, and of my brother, your cousin and godfather, who on occasion acted in his stead. Your mother tells me that she comes here at the behest of all the others, as always fearfully obeying the will of others, since she neither knows how to nor is able to do otherwise, though she forgets to pass on to me the messages she has been given warning me to be docile and submissive. She also tells me that she has been very concerned about your health and your strange habits – and tells me that your confessor complains about your not attending mass and other sacraments, and that even your father, after having dealt you harsh punishment that did not appear to have changed your behaviour, wants to have little to do with you now and has stopped making slighting remarks about how you slouch in your chair at the table or neglect your studies.

So you see, while it was my intention to give you news of what is causing me such concern, that serious love affair that you have certainly heard about, which weighs all the more heavily upon my conscience in that I know how thoroughly you have disapproved of any commerce with foreigners save that afforded you by your extensive reading of their works far into the night, I suddenly appear to be taking you in hand and questioning you as to your reasons for fighting so bitterly against everything and everybody – I who was your confidante once upon a time, to whom you would come with your secrets, resting your beautiful black head of hair on my lap. I know full well that I may die of the harm that has been done me, since I have never found any way to protect myself against anything that was being forced upon me save screaming and weeping. And the affection of the older sister that I have always tried to be to you should rightfully serve to protect me as well. But my beloved José Maria, what pain is this that has overcome you, news of which has reached my ears in bits and snatches, thus making the wound I have recently suffered all the more searing by reminding me of old wounds we suffered long ago in childhood? Why is it that you no longer invent plots and make up stories about the return of Dom Sebastião [25] as you once delighted in doing, that you no longer pay your girl cousins sly compliments and tease them about the way they wear their hair, that you no longer read books of chivalry and stories about our sovereigns of old, that you simply arise at the crack of dawn and wander about on horseback in deserted places until long after dark, refusing to eat or let anyone take care of you. What evil has befallen you, my little brother, that here in this rough cell where I have been imprisoned, where I have had a vain love affair now forever ended, I can do nothing to remedy, save to remember you forever in my heart, as I do my good Joana and that foreigner who roused my body and disturbed my senses. I know very well, though I now know that nothing is as certain as I once believed, that I should not speak to you of such things at your tender age, yet I discovered long ago that your understanding of everything and everybody has always been much less immature and your spirit more unyielding than mine. What did they do to you, my angel, what did they do to you? Come soon and try to see me at a more reasonable hour, and I will ask my brother to grant us this favour. For I do not know what I stand most in need of, being able even yet to feel a love of my kinsfolk through you, or being able to remember what you told me: that I should never, ever have been born a woman, or that everything is a tissue of lies and unfair differences. How true those words of yours have proved to be, my faithful secretary, so pure in heart.

The most chaste caresses from your cousin and sister

Mariana

5.5.71

Note in an Envelope Sealed with the Signet of the Alcoforado Family and Addressed to His Cousin Mariana by Dom José Pereira Alcoforado on the Day on Which His Body Was Found at Dawn Hanging from the Tallest Fig Tree Round About His Family's House

neither stranger
nor infant
nor hero to hail
with the body of your cousin
make a bell Mariana
that the Fatherland may toll

6.5.71

Poem by Dom José Maria Pereira Alcoforado Bearing the Date of the Morning of His Suicide

Angel of misfortune,
My sister Mariana . . .
Riding death
With its honour and sword

Piercing through my breast
With this blade
unmanning evil . . .
My sister Mariana

6.5.71

A May Love Letter and a Major Letter

'Joy and woe are woven fine'
WILLIAM BLAKE

'*et pourtant ça existe*'
LÉO FERRÉ

What did I wear pendent on my heart before you came
save the cleft that was the sign of my uncertain knowledge of you?

Neither visions borne in true light and hope in the greenness
(nor soft translucent skin of casual lovers, I
almost female
searching for clues)
nor knowing well the maxims of emotion
brought any peace or worth

and in emptiness
lost over you never finding you in our streets
caring for nothing but preparing your name
in pain I waited for you.

The forms were all imperfect
but sometimes in the focus of the mid-day heat
or on certain early mornings when the fear of all the no of night was
    suspended
the hen's white egg
or a cup of water
this calcareous hard city water
gave signs of an ending and I came to rest
and with a new peace erected against everything (even this)
I knew some coming was prepared.

And now we are?
This sweet flood of the nonsense of before in the lodging we offer,
                                you with your being in
me, I between your fingers   is it enough?

Homeless still, I hear your steps remaking me a trail
which till you came I disavowed and did not choose
to walk it was to follow you and keep my back tense for the no
and the hurried farewell of the smile of the no (I beg your pardon)
it was to let you come   (to yourself?)
it was to be at your right hand

the key to my outline grasped in your left fist
and without any limits at all

And so, love, you rewrote me like a long, long essay of some female of
    yours
which came to be my changing form
because you studied peoples, customs, places, languages, songs
to tell me yes so easily that I would know
that nothing I could search for was in vain
but only that.

7·5·71

Monologue of a Woman Named Maria, with Her Employer

Thank you very much I'm getting over it, it's not necessary to call the doctor, Senhora, I'm getting over it, I'm quite used to it, it's just attacks that come over me, I lose consciousness and can't breathe and then when I come to I'm all right again, I assure you, don't be concerned and please excuse me, I didn't want to frighten you, Senhora, how stupid of me to have an attack here at your house . . . I'm very much obliged to you but it isn't something that can be treated with medicine or prescriptions it's just nerves and people get nervous because of the life they lead and their bitternesses and sorrows . . . you know, I never talk about my life, or the way life has treated me, with everything turning out badly, the child God gave me, who's so sickly, poor thing, my marriage . . . But how could I have known! My mother was right when she kept saying 'Maria, be careful, you never know how a marriage is going to turn out, sometimes it's better for a woman to be an old maid . . .' But how was I to know that my António was going to come home from Africa a changed man, he used to be such a fine person, if you'll pardon my immodesty, Senhora, so good-hearted, but ever since he came back from the wars everything is all mixed up in his head and I'm frightened of him, he shouts night and day, he beats me till his arms get tired and I'm lying there stretched out on the floor. That was when I began having these attacks, one day he came home drunk and I called him a pig. 'You pig,' I said, begging your pardon, Senhora, 'where's the money for us to eat?' And he said: 'Shut your mouth you bitch or I'll kill you,' and then I started screaming and he lost his head and started to beat me with all his might, and the blows rained down on me from head to foot till I started gasping and spittle came dribbling out of my mouth as I lay there writhing on the floor and he kept beating me and beating me, and the only reason he didn't kill me was because my little boy, the poor thing, flung himself on top of me as I lay there and clung to my body and when he saw the poor child clinging to me like that, so frail and so terrified, he was ashamed of himself and went away, leaving me lying there unconscious, all alone with my little boy and then he came back a month later to beg my pardon, and apologized so politely that I forgave him, what else could I do, Senhora, everybody has his weak points and then after that everything went along the same as before at first, but then he started drinking again and keeping other women and not working and I had to go on doing housework by the day, and thank the Good Lord I always have places to work, the hardest part though is my little boy, they won't take him at the day nursery because he's always ailing, and I can't find anywhere to leave him, and not all the ladies I work for are as kindhearted as you are, Senhora, it was so good of you to tell me I could bring him with me, the others think he'd be a bother, but he never is, he just sits there quietly, his eyes following me, the poor thing ... the last time I took him to the lady doctor to have a look at him she said: 'This child needs a better diet,' but what can I do, Senhora, seeing as how there are times when I don't even have a mouthful of bread to keep him from feeling hungry ... When I think how affectionate my godmother Senhora Joaninha always was with me whenever I went to see her ... she urged me to come stay with her: 'Don't get married, Maria, come and live here with me instead, listen, there's nothing like a woman who's free because she doesn't have a man,' and I realize now that she was right, but it's too late. I was fated to be unhappy, it's no use fighting against destiny, Senhora, it's no use, a man can rebel whenever he pleases but a woman is tied to a man, to her children, and what can she do? Because my António really isn't a bad person at heart, he really isn't, Senhora, and he's the father of my Antóninho, who's been so frail ever since the day he was born ... and now with your permission I'm going back to work, Senhora, please excuse me for the worry I've caused you. To think that such a thing could have happened right here in the Senhora's house! I'm very much obliged to you for being so concerned about me, I almost feel embarrassed because nobody has ever cared that much about my troubles ...

but I must go back to work now, because I still have the dishes and the laundry to do and I can't take any more time out if I want to finish everything up today. So by your leave, Senhora, by your leave . . .

8.5.71

How Death Can Be Easier Than Love. The Lament of Mónica and Maria.

'Let me go away.'

Will I still have time? No one knows the way better than you – the short-cuts, the stones, the trees, the marks left by the years on places in these fields, on places on street corners in the city; no one can know better than you the hours that lie ahead of me.

Plus faim ni soif depuis dix jours avec la seule envie de toi, à crier.*

How the sun burns in my mouth.

I am suffocating, you can see very well that I am suffocating. This sort of torpor that is killing me, immobilizing me as I lie here at your side, these walls that I rub my hands across until they bleed, their brittle plaster gnawed by the centuries and the rats that have built their nests in them.

Your back. Your smooth, soft back: like the sea lashing my skin as I flee. Knowing that only you can help me. Listen: you have the key. The key that you turn with a sharp click in the oiled lock every day, and then th door silently swings open on its hinges . . .

J'ai rêvé. J'avais calé ta porte avec mon corps, pour te crier je t'aime parmi tes potes, cependant que tu étais retourné à d'autres décors.†

Oh, this window nailed shut with enormous nails that you went out to buy, and hammered as I watched into the wood

---

* Neither hungry nor thirsty for ten days now, wanting only you, so much that I could scream . . .[26]

† I had a dream. I had blocked your door with my body, so as to shout I love you as you sat there with your pals, but you'd gone back to other haunts of yours . . .

of the elegant doors on which I break my fingernails and scrape my fingers raw in the hope of glimpsing the sky and shouting for joy; the sky at least; the light at least.

I never manage to, I am unable to: this wind driving this sand before it, which piles higher and higher by the hour; it is gradually covering me up and bursting into flame, filtering into my eyes, my nostrils, my ideas.

Like hours, ideas slowly pass and die . . .

Ah, reviens, et tu verras avec quelle joie je vais piétiner tout, la résignée, l'indifférente, la putain, la crâneuse.*

Why do you not let me leave if there is still time?

Speak to me of hours, of nights; speak to me of your body so sheltered from the waves, from death; speak to me of the brightly lighted open city where there are pleasant carefree nights that fly swiftly by; speak to me of the heat waves on mountainsides, of heat waves on the houses in the south; my thirsty country, my red earth, my broad, broad beaches, the dizzying attraction that draws me to the edge of the abyss of nothingness as I breathe in the burning mist that forms along the shore, above and below my haunches already trapped in the sand.

O secrecy-security-safety and satiety: my intimate, lonely task as dawn breaks.

Speak to me, speak to me, speak to me until I fall asleep and forget you, hate you and leave you, abandon you or lose my mind.

Oh! Mon Amour! J'ai le fil, je suis désabusée! Impossible de t'expliquer encore, t'éveiller seulement.†

A jailor once and still a jailor: for how long?

You stretch your arms out to me and hold me fast in them, I am an animal to tame in your house with bread and a table and a son as well, and a door too. Let me go; let me leave and reject you and make you feel obligated and take shelter with you. Let me go; let me love you and call to you and spurn you. Let me go;

---

* Oh, come back, and you'll see how gladly I'll trample all my selves underfoot – the resigned one, the indifferent one, the bitch, the braggart . . .
† Oh! My love! I've found the thread – I'm not fooled any more! Impossible to explain to you – I just want to alert you . . .

let me accuse you and protect you and push you away and free myself and journey towards myself in you.

Ami, qui m'as fait mal et bonheur chaque fois un peu plus, je ne pleure pas. Même pas.*

What better plea can I send your way or use to hold you fast?

I bare my breasts and thighs, I caress your penis. How it grows harder and larger in my hand. I pass my tongue over it, slowly, lightly, and little by little it seeks out the warmth of my orgasm as I drink in yours, with its bitter acid taste. Then you move lower down, lower and lower, and begin to enter me, big and burning-hot and still erect. But I come immediately, I add to your self by becoming myself in you.

Ce soir, j'ai aimé en ton nom tous les hommes.†

Let me go away, let me forget you.

Stay. What can you possibly gain from my death, my madness, my restlessness, my suffering if you scoff at love and through one enslavement after another transform me into a more and more lowly creature, a creature more easily used and more useless with each passing day?

I am not yours, you have trapped me and regard me as your possession, closing your eyes to the truth; you do your best to own me body and soul and you know it – and I am a prisoner of your freedom.

How much time do I have left, I wonder?

You have some vague premonition, but you forget and impassively fall asleep at my side, as calm and peaceful as ever, gently stroking my hair.

Peut-être demain nous serons-nous rendus, peut-être jamais, peut-être la route, nous deux, qu'importe? Il n'y a pas de terre pour notre voyage.‡

---

* My friend, you who have hurt me and made me happy a little more each time, I'm not shedding any tears. What's the use . . .
† Tonight I loved all men in your name.
‡ Maybe tomorrow we'll have given ourselves up, maybe never, maybe the two of us will have taken to the road again – what does it matter? There isn't anywhere that we can journey together.

No, don't contradict me; I lay my head on your breast, and you hold me tightly, keeping me passive, wailing so softly that no one will hear my moaning, which you immediately seize upon for yourself, tenderly, greedily: and you lean down towards me: lean down over me. You watch me. You guide me. You dominate me. You imprison me.

*La mort même ne ferait pas ouvrir les doigts.**

I slowly open my legs, feeling the sperm trickle down onto the rumpled, wrinkled, loose sheets. Your lips gently rest on the burning wetness of my thighs.

Will I still have time?

Tell me: will I have time still?

See, love: I am going away now, taking possession of myself. The weapon pointed at your breast doesn't even seem threatening, merely cold, indifferent, watchful.

My love:

Will you be able some day to forgive me for this death?

Mónica

Maria is holding the revolver firmly in her steady hand, aimed straight at her soft, tender, vulnerable target. Only she sees the gaping hole through which the pain, the blood, all the world inside there, comes trickling out, slippery and sickly-sweet. Having traced a clean-cut, dazzling, burning-hot trajectory through her body, the bullet disappears somewhere inside her body, where it nestles, where it takes root.

She slowly falls, doubles over, falls, her hair over her face, over her shoulders, over her face again, on the floor now. As her fingers tense and relax, they clasp and claw the immobility that cautiously creeps closer and closer.

Meanwhile, the weapon is there in her hand (the source of power), still at the ready.

'How easy . . .' Maria thinks as she pulls the trigger.

15.5.71

* Even death could not pry those fingers loose.

The Prison

I walked up and down between those four walls with lumps of saltpetre and big dark brown stains, dragging my feet on the flagstones. I walked endlessly back and forth across that floor and also crawled over it on my hands and knees, and my not lifting my feet was due partly to exhaustion, but even more than that to the fact that it was an unnecessary effort when I knew every last inch of that floor by heart.

In one corner was the little brazier and the battered cooking pot, possessions acquired only with the greatest difficulty. Against the other wall was the cot, with its hard, lumpy straw mattress, covered with a single blanket, full of holes, thread-bare from so many washings and rewashings, now full of stains once again, with bits of dry earth and dung that had clung to his boots, since often when he came he would sprawl out there, adding to his other insults his deliberately irritating habit of rubbing his dirty boots on the holes in the blanket.

There were few other objects in that narrow space, and inside it a concern and preoccupation with everything and nothing, the slow coming and going of the daylight in the courtyard outside, a narrow space too, with a bucket of dirty water and a clump of weeds.

When he came in you could tell from his eyes that he was in a bad mood – one of those days when he would spew out new accusations, new suspicions, more of the usual insults. He sprawled out on the cot and left a new stain on the blanket, a gob of soft tar that would have to be scraped off with some dry stick picked up in the patio, and then scrubbed, but with what? – dry earth perhaps, to get out the sticky grease.

'This place is a disgusting mess, you haven't even washed the floor,' were his first words, followed by an order to bring him the cooking pot. 'Oh, you've been cooking potatoes, have you?' he said, and ate all the potatoes with his bare hands and then washed them in the water the potatoes had been boiled in, wiping the remaining traces of potato off on the edge of the blanket, and then – but why go into details about what happened next, it was all simply a provocation, a tactic to ferret out some reason for this stubborn silence so seldom broken, and still unbroken now, my eyes simply staring down at the empty pot and stirring the dirty water in the bottom, and then he said: 'Hurry up, throw this out, I won't allow such filth around here.' Words met with the same stubborn silence, and an acid, burning sensation in the pit of my empty stomach, and then him repeating: 'Hurry up, what sort of behaviour is this, how dare you drag your feet like that, I demand respect,' listening to the silence, watching my each and every gesture, searching for the slightest pretext that would allow him to step up the attack, to use brute force, and what difference would it make what gesture, what reply had provoked him, I might actually have used the word 'cop' or 'brute' or 'brutal cop' or something of the sort perhaps, but if that wasn't the pretext something else would be, and then would come the cross-questioning about my whole life, my comings and goings, my conversations, even my glances cast here or there, everything I did was suspect, evidence that I was involved in crimes and conspiracies. Then he leaped up from the cot and began to give me a series of careful, methodical kicks with his heavy boots, on the ankles first, then in the thighs, then in the genitals, his boots mounting up higher and higher as I doubled over, crouched down, curled up in a ball, the fire mounting also, the flesh opening to let in stinging jellyfish that settled down inside me, extending a network of burning pains that reached out like tentacles, with a fine line mounting from this wound in the flesh and thrusting itself up into my head, my neck, behind my eyes, my body now become a soft, unrecognizable mass held together only by pain, and the kicks continuing to mount up and up, along my belly, my ribs, my chest, my head, until finally my head touched the floor, exhausted, the limit of that inner collapse seemingly having been reached, but then everything became a sudden new shock, a new existence simply because of that draining and crushing within, with kicks in the eyes, in the mouth, in the nose, till everything went black, and I was simply a swollen, bleeding body lying there on the floor.

On coming to, I seemed to hear a voice repeating: 'So that's what you think, is it, so that's what you dare call me, is it?' – a monotonous sound that cast a magic spell over my descent into the abyss. My mouth touching the floor, my lips moving slowly, a whistling sound that told me that my two front teeth were broken – and suddenly I remembered everything, why I'd called him that, I remembered the night when José had done something, it's true, got into a brawl or passed out propaganda against the police or something like that, but I for my part have never had anything to do with papers or street fights, and why does he treat me like that – when I cook him his potatoes, take care of his clothes, and bore him the six sons that he made me?

17.5.71

Letter from Mariana Alcoforado to Her Brother-in-law the Count of C.

My Lord

How strange your visit seemed to me at first . . .

After having been a member of the family for so many years, why was it that only recently you troubled yourself to come pay me your respects and inquire after my health?

Calling me sister, something I do not understand since even my own sister does not call me that, you took my hand and your eyes sought mine as though in supplication, though your lips meanwhile forbore to utter words that must have been of the greatest import. Not daring to tell me why you had come, using subterfuges that demean the person who resorts to them, or displaying the sense of shame that suddenly overcomes a person who rightfully considers his actions to be wrong, you avoided any mention of the real motive for your visit, hurriedly and awkwardly attempting to say nothing about the message you were supposedly bringing or the reason that had brought you there, though certainly not out of shyness, since the look in your eyes was scarcely shy, my lord, as you clasped my hand in yours, your fingers trembling as they touched my wrist . . .

How bold you had become over all those years! When I knew you long ago, you were not dashing, nor were you possessed of a perfect talent for courtly compliments and gallant love poems. You appear to have learned a great deal from my sister, whom I also did not suspect of possessing such talents . . .

In the face of my calm composure, you tried to beat a hasty retreat, but it was too late . . . What an affront, my lord! What made you feel you had the right to insult me in that way, not even respecting this house of God? My unhappy love affair, doubtless, which must have caused a great deal of talk, at least within the family, as a consequence of which I have come to be regarded as the lowliest of women rather than the most un-happy, a woman to be bartered rather than an unfortunate creature who till the end of her days will be at the mercy of the man who enjoyed the right to sacrifice her, thus subjecting her, if necessary, to an even greater and more cruel humiliation.

I gave myself out of love, my lord, as a free gift, neither buying myself a husband nor selling myself as though I were merchan-dise. Out of love alone, and that must seem most strange to you.

I am not ashamed of, nor do I repent of anything that I have done, and you may so inform anyone you think may be interested in knowing such a thing. I never tried to keep my thoughts and feelings a secret, unlike Maria and my mother, both of whom are fond of masquerades and disguises. You surely must have realized this long ago . . .

I felt both pity and loathing for you at the same time, and I am revolted by your manners, which are those of a courtier astride a good mount, and by your intentions, which are those of a green youngster on the prowl. – What did you hope to gain by your visit? My favours and gasps of pleasure, rather than my total disdain and scorn? – you must have a very low opinion of woman-as-a-mistress, my lord, and you must regard loyalty as something of very little value, as you likewise must have little respect for suffering. Did not my pallor and my gauntness tell you what torment I am living in ?

Let me be buried, let me rest in my grave in peace, since they have shut me up here inside these walls as though I were being punished for a sin that I did not commit and do not even know the taste of. My mother demands that I silence my heart and put an end to my rebelliousness, perhaps because of her hatred for me; my sister, for her part, together with my brother, enjoins me to fulfil my duty to the letter and destroy myself, in the name of the vow of chastity that was forced upon me. My uncle also threatens me, unsheathing his sword . . .

Is locking me up in this convent not enough for my family? To what further humiliations will I be subjected?

Do not persist in your efforts to hurt me, to persecute me; the purpose of this letter is to inform you how useless it will be to try to see me again, and to tell you that Joana already has orders to explain to my uncle precisely what has happened on this occasion should such a thing ever recur and should you ever again summon me to the parlour, under the pretence that you represent the family.

You have now had your revenge for the scornful, mocking way I treated you in the splendid days of long ago when I was free, since the words that you failed to utter were most clearly expressed by your eyes, as your intentions were most clearly expressed by your hands.

Mariana Alcoforado

17.5.71

The Body

The body lay there asleep, nestled in its repose, in its rest, so
tranquil, so present in the yellowish light, defining itself by its
weight and by that state of quiet, all bathed in light, with no
outline separating the body and the light, the smooth muscles
beneath the skin, so languid in their silent presence, almost dis-
solving, the nest of their own repose, almost an extension of
the rumpled sheets and their drooping folds, and the warm hollow of the mattress, and the light as soft and thick as a yellow
skin laid over the other one, filling the room to the ceiling, from
wall to wall, enfolding like friendly bodies within its slumber
the lamp and the night table and the books and the clothes,
turning the entire room into concentric circles of light and varied
substances surrounding the centre, a nucleus of very soft breathing, communicating to everything round about this single, very
gentle movement, the golden skin stretching a little across the
chest with its swelling curve and its almost pink nipples, and the
ribs also moving with the same smooth, steady, gentle ebb and
flow of calm water, the broad, well-formed back tapering to the
waist with the clean-cut lines of hewn stone, but stretching out
from arm to arm in a high, gently rounded curve, with a sharp
hollow in the middle like the bed of a river, and the delicate,
angular hip bone still moving, abandoning its usual discreetness
and jutting out now from this body lying on its side and leaning
over slightly, a little hollow thus forming at the waist, hiding the
belly and the dense softness of the warm hairs, and a little bit of
the genitals, emphasizing the roundness – though it remains a
severe, chiselled roundness – of the two narrow buttocks, the sex
organ then appearing between the two legs that open, one of them
stretched out on the bed and the other one slightly flexed, the
thigh of the raised haunch resting on one knee on the bed almost
disappearing, and the lower leg sprawling out on the sheet,

almost crushing it with its weight, and between the thighs, being reborn of the shadow of the hidden belly stretching out like a burning plain, trapping within itself the yellow of the light, in the nascent curve of the buttocks, in the thighs, in the legs, between the thighs, the genitals, the two little apples whose firmness is outlined beneath the soft skin and the folded corolla of his sleeping penis.

18.5.71

Letter from a Man Named José Maria to António, His Childhood Friend

António:

I hope this letter finds you in good health, and also your mother, who's my godmother, and your sister Joana. I for my part am worn out but have no worse complaints, thank the Good Lord.

Like I promised I would, I'm sending you a few lines to tell you what to expect if you ever land up here in these parts, which could be better, I must say, because when we go out on mission we find ourselves slogging through mud up to our balls and it's hard going with our heavy weapons, not to mention our fear of being ambushed. The other day there was a guy who got his nuts shot off. And Francisco, the son of Aunt Maria from Abelha, do you remember him? His face wasn't even recognizable when we found him. And to think that he was about to leave for home because when I got here he had only a few more days before his time in the service was up, and then on the very last day he was sent out into the bush and got blown up by that land mine!

They say you have to accept your lot in life, but I just can't resign myself to the prospect of staying here for so many years and lots of times I get to thinking things you can't even imagine, and at night it's even worse. In the beginning I thought it was because of the heat that I couldn't sleep, but I can tell you it isn't just the heat, and then I tell myself 'you have to have a little fun, man,' but where the devil is a guy supposed to have a good time in this hellhole? There's no lack of women, but as you know I'm not really the kind to go in for that sort of thing, and besides I'm scared of catching some disease from them because all the other guys sleep with them. Some of the chicks are quite good-looking, with nice, firm, bare-naked tits, and sometimes you get so crazy in the head you couldn't care less what they smell like

189

or what colour they are . . . we're all the same, I know . . . but it upsets me and I keep thinking about these things after I've screwed them . . . Then there's all the shooting – it almost drives me crazy, and all I want to do is get out of there, so I crouch down as best I can, and if I'm telling you exactly how I feel deep down it's because I can't help writing you these lines – not only because we're old pals, but also on account of your sister Joana.

That girl makes my blood boil. She's got a mind of her own, damn it all. She's so stuck-up and stubborn that she's taken it into her head that she doesn't want us to get married now – 'It's better to end the whole thing,' she says in her letters, and all sorts of other nonsense like that. She's putting on airs now that she's got herself an education and it seems I'm not good enough for her any more because at one point I said to your mother, who's my godmother, 'Let her learn dressmaking if she's in such frail health and thinks she's too good to work in the fields the rest of her life. I'm not in favour of her getting herself an education.' But Joana insisted and Dona Mariana, who's such a great lady, so refined and so clever, sweet-talked her into coming to live with her, and dressed her up in fancy ribbons and laces and gave her books . . . spoiling her in all sorts of ways so that she's never been the same since. We've always been sweethearts, as you know, ever since we were kids, and now your sister's started sending me those letters telling me it's all over between us.

I'd like to ask you to try to get her to change her mind – the best way to deal with her is to be gentle with her and not go after her hammer and tongs, because as you know she's terribly pigheaded and it's hard to get the better of her.

António, Manuel das Vinhas will be bringing you this letter, because it will also give him a chance to talk to you about selling a little piece of land he wants to get rid of. Now that he's finished his military service and is through fighting, he also wants to stop farming.

I won't pester you any more for now – except to ask you to give my very best regards to your mother, who's my godmother. So good-bye for now, with a handshake from yours truly

José Maria

18.5.71

Of Walls and Flowers[27]

of words delaying (touching) sorrows
and of walls surrounding flowers

of flowers arming words
sending up fires
and of bastions growing higher
around the places of love

of sorrows sheltering
words like flowers
never freely spoken
because walls listen

which of us of sap (in blood)
walled-in flowers

20.5.71

Letter Sent to Mariana Alcoforado by Her Nursemaid Maria

Dearest Little Miss Mariana

I call you my little miss because that is the way I remember you and pray for you every night in my prayers, because I have never stopped missing you since the day you left this house, you poor little thing, nothing but skin and bones because you were so unhappy, yet still trying your best to console me, as though it were I who were being banished. May milord your uncle and milady your mother forgive me – both of them scold me when I shed tears for you.

Little Miss Mariana, I am writing you these lines because I am so concerned about milady your mother. For some time now, Miss Mariana, she has kept very much to herself here in this house, and has begun thinking about leaving for the villa in the country, with only me to keep her company while Miss Maria is in Lisbon with her husband, who, just between us, is a bad lot. What one does one pays for . . . and your sister . . . but it is best for me to hold my tongue, for otherwise I might let some truth slip out that is better left unsaid since nothing would be gained by revealing it.

But as I was saying, milady Dona Maria das Dores has been keeping to herself and brooding, scarcely eating or sleeping, and spending the entire day out in the burning hot sun. And once last week she stole out of bed in the middle of the night, went downstairs, and fell into a fit and collapsed on the floor of the little drawing-room. Froth suddenly began pouring out of her mouth and she started babbling words that made almost no sense. When I discovered her in such a state, I began to scream but since no one came to help, I stopped screaming and left the poor thing there on the floor with her head propped up on a pillow.

And it was then that I heard someone stealthily close the front door, and the sound of footsteps in the garden. I thought it very strange, and went to have a look around, since as you know I am not easily frightened. But whoever had been there was already in the street. As I was saying, I went to have a look and saw a man wrapped from head to foot in a cape, Miss Marianinha, running in the dark as though he knew precisely where his feet would land. I had sudden forebodings and ran to Dona Maria's room and then to all the other rooms in the house, but they all looked the same as usual and nothing was missing as far as I could tell at first glance.

For Dona Maria's sake, I said nothing of what had happened. And then when your poor mother came to her senses, she clasped my hands in hers and said, in a soft, subdued voice that I had never heard before, since she is always so haughty and harsh-spoken: 'I beg you, in the name of heaven, Maria, don't say a word about this to anyone.' But I thought I would burst if I didn't confide in someone and I knew that only my Miss Marianinha will understand and keep all this a secret, and at the same time counsel me as to what I ought to do, for I spend my nights thinking that I hear footsteps and running to Dona Maria's side, never knowing whether I shall find her with the whites of her eyes turned up and about to depart for the better world beyond. And to tell you the truth I have never known what to make of all this: I have no idea what that man was doing here inside the house if he was not a thief, nor why milady your mother had come downstairs at that very late hour, dressed only in her nightgown, when it was so cold, nor why she collapsed on the floor of the drawing-room with such a thud that it woke me up, nor why she refused to allow me to summon the doctor or write to Miss Maria to come. Heaven help me if my mistress should ever find out what I have written in this letter, Miss Marianinha, but I know how good-hearted my little missy whom I nursed with my own milk is, and since I can no longer bear to keep silent, I am seeking your counsel in the face of this train of events that has left your mother so troubled and so overcome with fear that she often breaks into a sweat, whereupon I take a cloth and carefully dry her contorted face and her sweat-drenched hair that clings to her head.

She will not live long, my child, if these fevers and anxieties continue. She can no longer leave her bed, or even lift her head from her pillow.

May God forgive me: it is only now that I can feel pity in my heart for her, and at the same time I find myself thinking that this is her punishment for having been so hard-hearted and done what she did to my missy.

And despite everything that has happened, she is still as hard-hearted as ever. In speaking to her of you just yesterday, she immediately bade me hold my tongue, in her usual voice, a voice of stone: a voice as icy and stony as the look in her eyes as she stared at me then, as white as chalk, her teeth clenched.
... I swear by all that's holy that her strange behaviour almost makes me think that she has gone raving mad ...

What ought I to do, Marianinha, whom can I trust to help me?

I beg you to forgive me, missy, if these lines have made you even more distressed than you doubtless are already.

I ask your prayers for me and beg you to accept the same fond kisses as ever, Miss Marianinha, from your faithful servant

Maria

23.5.71

Letter Found in a Sealed Envelope Among the Papers of Dona Maria das Dores Alcoforado

Senhora

Do not call my demands upon your body a form of extortion whereby I keep my knowing you intimately a secret by feigning to ignore you – I who have had my way with you for so many years now, having once possessed you as a means of avenging myself for long-standing quarrels and hatreds – when what is truly extortion is my having been unable to rid myself of the vice and the desperate need to keep you for myself, even though in secret, much more mine than if you were truly mine, inasmuch as even today, after all these years, I still prefer you to any other woman, though I do not really know whether what feeds this desire is merely your body or also the immense pleasure of betraying the person who craftily entrapped me and led me to have nothing but contempt for everything that I had previously respected.

I have already told you all of this long since, immediately after having made you mine, when you still thought that I had done so because we loved each other. I disabused you of such a mistaken notion forthwith, Senhora, by telling you what had led me to court you and pretend a love for you when the one thing I could possibly feel was hatred. You were merely a plaything, and at the same time a woman who belonged to my enemy whom I would never forgive (and never shall forgive), an innocent victim trapped in the web he was weaving, a pawn in the deadly game that he and I were playing, and hence a woman I coveted both in and of yourself and as his lawfully wedded wife. By winning you, I would crush this man's pride and destroy his honour, which he had always prized even more than his life and even more than you, Senhora, since I believe that your husband was less passionately in love with his wife than I, whose one aim in the beginning was simply to destroy him. But in the end you may rest assured that I destroyed myself as well, since I cannot do without you, ever since that day we first made love to each other, you full of illusions and I benumbed by my desire for vengeance, that day when I made you mine by promising never to reveal that I had possessed you.

And when have I ever possessed you?

What irony, Senhora: I won you by feigning a love I did not feel and came to care passionately for you, and what was then false is today true. And yet the only thing you now grant me is your hatred and scorn, together with the heat of your body, over which I run my fingers with the same bedazzlement as when you were still almost a child and ignorant of the world and its evil ways.

You became bitter and hard-hearted towards everyone, to the point of despising one of your daughters, who, poor thing, has never known why she has been the object of such vengeful fury on your part. For even though I have never been able to wrest from you the secret that you have kept so carefully hidden in your raging hatred against me, I nonetheless have reason to suspect that Mariana has my blood in her veins ... even though you deny it, you nevertheless give proof to the contrary, through the evil you have done her, as though she had not been conceived in your womb in the same way as her older brother and sister ...

Do not call my demands upon your body a form of extortion, but rather a vice and a desperate need, Senhora, for today it is you who are the extortionist, keeping me a prisoner of my fear of losing you, condemning me to endure forevermore the pain of knowing how much you hate me, and of being forced to forbear expressing my love for my daughter in order to keep her mother ... if only I might be permitted simply to speak to Mariana just once ...

What cruelty, Senhora!

Even if this is your way of punishing me in my very blood for having one day humiliated you, leave our daughter in peace, for she is guilty of nothing save having allowed you to make her unhappy!

In the end, which of the two of us, do you believe, has proved more monstrous, more relentless in our search for vengeance?

Very well, then, Senhora, I withdraw from the game and forfeit everything. As I said to you yesterday:

I shall thus lose you

Hence I free you at last of the humiliation of seeing me, of belonging to me, of waiting for me in the silence of the night. ... But by way of this letter I lay down my final condition, Senhora: in exchange for losing you, I demand Mariana's happiness.

Take her back home, deliver her from the bars behind which she is serving a prison sentence that she does not deserve.

I await your reply, inasmuch as you were unable to give me one yesterday, having suddenly been overcome by some terrible seizure on hearing my proposal, for reasons which I still do not understand, since it ought instead to have filled you with joy.

Or was it indeed happiness that made you feel faint, turn deathly pale, and stare fixedly into my face?

I would be tempted to say that it was as though you loved me, were I not so intimately familiar with your rancour, your nature, your soul that is even colder than your body ...

You have totally avenged yourself at last, Senhora, after all these years: or can it be possible that even this is not enough to satisfy you?

24.5.71

First Letter VII

I am thinking of both of you and making a distinction between you, though not distinguishing you from the totality we form. I cannot find the words, however, to tell you what role all of this – our project and our meetings together – has played in the upheaval that seems to have turned my entire life topsy-turvy recently. I feel that despite my respecting the rules for our meetings – our lunches and our evenings together – I have said nothing, and I confess I don't know whether or not it is because I feel completely apart from all of this, or whether on the contrary this is one of the tunnels that has opened up and shown me a way out; nor do I know what sort of life awaits me, and my bone-deep fatigue tells me that it is death I'm heading towards.

What sort of mother have we been to me: was that what it was all about? I paired the two of you off with a cavalier in a cell and gave birth to myself and am drifting aimlessly and helplessly along with you (with us), and I don't understand what is happening to you (to us): I cannot decipher texts or read signs. Or is it that I really can – but am afraid to? Is what is happening my fault (*j'accepte le meurtre*),* or do I consider myself the focal point of the disruptive differences I sense between us even when we are working together? But do such differences really exist? Let's take a closer look:

The last thing that you, my one sister, contributed to this written text was a section entitled 'The Prison', in which the reader was not supposed to be able to tell at first who is keeping whom a prisoner. *Et j'ai découvert ta fragilité et ta tendresse de grande pequena irmã*,† both across a great distance (that episode in our

* I admit to murder.
† And I discovered your fragility and your tenderness of a big little sister . . .[28]

professional lives involving the visit of a French 'specialist', during which I played roles ranging from that of 'housemaid' to 'Portuguese queen'), and in the closeness of working in the same place with you every day, in your bearing witness to the fact that I was approaching a turning-point in my life, in this sort of fear, in this feeling of imminent tragedy which always casts a dark shadow over times when everything is changing with frightening suddenness. You helped me. I help you. I tell you some things, but keep others to myself.

As for you, my other sister, it grieves me or frightens me to tell you this, but you hurt me.

Or is it the pain you feel because of this whole experience of ours that hurts me? You are the one who has written the most of our 'exercise', the many characters, the blood, the sex, the screams were your creation, and more recently you have invented this wanton, libertine Joana – you who knew Mariana the best. I see you in the night/day of your book in a bright red dress, at times furious with others, at times self-absorbed, at times voracious, and I feel your hostility – towards what? Towards the death in me, towards what was one day forever begun and has not yet been ended, towards this sort of apathy or a sort of mesmerized impatience that overcomes me when I see the energy with which you take control of everything and moisten it with something that is warm and vaginal, flowing down over the dry rod, the narrow haunches that you celebrate in verse, not wanting to destroy them. Why did you choose *me* to to exorcize yourself of yourself/of us? Why do I say such things? *Tu ressembles à ma mère et tu n'aimes que l'autre; voilà ma plainte devant toi.**

But the other, the one with the serene face, also shares our lives. How peaceful and warm it would be for me to be able to speak of the two *yous* as a single *you*. and now that I have written/ said this, it seems to me that I can do so. You identified me with Maina and left me room to defend the chevalier, whom I felt had been too harshly dealt with, and just look in what direction I am headed when we meet now – towards Mariana, sealed up within herself, fashioning a de luxe coffin for those of her own

* You resemble my mother and love only the other one of us; that is what I reproach you for.

kind, without faith like you, my one sister, who have faith in nothing, and without determination, like you, my other sister, who are determined to change everything; without your magnificent body, my one sister, and without your magnificent face, my other sister. In the end I am a 'signal gently raised on high', more smoke than phallus – can it be, my friends and sisters, that I am becoming a phantom at your/our command?

24.5.71

Letter from a University Student in Lisbon Named Mariana to Her Fiancé (?) António, Who Has Taken Off for Parts Unknown

How many thousands of years do these three months add up to? And yet when you split, I wasn't sure of anything (and will I ever be?). They say that absence makes the heart grow fonder – can that be why I mope around, feeling as though I'm all by my lonesome in a total vacuum? Or is it because you're so different from all of this, from everything that's left, from the silence that's set in, from these nights loafing around doing nothing, from listening to dumb lectures by dumb profs, from the Movement that's turned into nothing but bullshit they sell on records and posters. And what am I doing here in the middle of this whole zoo, I keep wondering – even though I don't have any reason to desert. On the contrary: I simply fall in ranks, get in line, and go along with the whole thing: but it's all such crap.

How far did we get? We read this and that, we took walks together and felt sorry about everything and everybody, we had some great lays like the little fuckers that we are, you made me come and all that whole bit, and you know the only thing that really sticks in my mind? That last night, the last two nights – me with my hair needing washing and not caring a bit and you with your face all battered, saying, 'Damn, I've got to desert,' and the two of us standing there looking at each other as though we'd just realized for the first time what the score really was, and still not being able to say one word that wasn't out of books, some book or other from that whole mess of books, after we'd taken off under full sail for our first honest to goodness confrontation with the cops, because up to that point it had been the same as with all the rest, we'd 'protested' exactly as we were expected to, with your father 'having dialogues' with you about Marcuse and my mother paying for my boots and my miniskirts and even being ever so tactful and 'understanding' and slipping me dough for 'the pill'. *My* mother, that is. There's no such thing for me any more as *the* old lady and *the* old man – that definite article that the gang uses to designate/define their parents, since all of us had exactly the same kind. The Father and The Mother, in capital letters – like the Reverend Father and the Reverend Mother in the last century in those schools run by priests and nuns for kids from all the well-known families (and well known to each other, down to the last skeleton in the closet and the last cent in their bank accounts), the definite article defining them as part of the original magma out of which people crystallized (and still crystallize today): either this or that, male or female, son or daughter of so and so, and that was enough (and still is enough today). But I don't understand any of it, and don't even know what to say *no* to, because today even saying *no* is just something that keeps the cash registers ringing. And I look at them and my so-called brothers (because when you have real brothers it's something you keep hidden), and it seems to me that everything I have to do with them, with their rites and their rules (even the cultural ones) has all turned to dust, now that I'm faced with – what? With your being gone, you who were such a great pal of mine (but what else were you besides that?), or my loneliness after you decided to desert, no doubt because you'd been bashed over the head in the canteen that Friday and told the gang you were going to skip the country, or maybe because of who you really are after all. In the middle of this zoo, this soap opera, we can only know who we really are by lighting out for somewhere – you for foreign parts and me deep down inside my loneliness for you.

I'm falling apart, having been ripped to pieces by the struggles involved in the cycle that's taken me from being educated to being informed to being amused, with the 'right crowd' of course: this feeling that somebody has planted his foot on my neck when I realize that you had all the same vices I did and yet, maybe because the needle that indicates who the 'right crowd' is simply didn't register properly in your case or because you had so many gifts that the Establishment refused to put to use, you left all that behind by leaving me. And poor little me: I can imagine you so well there in Paris, meeting up with someone, perhaps at the Joie de Lire bookstore or some other favourite haunt of yours these days, who will latch on to you and take you to chic dirty parties, and I can see myself taking up tearful love laments inherited from genteel ladies in Galicia and Douro, and because I'm educated, also discovering that in Alexandre O'Neil's famous line, '*não é para mim este país*'* (do you remember how all the gang devoured his poetry?).

Jorge Listopad staged António Patrício's *O Fim*, written in 1909, at the Casa da Comedia recently. I went to see it with the gang. It began to steal inside me through my eyes and throb in my head and at that point all those ragged costumes and the text suddenly began to seem not just clever staging and a well-written play but amazingly *pertinent* to the whole gloomy situation today, and crept into my vitals and stayed there: 'The only thing left to us is our inner feelings, only our innermost feelings.' Some of the gang can't understand why Listopad chose that particular play, and claim it has nothing to do with what's happening today – the vague 'foreigners' crossing the bar and entering the city, the population of Lisbon snatching up ridiculous arms and allowing themselves to be massacred 'in the name of our people', and the queen, ah the queen – you would have had to see the play, but believe me, she's part of us, we all have her inside us, and that's what makes Patrício's interpretation of that sort of woman perfect, absolutely perfect – you know the type, the little lost soul whose heart is broken, a foreigner in rags, the dim memory of her former glory stamped upon a body destined merely to be stripped bare and to endure her fate day by day until the bitter end, the *fim* of the title – a chick pretty much like me, really, tiny and refined and oh so sensitive, saying softly: 'I'm hungry.'[29]

António, I want so desperately to go away and I want so desperately for you to come back. What harm did we ever do that made them bring us up to be little kings and queens sitting on thrones for sale, what harm did we ever do to be forced to suffer all this dissension and all these separations on account of the African question? *Je t'aime, je t'aime* – how can you say a thing like that in Portuguese? – *je t'aime*

Mariana

29.5.71

* 'This country is not for me.'

Text on Solitariness

'You are beautiful,' the man said, running his hands down her body lying naked and exposed on the bed, one of her legs bent back, and the other stretched out along the sheets.

'You are beautiful,' the man said again, following the curve of her breasts with his fingers, noticing her tensed lips beneath his and the profound, acid revulsion reflected in her eyes.

'I love your hair, your concave belly, your thin hips, your arms, your thighs, your smell, your tongue. I like it that you feel revulsion for me but still come to bed with me.'

He leaned down then, running his mouth over her as though he were trying to breathe her in, leaving on her skin a wet scar of saliva; his flaccid body voraciously attempting to take on firmness and hardness inside that of the woman who was struggling, though still motionless and rigid. But struggling nonetheless.

Mónica thought: 'I'm going crazy.'
Mónica thought: 'I'm going crazy.'

The man was eager to possess the soft velvety terrain of her skin and devoured her freshness with thick kisses, drank in the motionless fragility of her neck and her brief gesture, in order to prolong it. With a brusque motion he pinned her thin wrists to the sheets.

Petrified, Mónica felt him start to enter her, slowly at first, his sex organ still soft and hesitant in its semi-impotence, and then larger and hotter, impatient, clumsy. A small, atrophied penis inside her deep, soft woman's vagina enlarged by love-making and amorous bouts in bed and profound orgasms.

He saw her hard, staring eyes, as acid as transparent stones, of a translucid, rare blue, like water or the sea, but above all else: harsh, unyielding eyes.

Mónica saw the man's eyes, tiny and bloodshot, dark brown with little dirty yellow specks, lost in hers.

Mónica heard the man's groans each time he came and went inside her.

She felt the man's sticky sweat and the flabbiness of his belly as it spasmodically sprawled across her hips and belly.

Then her revulsion let loose, like a spring; it mounted, scaldingly, overwhelmingly: a giant wave clogging her throat, concentrating there in a lump of vomit that she swallowed, stunned, nauseated.

The man strained to come, exhausted, his organ lost within that dry, hostile, inhospitable vagina. He strained in that spongy flesh, ragingly, the palms of his hands stretched out flat on the bed. In a rapid, pendulum-like motion, he moved in and out of her, to hasten the orgasm trapped in his empty, spermless testicles.

Mónica thought: 'I'm going crazy.'
Mónica thought: 'I'm going crazy.'

thinking from the beginning of her husband and her love and desire and passion for him that refused to remain silent, that would never remain silent, becoming an enormous scream.

Mónica screamed:
slowly, intermittently. A monstrous scream like a monstrous, stabbing pain.

Lost in that scream, the man became excited, pinned the woman down, forced her over on her back, and gripping her with firm knees, his fingers digging into her pendulous breasts, forced her anus open and entered it, tearing her, and climaxed immediately filling her with his watery, tepid milk. And then he became excited again and came at her once more to wreak his vengeance upon her; immediately dirtying her with his sex organ, clamping his mouth shut to make her aware that he was savouring the taste of his victory.

Mónica waited for him to go to sleep. She listened attentively to his breathing, and then with slow, careful, deliberate movements she picked up a pillow, put it over his face and with all the strength of her desperation pressed down on it, struggling against the convulsive grasp of the man's arms, lying on top of his body, her legs pinning down his as he fought to throw her off, the two of them remaining thus, locked together, until she stopped feeling him move, and even long after, lying stretched out for hours there on top of his already-cold body, sleeping, her head resting on the pillow over his face.

29.5.71

Letter Written by Mónica M., on the Morning She Committed Suicide, to Dona Joana de Vasconcelos

My dear Joana

I felt so at peace in my house that I awoke from my silences with a start, wracked by a pain more piercing than if I had been run through with a sword or a keen-edged dagger drawn from its sheath.

'Mónica, you are sleeping, you are sleeping,' you used to say to me, digging your fingernails into my arms, and I would smile dreamily, not understanding you, but believing those who had told me how outrageously you behaved.

Having married out of passion, I was inflamed by it and blinded by it, forgetting myself entirely, my hair lying loose on the pillow, simply waiting for my husband to take me, neither caring nor noticing whether he was taking me out of love or merely making use of me.

Did I ever ask whether he loved me?

Did I ever ask how much my dowry had been and what was written in the marriage contract? Did I ever ask if my father had bought me a husband, giving me to a man for whom I was not a woman to his liking? – I was so madly in love that I always took his silences for mere passing moods and his rages as fits of jealousy, and in my ardour even regarding his coldness as of little consequence.

How blind with passion I was, Joana, never imagining that anyone was deceiving me.

'Mónica, you are sleeping, you are sleeping,' you used to say to me, and today I see, I know, that you were on the point of revealing to me what I had failed to see.

207

That is why I am writing to you, sharing my weeping and wailing only with you, a woman who grew up with this sound continually ringing in her ears, though never resorting to such behaviour herself, being unhappy without ever bemoaning her fate, making her own life a weapon, a battle. I marvelled at you. And it is your courage that even today serves me as my example as I make a person of myself.

How many times we talked about ourselves, and I used to laugh at all the things you said, never taking you seriously, refusing to take Mariana's place and faithfully follow you and adopt your principles as my own.

How blind I was, lost in my own fantasies and my gentle dreams; and how terrified I became as little by little the truth made me cold and indifferent to everything . . .

Do not weep for me, Joana, for by doing what I am about to do I am regaining my self-respect. I can no longer tolerate his treating me in such a humiliating, perverse way, thinking up new tricks every day now that he knows that I am aware of his true nature, and I can see no other way for a woman to free herself (what other way is there, Joana?), for what other path is there to follow save this one, my every gesture calm and deliberate and as joyless now as life itself . . .

I was traded for another and never loved even when I was possessed: this enrages me, humiliates me: surrendering myself to him, hiding none of the pleasure I felt, my soul stripped bare and my body exposed in all its ecstasies, all its frailties, all its innermost tortures.

'Use him,' you said to me yesterday. 'Use him if all that pleases you so much, if that man gives you so much pleasure.'

I had not told you of my torments, Joana: his contempt, his refusals, his cold, inert body.

How I reproach myself for not listening to you, for sleeping while you did battle, my sister. But the future does not yet belong to us, nor will it belong to my daughter, nor even to her daughters.

I entrust Mónica to you; her father will surely abandon her to you with the greatest of pleasure. Take her for yourself; you will know how to guide her far better than I.

I kiss you forever and always, and remember, Joana, do not weep for me, I beg you.

Mónica

Before overturning the chair, Mónica slowly passed her hands over her naked body which would hang in front of the open window exposed to the bright morning light.

Outside, she could still see the branches of the trees moving restlessly, stirred by a wind heavy with rain.

30.5.71

Third Letter V

My sisters:

But what can literature do? Or rather: what can words do?

1.6.71

Extracts from the Diary of Ana Maria, Born in 1940, a Direct Descendant of the Niece of Dona Maria Ana

My ancestor Maria Ana, the philosopher, what point have we reached: if the woman still has nothing, if she exists only through the man, if even the occasional pleasure she receives from him is meagre and perverse, what does she risk or what does she stand to lose by rebelling? Revolution is a dangerous game, and the bourgeois citizen taking part in the French Revolution risked everything, even though the objectives of his attack were limited; but what does a man risk or stand to lose, if none of her needs are satisfied? What, then, were you complaining about? I am well aware that this is not the real problem; I know that this is a false argument; but this whole question is an important one nonetheless.

I am well aware that revolt on the part of the woman is what leads to disruption in every social class; nothing can ever be the same afterwards, neither class relations, nor relations between groups, nor relations between individuals. The very roots of repression must be destroyed, and the basic repression, the one which in my view lies at the very core of the history of the human species, creating the model and giving rise to the myths underlying other repressions, is that of the woman by the man. So long as this situation persists, no understanding between men and women will be possible; even the way we want to bring up our children will be a matter of contention. Everything will have to be entirely different, and we are all afraid. And amid all this, the woman's real problem is not whether she is going to win or lose; it is, rather, the problem of her identity. There is little doubt that in this society there are many things she finds satisfying; but there is even less doubt that the woman (and the man as well) are not aware of how they are manipulated and conditioned. Perfect repression is the sort that is not felt by the person suffering from it, the sort that is unconsciously accepted, thanks to a traditional upbringing spanning many long years, with the result that the mechanisms of repression come to be internalized within the individual, and hence become a source of personal gratification. And if perchance a woman becomes conscious of her enslavement and rejects it, with whom can she identify herself, how can she acquire an identity of her own? Where can she relearn how to be a real person, where can she reinvent the model, the role, the image, the gestures and the words of her life from day to day, the acceptance and the love of others, and the signs of acceptance and love? I am very much aware, Maria Ana, my ancestor, of what you were complaining of, of what you were incapable of: of inventing, all by yourself, the mother, the heroine, the ideology, the myth, the matrix that would give you substance and meaning in the eyes of others, that would open up a path leading to others – if not a path of communication, at least one of shared concerns and anxieties.

And what did you invent in your endeavour to reshape your presence, in your own time and place? You refused a husband, you refused a man, and what this gesture means to us is that you were a spinster, a frustrated, hysterical woman, like all women without a man, writing pretentious texts, just as you would pamper a poodle or take an active part in organized charities were you alive today. And that is the particular coloration you have in my mind's eyes, too, I think that is how you were, at least in part, or perhaps fundamentally, despite the fact that I understand you, and despite the fact that I recognize that I therefore also fear you. Where is there a place to reinvent gestures and words? Everything is permeated with time-hallowed meanings, including our own selves, down to our very bones, our very marrow, even in the case of us women who are attempting to bring about a revolution. Looking at you, Maria Ana, I recognize reluctantly, like everyone else, various facets in you whose colours blend, despite the fact, or perhaps because of the fact, that a number of them were contradictory: the woman who refused to confront others directly, who feared shared pain and experience, a spurned woman whom nobody wanted, perhaps because of your refusal, perhaps not; but in any case a spurned woman is a figure whom society scorns and detests, and in this contempt lies the punishment that we try to escape by surrendering ourselves, without seeking another alternative, since this contempt is more than ample reason for us to cast aspersions on the refusal of a woman to accept a man and instead live by herself, either out of natural inclination or through deliberate choice on her part. Hence we suspect such a refusal of being tinged with bitterness, puritanism, or frigidity, and attach great importance to the consequences of this refusal – loneliness, aridity, frustration – using them as threads to begin weaving the whole pattern all over again: the blame heaped on the woman who lives by herself (if you don't have a man it's because you're puritanical or frigid, and so you're frustrated – and why is it that I presume that you are a virgin?), while at the same time the man who rejects women is surrounded by a certain aura of absurd but haughty superiority. We accept his rejection of what is all too familiar, the exercise of his sex drives on the body of another, his sexual desire that is never questioned (no one will ever presume that he is a virgin even though he may well be one), his sex that is ever visible and complete ,whereas the woman who rejects a man always seems to us to be inferior and ignorant, evading an awareness of her sexuality, such as it would be revealed, shaped, and taught to her by a man, fleeing the power of the male as though he were an adversary long since vanquished, avoiding the inevitable defeat that in our heart of hearts we all consider quite natural. Maria Ana, my ancestor, that is how we see you, that is why I am hostile to you despite your being my sister, in this era which many call an age of equality, when women's work is now worth money (though very little) and women's words are now being heard (and misunderstood). Will the day ever come, Maria Ana?

13 April, 1971: a day not purposely chosen – reading articles in an evening 'progressive' paper, thought-provoking, instructive reading:

The fashion game – how long are skirts going to be this next summer? Will they stop at calf-length? Professional buyers are playing the game – and placing their bets – the world over; what is at stake is the industry that answers one of the three fundamental needs of humanity – food, clothing, and shelter; the textile and clothing industry brings Italy a billion dollars annual revenue; the fear of buying the wrong thing; a problem that has come to complicate the summer fashion picture is that of 'hot pants'; if a daring offensive is not mounted in the field of fashion, these tiny little enemies may well seize this opportunity to strengthen their hold.

A 'new chapter' in the special *cinéma-vérité* series – a story that has happened yesterday, that is happening today, and will happen tomorrow, so long as there exists a 'market' for buying and selling happy hours. This episode was about a lady pianist; her 'calling' was to find love without ever becoming attached to a man; but there was one man for whom she was different . . .

The television critic insisted that it could just as well have been a 'doctor' or a 'journalist' or an 'actor' or a 'manu-facturer' or a 'factory worker' as a pianist; anyone who is alien-ated, turned into a consumer product. In the film Catarina, the pianist, sees the possibility of making a new life for herself, of refusing to be turned into an object in such a cruel way, she will stop giving concerts and just make records, and at Christmas-time she plans to return to her catalyst-journalist; but she is never reunited with him because the plane that she takes ex-plodes. There had been a discussion following a showing of the film – a male critic, Ramos, had wondered whether a *wanton woman* could ever aspire to love, and a woman critic, Horta, had said that it was called a love story because it was the story of a *lady* pianist rather than a *man* pianist, but the critic maintained that it could just as well have been a 'doctor' or a 'factory worker' as a pianist (male or female), since the real problem was that of the consumer society, and so he reported that the dis-cussion had turned into a '*dull exchange of banal remarks by ladies sitting eating their little teacakes and drinking their little cups of tea*' (all it takes is to substitute the word 'ladies' for 'doctors', 'journalists', 'manufacturers', 'factory workers'); you are quite right, Dona Maria, that's terribly ill-bred, isn't that something though, just imagine, won't you have another teacake?

A model is practically a synonym for a candidate aspiring to movie stardom. And this is precisely the case with the young girl (shown in the photograph above, in a bikini) who got herself a role in a film, even though it is a non-speaking role; she will not be required to say a single word; but she's on her way to becoming an actress.

Miss Mozambique arrived in Lisbon wearing a 'native costume' (a photograph of the aforementioned beauty with a large group of smiling girls also in native costumes posing on a flight of steps).

Ministry of Finance, General Accounting Department, Personnel Division ... announces a competitive examination for Grade 3 administrators, *open to male candidates only* ...

The automated kitchen, the invention of a harried man – his wife was in the hospital, and he was staying home to take care of the couple's four children. Markus Beck (a mechanical engineer) tried his best to do all the housework and look after the children, but the dirty dishes in the sink kept piling up higher and higher; foundering in this sea of troubles and tasks (and why did they describe him as 'a mechanical engineer whose wife was in the hospital' when they might have said 'wife who was pregnant for the fifth time'?), he invented the automated kitchen.

To sum up:

The fashion game to cover or not to cover the knee
that is the question: an industry fundamental needs
providing food, clothing, and shelter for humanity
brings in annual profits of millions of dollars
buyers from all over the world are playing the game
clothes designers fear the tiny 'hot pants' enemy
giving fashion sales a world-wide shot in the arm
with long skirts
the latest chapter in the special truth series
happening today, happening tomorrow
as long as there are such things as movies markets
the buying and selling of happy hours her calling was to find a
    man
and the piano and the market and the journalist as long as there
    is
one for whom she was different and love
the critic is satisfied to substitute the word lady pianist for
    journalist
or doctor or factory worker and substitute Dona Maria
for the lady pianist and replace rebellion

by teacakes and can you imagine such a thing
being a critic is ill-bred
model almost synonymous with a role
she won't be required to say a single word she's on her way to
    being
Miss Native Costume in the general accounting office
grade 3 administrators belonging to the male sex
needing only a certificate
of proficiency a harried engineer invented
four children and the automated
kitchen
while his wife was in the hospital.

An electronics industry is being developed. Women are being recruited, for their fingers have a delicate touch, thanks to the fine embroidery, the lacework, and other domestic and regional crafts that they have been taught to do – the best possible fingers for assembling electronic equipment. They are paid a mere pittance, since naturally they are unskilled labour, with no specific training for their present jobs as factory workers; it is easy to exploit them, for they are unaware that industry will profit from their already-acquired skills without paying a single extra cent for it; they do not even know that their fingers have been trained, and it seems to them that their lot in life has already changed for the better if someone puts their insignificant female talents to use, being powerless creatures who heretofore have not been good for much of anything, since bearing children doesn't count. Jobs in industry are becoming available for women; that's fine, that proves they're making progress. Equal pay for equal work; but the work is not equal, how is it possible to compare jobs, when men do different things and only women are used for this difficult work in the electronics industry? Young ones, preferably unmarried ones, so that they won't miss work because of family problems. Later it is all quite simple: when they are old enough to get married and have children, or at any rate after having worked for five years or so, they quit; hence the problems of absenteeism, promotions, demands for higher wages are reduced. Replacing personnel is not a problem either; on the contrary, women are already skilled workers when they are hired, and they leave once they're no longer useful, that is to say, when they are exhausted, their eyes ruined, and their nervous systems badly damaged.

Women – and blacks – are also turning up nowadays as workers on road-construction projects and as city street sweepers. Up until recently, these jobs were not regarded as suitable for women. But now that men – white men – no longer want them, because they are backbreaking and pay very badly, they are becoming woman's work.

Merely an example, from which no generalizations can be drawn? On the contrary: this sums up the history of the so-called improvement in the condition of women through access to jobs. But there is also the example of the accountants' jobs for males only; the rules governing competitive examinations for the filling of vacancies in almost all state agencies, where preference is given to men, except for those jobs that they do not want; the various ads in the papers 'company seeks female employees . . .' When we read or hear that 'Nowadays women work side by side with men in the most varied sectors of activity', this means, when translated into the terms of the real situation: women today are being utilized in sectors of the labour market, professions, and functions that men have now rejected in favour of others that offer them better working conditions and better pay.

How has the situation of woman changed? Today she is FREE OF LAUNDRY PROBLEMS WITH A WASHING MACHINE. And there are female beauty contests, with the beauties in bathing suits – practically bikinis – turning to the front, to the rear, to the right, to the left. And there is not a single protest from the television critics, some of whom pride themselves on being so 'progressive'. That's not what people are concerned about, there's no 'woman's problem', the real problem lies elsewhere, so why all the fuss? The great majority of middle-class people, who nowadays are no longer landowners, have no appreciable power; the great majority of them make their living by doing intellectual work, by engaging in their liberal or non-liberal profession, lost in a mass society. So who's afraid of an attack on private ownership of the means of production, of an attack on the power elite or pressure groups? Only the very few who would be directly affected. But they all 'have' women; and THEREFORE there is no 'woman's problem', that's just so much nonsense; that's not the real issue at all. As for the exhibition of human females, not a single protest has been forthcoming from the television critics. It's even a step in the right direction, one of them has said: beauty has ceased to be a sin and ugliness a virtue; it's a public homage to female pulchritude. A woman can buy a washing machine and enter a beauty contest to show off her arse and her legs. How has the situation of the woman changed? Once an object that was a producer, of children and so-called domestic labour, that is to say non-remunerated labour, she has now also become an object that consumes as well, and a consumer product. Once upon a time she was like a piece of farmland, something to be made fertile, and now she is commercialized, something to be distributed.

And eroticism, gentlemen, what about eroticism? In almost all the so-called erotic books that are everywhere today, *il n'y a pas de femmes libres, il y a des femmes livrées aux hommes*: there are no women delivered from their bondage, only women delivered over to men. That is the sort of liberation that men offer us; after being the warrior's repose, we are becoming spoils of war. The charwoman who used to clean the office where I work died of septicaemia after aborting herself with a stalk of celery, and a few days ago I learned from one of her co-workers that it had been her twenty-third abortion. And a number of years ago a woman friend of mine who is a doctor told me that women who entered the hospital emergency ward with their uteruses perforated, torn to shreds, ruined forever after attempting to abort themselves at home with knitting needles, sticks of wood, cabbage stalks, and anything else they had at hand that would penetrate and scrape, were treated with the greatest of contempt, and that the curettages they were then subjected to were performed without any anaesthetic whatsoever, coldly and sadistically, 'so as to teach them a lesson'. To teach them what lesson, for God's sake?! To teach them that they have been the victims of the contradiction (concealed beneath the mask of what is supposedly

218

their inevitable fate) that society has created between the fecundity-demanded-of-a-woman's-womb and the place-denied-women-for-raising-children? Ever since the destiny of the man and the woman irremediably branched off in two opposite directions – but when, O when, did this happen? – the woman has fallen victim not only to all the existential anguish and all the forms of social repression that are the common fate of both men and women, but also to the anguish of her biological destiny, become her drama alone rather than a dramatic experience of our entire species, thereby falling victim to a repression whose instrument is this biological destiny of hers that has been turned into an individual drama. Lovers pass by in pairs and we know that they are irremediably separated one from the other; there is no love between a man and a woman that is worth the pain, for in the love-experience the woman is at the very limits of the agonizing, repressive, and lonely fate that society has invented for her. What good did love do Romeo and Juliet?

1.6.71

Mónica

Mónica awakens.

She awakens as though she had been wrenched from sleep by a sudden, unexpected noise: a cry, for example, or a chair falling over on to the wood floor without a rug on it: a chair falling over all of a sudden on to the slippery waxed floor, a chair that has toppled over because of someone's clumsy gesture, or been overturned on purpose, in despair or icy indifference or great agitation.

Mónica doesn't know. She opens her eyes, and realizes that she is in her bed: her heart is pounding wildly; her hands clutch the sheet and pull it up towards her bosom.

She listens:

Silence envelops the house in its heavy veil. She keeps listening, as though she cannot believe this quiet that she feels is attempting to deceive her, to take possession of her by way of her vitals, her dark, rough womb. She tries to look around the room, but because the oil in the little lamp is no longer feeding the wick and the flickering light that normally disturbs her at night, projecting threatening shadows, stealthy, fleeting phantoms on the walls, has gone out, she is unable to make out the pieces of furniture, the familiar objects, though she sees them in their usual places in her mind's eye, knowing precisely where they are, having decorated the room herself with objects made of porcelain, metal, brittle old wood, or new wood with a sharp, acid odour that obsesses her.

She gropes about: her fingers feel the thin fabric of the bed-spread, which she pushes away. She slowly puts her feet on the floor and with outstretched hands, feeling her way like a blind woman, walks in the direction of the window, thinking that she can see a frayed, dirty streak of light through the cracks of the shutters, the first light of dawn, still diluted by the darkness of the night. First her fingertips touch the high window-sill and then she stretches on tiptoe to reach the iron bolt that is firmly fastened. She climbs up on the narrow ledge and, though she cuts herself, she manages to slip the bolt, which slides open with a squeak as it rips her skin.

Mónica licks and sucks the acrid blood until she feels the cut stop bleeding; then with great effort she manages to open the huge heavy shutters over the window; dawn is really breaking now, at once hesitantly and rapidly. She runs her hands over the clouded window-panes, wet with feeble little trickles, trapped somehow on the smooth surface of the glass and listlessly cling-ing to the skin of her wrists as they trace enormous circles in that cold sweat, in that steam laden with moisture: a sort of saliva and mucus.

The morning filters in through the ragged openings in the trees and settles on the walls of the house, casting intense, mo-tionless reflections in certain spots, and in others spreading out in dull, torpid patches.

Mónica watches the scudding clouds heavy with rain, her eyes following them as though she were trying to impress them on her memory forever. She slowly shakes her head, with a tense, restrained motion. Suddenly she halts, petrified. She listens again to the emptiness spreading through the house, penetrating its rooms, searching through them in order to suck people into its treacherous belly.

Mónica knows now that something is really moving there in the house, something threatening: an almost inaudible creaking sound reaches her, a creaking that seems to have been labori-ously expelled from her own vitals. A creaking that only she hears, shivering with terror, her hair standing on end. She curls up in a ball, out of a sort of self-defence; she stifles her unbear-able desire to scream, to hide herself in the bed and scream and scream until someone comes to help her.

Mónica digs her fingernails into the palms of her hands and walks towards the door, which has suddenly opened, and then the creaking sound becomes clearer, more precise, much closer. She walks slowly down the hall, tripping on her long nightdress; a huge hall, lined on each side with doors, all of which are closed at this hour. Mónica halts: the door to her mother's bedroom is standing wide open, but the room is empty. Mónica staggers, and is about to scream; she looks at the unmade bed, and is about to scream. But suddenly she begins to run up the stairs, slips and falls, gets up, and begins running again. She knows that danger lurks; the dull, thudding noise, the regular, pendulum-like sound continues, seeming to dominate, to devour the entire house.

The chair has fallen over backwards in the middle of the little room; Mónica does not understand: her mother's hair is hanging down, and the rope which she is dangling from, the other end of which is fastened to a hook driven into the ceiling, seems to be made of her hair too. Mónica then clings to that naked body slowly swinging back and forth in front of the window. The white body, still warm, in which she buries her face, on which she rests her head. The body that she cradles in her arms, with neither despair nor grief. Her mouth glued to that soft, familiar skin, as though to drink from it or conserve in it, to breathe from it, to breathe into it her own warmth.

5.6.71

Letter Left by Mónica M. for Dom José Maria Pereira Alcoforado

José Maria

How to explain to you the reason for my death and for my not loving you . . . the growing despair that drives me to abandon life, I who have traced its imprint on my body with my own hands and my own voracity.

I refused to surrender my mouth, my breasts, my womb to you, without having first told you that my thoughts and desires were directed towards another. But I never confessed to you that it would be impossible for me to one day come to love you, to not push you away, suddenly turning deathly pale and overcome with loathing at having given myself to anyone save him: my eternal obsession and the object of my contempt, but also my love – your one role, José Maria, having been that of a means of avenging myself or forgetting, of benumbing myself, of venting my fury.

You did not deserve that, I know, and I am sorry: for you, not for me, since I have always known myself to be weak and foredoomed to unhappiness and anguish.

Forget me, I beg you!

Forget me, even if in order to do so you will be obliged to hate me, but forget me, I implore you!

In the end, what difference can my absence from this world make to you, if all I gave you was my absence from myself . . . For I was always far, far away, even when I lay sleeping in your arms . . .

Mónica

8.6.71

Paper Found Between the Pages of a Book Belonging to Dom José Pereira Alcoforado

How, my love, can I explain to my heart and my body your death, your absence, your remoteness from yourself, your violence directed against your own flesh?

You made your blood run dry, you made it sterile, a captive, so as to turn your veins into places where nothing breathes and everything is lost . . .

How much of the fault lies with me, how much am I to blame, I ask myself, having obliged you to follow my mad rambling trains of thought, to which you listened so attentively, with a vacant, faraway look in your eyes, remembering the pain that you were suffering.

And even if you never loved me, nonetheless . . . you held out your arms to me and were my haven and my comfort, my only safe anchorage in this life.

But what use is it now to think of you and think of us, the taste of your mouth melting on mine, the soft contours of your body dizzying my senses . . . The soft contours of your body, my love, that body that I never truly knew, even when I ran my hands over every inch of it or held it beneath mine, fragile and almost fluid, pale and lithe in the desire that I knew beforehand would be carefully restrained or only reluctantly expressed as you lay in my arms, so distant and remote, and surrendered yourself to me.

Indeed, what use is it to think of you, when you are lying rotting in the ground, Mónica, and when I leap over the wall of your garden in the middle of the night, instead of finding you there, I find only the terrible secret of despair, the deep cavern of silence where everything is irredeemably lost forever . . .

The only thing I find round about me is hatred and hypocrisy with its artificial roses.

Loneliness.

I feel no attachment to anything or anyone, for you were the only one I ever cared for, and I surrendered to you in the heat of passion, with none of the little games or gallant compliments or flowery words that a suitor says to his ladylove in a drawing-room.

The only caresses I was ever given were those of my cousin-and-sister, today locked up and 'dead' in a convent; she stroked my hair as I rested my head in her lap, as I did in yours only a few short days ago. Your fingers felt quite different to me, however, and the burning warmth of your legs and your perfume.

My bright flame of love and hours lost in mad ravings and suffering . . .

. . . wasted hours, my love, what an outrage! With no hope of ever seeing you again, time itself is nothing but a waste now . . .

At night I mount my horse and ride and ride through the darkness, seeking the oblivion of madness, the self-annihilation of utter exhaustion; yet daybreak finds me still alive and lucid, perhaps because I am already forgetting your contours, imagining you now rather than living you.

Rather than keeping you . . .

My angel of unhappiness, my sister Mariana . . .

9.6.71

The Daughter

Mother:

António came to ask me to go to see you and forgive you . . .
Will you too ask me to forgive you? Will you expect me to lean
down over that bed where you have already begun to rot away,
and kiss your forehead so that you may die in peace?

But what right do you have to die in peace, to quietly close
your eyes and end your life without the knife blade of remorse
turning round and round in your breast! It is not enough to be
a mother: it is not enough to have borne a child in one's belly
for that child to come to love us; but in order for a child to hate
us how much harm we must do him . . .

You know nothing, I am certain, of the weight of my hatred,
not because I have kept that hatred hidden from you, but because I could never sharpen it to a keen enough edge to wound
you, and hence it was powerless; you are aware, however, of the
crime that you have committed: you refuse to allow me to have
my son, who regards me merely as a mad woman whom he
pities. I can imagine what you have told him, how you have distorted what has happened. With António's help, you have
brought him up in your own way, gaily laughing at my despair
and my eagerness to hold in my arms this son that the two of you
have taken away from me, acting both as my torturers and my
judges, plotting and conniving together to make me suffer and
keep me shut up here in this mental asylum, completely within
your power – and now I've been summoned to come and forgive
you for the 'punishment' you inflicted on me . . .

Punishment? But what crime did I commit and what punishment did I deserve?

Is a woman necessarily obliged to suffer every sort of humiliation from a man simply because he is her husband: her lord and
master? Or does being born a woman perhaps automatically

mean being unhappy and being forced to bear a burden too heavy for her to carry?

You were mistaken; you will never hear a single word from my mouth that bears the slightest resemblance to forgiveness. On the contrary: my hatred will pursue you till death and perhaps even beyond: for didn't you condemn me forever to this prison to which you had me committed as a madwoman?

And may I ask, Mother, how it is possible to seek the lucidity of true forgiveness of a woman who has gone out of her mind?

Forgiveness for what, and for what reason, might I ask? Weren't the two of you sane whereas I was mad? Aren't the two of you normal whereas I am demented? In that case, I have nothing to forgive you for; you may die with my hatred without its troubling you in the least, as has always been your habit, isn't that so?

You may rest assured, however, that since I allowed myself to be imprisoned behind these bars in order to free myself, I have no remorse . . . only how imprudent I was not to take your sharp claws and the weight of the law into account! I refused to use slyness, the only weapon that a woman is allowed; instead I battled openly, in a struggle that always ends with a knife in one's own back.

And I have once again come off badly, Mother, in the unending war between the two of us: I know full well that this letter will never reach your hands . . .

But what a strange letter for a madwoman to write. António . . . will you too not seek my forgiveness some day? At that moment I shall make you the object of all my hatred, whole and entire, a hatred filled with even more hatred, as today its object is my mother, to whom you will never read these clumsily written lines traced by my hand that has lost the habit of holding a pen.

There is nothing to stop you, I know, from dragging me by force (the way you brought me here) to the bedside of that woman who is now half-dead so that she may see me and consider my presence there an act of forgiveness. But you may be certain, António, that as I spit in her face, it will be with sincere thanks to you for having given me the opportunity to do so.

Mariana

10.6.71

In the Morning – Mariano;
In the Afternoon – Nothing

In the month of March, Mariano chanced to discover that he
was mediocre. It was not a sudden fit of depression: he wasn't
tired of his wife; he hadn't recently asked for a raise behind his
colleagues' back; he hadn't had a falling-out with his pals at the
café or been rejected by his girl friends; he hadn't been turned
down by a whore on the street; no policeman had put a ticket on
his Fiat; he hadn't cut his hair short; he hadn't dropped out of
school; he hadn't pawned the watch his aunt had left him; it
wasn't the end of the month; it was the middle of March; it
wasn't raining; no one had told him so – but he was mediocre.
He woke up in the morning with this word on his lips; he looked
in the mirror and could still hear the word. When he brushed his
teeth, the beat of the word 'mediocre' speeded up, so that first
it became 'meocre' and then 'mocre, mocre, mocre'. As he
shaved himself with his electric razor it sounded like 'meeeeoo-
oooccrrreee'. And so on. He buried himself in the morning paper
as his wife did the dishes, with a great rattling of plates and clink-
ing of silverware, and he spied the word 'MEDIOCRE' in
heavy type – it was a Thursday, the day he always bought the
Diário das Notícias. There was a review of a new edition of Camões
and he read what the critic had to say about Camões. And there it
was, the word, or him, his case exactly – mediocre. One of those
coincidences. At work he did everything he had to do during the
day, except that he said very little, but nobody made any particular comment about it to him, since he hardly ever said very
much, except when he was annoyed with everybody around the
place, and today he wasn't. The rhythm of the word 'mediocre'
turned into a sort of Morse code as the typist tapped away at her
machine – me me me di dididi o oo crrrree cre didi o.

When he went past the shoe-shop he decided that at the end
of the month he would buy one pair that was in the window.

They were a little bit out of the ordinary, but not too much so. He was reading a nameplate that said '*medicodecrianças*'* when the bus struck him square in the chest. Before everything turned from a dull green to a thick vermilion, he could still hear the words 'All men are mediocre, Mariano is a man, and therefore ...' and the voice of his wife saying that it was a good thing he'd already paid his final exam fees on the seventh. Heavens! He was a most unusual corpse.

17.6.71

* Paediatrician. (*Translator's note.*)

Letter from a Man Named António, for Twelve Years an Emigrant, Residing in the Town of Kitimat, on the East Coast of Canada, Opposite the Queen Charlotte Islands, Close to the Alaskan Border, to His Wife Named Maria Ana from the Town of Carvalhal, Parish of Oliveira de Fráguas, Circumscription of Albergaria-a-Velha, District of Aveiro

My Good and always remembered Wife Maria Ana, thank you very much for the letter that I have just received from you, and for the sweater which has also arrived, even though I didn't really need one because wool clothes like other things necessary to live comfortably are of good quality here and not much more expensive than they are back there. I'm in good health, thanks be to God as people say back there and I'm thinking of quitting working as a lumberjack and setting up a grocery store in Montreal which is a big city here in this country I don't remember whether I told you about it or not when I was there. I know some nice Portuguese people there, a man that was in the army with me Fernandes who's settled there with his wife and his sister-in-law her name is Maria Adélia they're very nice to me and treat me like one of the family.

As for what you wrote me about the boys and our girl it seems to me you're fretting and fuming too much as usual they must be pretty well off what with all the money I've sent seeing as how I got along with much less when I was young and the army never did anybody any harm and you can also make good money in France and besides the passage here costs a lot more. With this business of the grocery store I may not be able to send you as much money as usual for the next few months and then we'll see because you seem to have lots of money stacked away by now. This is a big country and anybody who gets used to living here never gets used to living anywhere else. I remember all the misery I saw in Portugal, even among those who had made good money in France or Germany, where there are all those grey houses without ventilation and the women are all bundled up and

sickly-looking. Goodbye Maria Ana, give my regards to everyone and I'll be sending a money order soon so you can buy some
more gold pieces and a friendly hug to you from yours truly

António

18.6.71

Letter from a Soldier Named António to a Girl Named Maria, Employed as a Housemaid in Lisbon

Miss Maria:

I hope with all my heart that this letter of mine finds you in good health. I'm feeling all right these days, thanks be to God, and so are all my buddies except Aunt Maria Ana's Júlio, who was the one who told me where you were living now. He's lost a leg and is in the hospital and I don't know what's going to become of him when he goes back home to Carvalhal, because you need two legs to till land and that's the only thing he knows how to do because he's never been trained to do anything else and he's in such despair over the whole thing that he keeps crying all day and all night long and the only thing he'll talk about is what's happened to him.

But this letter isn't about Júlio poor thing, and please excuse me for bothering you and for being so bold as to write you but I feel so lonely that I wanted to find somebody who would drop me a line once in a while to help me forget this awful life I'm leading. It's so sad and dreary that it scares me and I'm not ashamed to admit it. The real reason why I'm writing you this letter, Miss Maria, is to ask you a favour – would you be willing to be my pen pal?

It so happens that all my buddies here get mail and I never get any, so Aunt Maria Ana's Júlio thought of you and said to me if I were you I'd write to her, she's from the same home town as we are and she won't say *no*, but I kept putting it off because I was too shy to write you right away.

So if you ever happen to have time and would send me an answer, I'd be very happy. As you can perhaps imagine, I'm very homesick and the nights are long without even one photo of anybody or any news about what's happening in the outside world or about other things so as to forget this war and how unhappy it's making us and our families. Júlio's father has emigrated to Canada and wrote him to say that there's no way for cripples to earn a living there and that he should try to wangle some money out of his mother to get by on and the poor boy didn't even finish reading the letter and tore it up before my very eyes when I went to visit him in the hospital to cheer him up, because everybody's forgotten him and he's all alone with his troubles.

To tell you the truth, Miss Maria, everybody that gets sent down here gets scared and we never get over it. It's a fear that never stops gnawing away at us somewhere inside. It's not very hard for anybody to be brave when they're far away and don't hear the bullets whizzing past, trying to snuff a man's life out.

I've seen lots of my pals all hunched over vomiting and falling to the ground as white as a sheet and we have to drag them along by brute force to get them out of there.

It's on account of all this and how sad it all makes me feel that I need letters to cheer me up, and so I thought that you might not mind writing me, Miss Maria. We could tell each other about the sort of life we're each leading, because a housemaid's life must not be a very happy one either.

To tell the truth, I've never been happy, even when I was small. My mother, God rest her soul, often used to tell me that I was so highly-strung that I'd never get anywhere in life.

And I've decided now that she was right.

I don't want to put you to the bother of reading a longer letter, so I'll close now, with my very best regards to you.

Yours truly,

António Mourinhas

19.6.71

Second Letter VII

Sisters:

One of us asked:

'But what can literature do? Or rather: what can words do?'

And today I answer (us) with this sentence from Reynaldo Arenas:

'At that time I felt all alone and took refuge in literature.'

What time? Our time. And what weapon, what weapon are we using or are we scorning to use? Where can we take refuge or how can we fight effectively for our cause as long as we are carrying on the battle in the realm of words alone?

How can we use words to help us and talk to each other, woman to woman, and tell each other how we are still the property of men, the spoils today of warriors who pretend to be our comrades in the struggle, but who merely seek to mount us and be cavaliers of Marianas who are prisoners in other prisons and nuns in different convents, without realizing it?

Here in Portugal we are in the midst of the era of women's liberation:

women vote, women attend universities, women hold jobs; women drink, women smoke, women enter beauty contests; women wear mini-skirts, maxi-skirts, 'hot pants', Tampax; women say 'I'm having my period' in front of men, women take 'the pill', shave the hair on their legs and under their armpits; women wear bikinis; women go out at night by themselves, go to bed with their lovers; women sleep bare naked; women now know the meaning of certain words such as orgasm, penis, vagina, sperm, testicles, erection, frigidity, clitoris, masturbation, vulva; among themselves, behind closed doors, in the intimacy of the lavatories of government office buildings where they are employed, during recess periods in schools, in universities, in bedrooms, in living rooms, they are even going so far as to tell dirty stories, to share certain intimate details about their experiences in bed, and to take certain liberties of language; and thus they are becoming modern, becoming liberated, improving their lot . . .

So here we are, sisters, in the midst of the era of the liberation of the Portuguese woman . . . and the man rejoices and says proudly, 'We're all for improvement in the situation of women, we're helping women get ahead, we're loosening their shackles, we're freeing them from their slavery.'

And the man rejoices, sisters, and aids and abets the woman in this farce, in this delusion, in this false and shameful 'liberation' which has made her even more of a prisoner (a prisoner of herself), caught fast in the meshes of a society that uses the woman, dominates her, enslaves her, takes her in hand, exploits her, manipulates her, consumes her. A society in which texts such as this one, entitled *The Woman and Work*, have suddenly begun to appear:

. . . and since it is jokingly said that 'woman is man's last colony', it is perhaps worth taking the risk. *Even though that phrase in quotation marks may be an exaggeration and in bad taste, it nonetheless is indicative of the fact that the professional status of women is still subject to numerous inequalities.*

Note here a certain tone with which we are all too familiar: 'it is jokingly said' (jokingly, my sisters?) and farther on: 'Even though that phrase ['Man's last colony'] may be an exaggeration (an exaggeration, sisters?) and in bad taste' (naturally it's in bad taste, sisters . . .).

The woman the man's colony? What an idea! What an exaggeration . . . !

What power does literature have, do words have, sisters, against all of this? Not to mention the fact that we are confronted with an age-old situation that has not changed in the slightest: 'Woman does not have a culture of her own. She exists in a culture where power belongs to men, and therefore, within this culture, she is alienated . . .'

20.6.71

Sonnets from the Portuguese:
Elizabeth Barrett Browning 1850

VI

Go from me. Yet I feel that I shall stand
Henceforth in thy shadow. Nevermore
Alone upon the threshold of my door
Of individual life, I shall command
The uses of my soul, nor lift my hand
Serenely in the sunshine as before.
Without the sense of that which I forbore –
Thy touch upon the palm. The widest land
Doom takes to part us, leaves thy heart in mine
With pulses that beat double. What I do
And what I dream include thee, as the wine
Must taste of its own grapes. And when I sue
God for myself, He hears that name of thine,
And sees within my eyes the tears of two.

XLII

How do I love thee? Let me count the ways.
I love thee to the depth and breadth and height
My soul can reach, when feeling out of sight
For the ends of Being and Ideal Grace.
I love thee to the level of every day's
Most quiet need, by sun and candle-light
I love thee freely, as men strive for Right,
I love thee purely, as men turn from Praise.
I love thee with the passion put to use
In my old griefs, and with my childhood's faith.
I love thee with a love I seemed to lose
With my lost saints – I love thee with the breath,
Smiles, tears of all my life! – and, if God choose,
I shall but love thee better after death.

20.6.71

Composition by a Little Girl Named Maria Adélia, Born in Carvalhal and a Pupil in a Convent School in Beja

DUTIES

There are many sorts of duties and everyone must do his duty. There are two main kinds of duties: men's duties and women's duties. Men's duties are to be courageous, to be strong, and to exercise authority. That is to say: to be presidents, generals, priests, soldiers, hunters, bullfighters, soccer players, judges, and so on. Our Lord gave the man the duty of watching over others and being in command, and even Jesus Christ was a man and God chose to have a son and not a daughter to die in this world to redeem our sins which are many, and in the hour of his death He said 'Father, forgive them, for they know not what they do.' So it is men who organize wars in order to save the world from perdition and sin (the Crusades, for example), fighting to save the Fatherland and defend women, children, and old people.

Then there are the duties of women, the most important of which is to have children, protect them and take care of them when they are sick, teach them good manners at home, and give them affection; another duty of the woman is to be a teacher and other things such as a seamstress, a hairdresser, a housemaid, or a nurse. There are also women doctors, engineers, lawyers, and so on, but my father says that it's best not to trust them because women were meant to keep house, which is a very nice duty because it's a pleasure to keep everything neat and clean for when the husband comes home to rest after working hard all day to earn money to support his wife and children.

Since the cost of living is very high and it's so hard to make ends meet, my mother says that the woman ought to help her husband, but I wouldn't like to have to help my husband and I won't marry anybody except a rich man who can buy me nice dresses and a car, take me to the cinema, and keep two maids, and my mother says you're right to think that way, daughter, don't ever marry a good-for-nothing like your father, who doesn't earn enough for us to keep soul and body together: we left our land and moved down here because he's such a fool, but he's your father and you must respect him. We moved here and there's hardly anything to eat because nothing comes out of the ground except stones and I'm here in this school. Where my mother came from, there was always my grandfather to help out, and more things grew out of the earth to keep you from going hungry. But my father decided to move to this part of the country to work as a stone-cutter, and since one of the duties of the woman is to obey the man, that's what my mother did, and what helps keep the family alive is that she does day work for a rich lady, the relative of another rich lady who had a daughter here in the convent, because once upon a time one of the duties of women was to enter a convent and maybe it's still one today, but nowadays a woman isn't forced to enter one. The Father Superior says that it's a vocation but I don't know what that means and so I call it a duty because it sounds nicer. One day the rich lady asked me if I didn't want to become a nun (in her family the girls can hardly wait to become nuns) and I said no thank you, Senhora, and stood there looking down at the floor the way my mother taught me, and she said what a charming little girl and patted my head and I saw the sparkling rings on her fingers. Rings with beautiful precious stones, and I thought that being a rich lady ought to be one of the duties for women; and I wanted to be a rich lady then and kissed her hand all of a sudden, just to see what the rings felt like when I touched them with my lips, and she thought it was because I was fond of her and said poor little thing and gave me five *escudos*, but when I wanted to go to the shop to buy lollipops with the money, my mother took it away from me, screaming don't waste money like that, that's enough to buy a little rice and potatoes, and I gave the *escudos* to her because children also have their duties and one of them is to obey their parents, but I thought to myself that I'd never tell her anything about my life again or show her anything that anybody gave me: people have to watch out for their own interests in life and it's their duty to be smart, and one of a woman's duties is to be deceptive, the way I see my mother being with my father. Once she even said to me listen, daughter, a woman has to know lots of tricks to get what she wants, because we're all weaker than men, so men make fools of us, that's simply the way things are, but we have to look out for ourselves. So one of the other duties of a woman is to be sly.

We must not be led into temptation, the Father Superior says. I don't know exactly what he means but I don't see anything like that here in the convent school, and all I know is that when I'm grown up I'm never going to be unhappy like my mother, always having to clean up the messes my father and the rich lady leave. But at least the rich lady keeps on giving us leftover food and old clothes instead of throwing them in the dustbin. Because there are also duties of poor people and duties of rich people. One of the duties of rich people is to be charitable and that of poor people to beg and to accept what's given them and show their gratitude.

The world has always been like that, the Father Superior preaches in his sermons, some people with everything and others with nothing, it's God's will. Doubtless it's because He was never hungry like us, but the Father Superior said no, that wasn't the reason, it was because you have to be poor in order to go to heaven afterwards and rich people won't go to heaven, and then he told a story about a camel that went through the eye of a needle and I thought it was funny and started to laugh, so he punished me. Because it's one of the duties of children to be punished, just as it's one of grown-ups' duties to punish children so that they will learn to like punishing others, since punishing someone is a rather frequent duty and a necessary one in life.

Just last week my father's boss punished him because he was going around telling the other men that work with him that they ought to ask for more money because the wages they were getting weren't enough to buy food and pay their rent. And my father's boss laid my father off for a week and I was the only one who had anything to eat, if you can call it that, because I was here at the school, except that I don't sleep here.

And my mother wore herself out scolding my father and crying and saying listen, you, don't get mixed up in things like that, just look what happens, here we are dying of hunger when other people have full bellies, since you were the only one the boss punished because you were the one who got ideas in your head.

Because one of the duties of bosses is to punish their employees, and it's the duty of employees to work for their bosses so that they can get richer and more powerful. Maybe I'll marry a boss some day.

But that wouldn't really help much, because when my father gets drunk and beats my mother up, he always screams: I'm the boss around here! And she shuts up and begins to cry very softly.

And this is about all I'm going to write, because if I were to list all the duties there are in the world it would take me the rest of my life. I just want to mention one more duty though – that of the woman of ill-repute who is said to lead a bad life. But I don't know what's meant by a bad life because my mother and all women like her lead a bad life.

The Father Superior says in his sermons that such a thing is a great sin and that any woman who fulfils that duty will go to hell.

The Father Superior says that one of a woman's duties is to be virtuous. But even though I don't know exactly what being virtuous means, I don't imagine it gets you very far.

I like duties very much.

Maria Adélia

20.6.71

Composition by a Little Girl from Lisbon, Named Mariana, a Fourth Grade Pupil in a Convent School

WORDS

There are good words and bad words, pretty words and ugly words. The word 'Portugal' is a very pretty one, but the word 'Trancos' isn't.[30] There are words that don't go with the things they're used for. 'Moon', for example, is all right, it couldn't be any other name because then it wouldn't be that thing, but the word 'notebook' isn't like that. It reminds you of 'winter' and 'hell',[31] and notebooks all depend, not all of them are horrible, only the maths one is for me. The word 'leaf' is also used for many things, but it must always be a leaf of something, of a book, of a tree, of tinfoil, and there's no way of knowing which, a leaf can't just be a leaf all by itself.

Words are also used for talking and consoling and suffering. Words like that don't mean anything one by one, like the ones I wrote before, they only mean something in sentences, that is to say, when you put them together with other words, all in a bunch.

The word 'good', for example, is good, it seems like a gentle word, but if somebody says 'this young lady isn't a good girl', with a shake of the head, it can hurt you a lot. When you put certain words together, some of them turn out to have exactly opposite meanings. The word 'fresh' for instance. If it's used for a fruit it's good, but if it's used for people it's not. And the word 'sad', for example, is a blue word, because almost all words have colours, and it seems to be asking people to keep quiet, and the word 'laugh', which is yellow, doesn't make people laugh all by itself. The word 'mother' is too heavy for what it stands for and the word 'father' too clear and too light.

And now I'm going to invent the word 'disintelligent' seeing as how that's what I feel I am because words confuse me and because I never say anything. When you write, words are made up of letters, and you only hear them as words in your head. The end.

Mariana

22.6.71

The Struggle

Maria lets go of his arm and starts running.

The man tried to grab her, to pull her towards him, to call to her, but then he just stood there watching her disappear among the crowds of people gathered on the pavements in front of the shop windows, jostling each other as they waited to cross the streets.

Maria:

I stood there watching you disappear, dumbfounded, thinking that you had gone mad and overcome with a terrible fear that kept me from trying to stop you; fear of losing you or fear that you were being badly led astray by that imagination of yours which, as you well know, has always displeased me. You are scatterbrained but I never thought you were wayward.

Your husband

António

Maria runs among the crowds gathered on the pavements at that hour, she runs without seeing where she is going, without knowing if he is chasing her in order to try to take her back home. To beg her to return like the other times. This time Maria feels that she will not give in.

She will never give in to him again:

Neither to pleas nor to threats; neither to tenderness nor to physical torture. She is determined to fight and she runs: she flees, carrying with her the emptiness that her life has been, like return luggage.

Maria:

I can still see you running as though trying to escape something: your skirt was a red patch of colour that my eyes followed:

for whole minutes, for a few seconds, or for centuries of parched thirst?

I tried in vain to forget you and even now that I've come to hate you, here you are, still intact in my memory. Your fragile presence here in this house where you belong.

I will do anything in my power to make you come back.

Your husband

António

Maria runs. The people clustered on the pavements bar her way and she pushes her way through them as fast as her legs can carry her, though they grow heavier and heavier as she continues on her way.

She raises her hands to her breast, looks for a place to rest. But isn't that precisely what they'll be waiting for her to do: try to rest?

Maria:

Don't think I'm being vengeful. You know I love you. But my mother writes to me and says: 'How can you go on brooding about that madwoman who left you?' I sit there not saying a word and I can still see you. I keep following you step by step in my mind's eye as you run, fleeing me.

What do you expect me to do?

Don't think I'm being vengeful. You know I love you. But I'm taking another tack now, and my ways of proving to you that I love you are different.

Your husband

António

Maria realizes that she has stopped running, her body is drooping with fatigue, overcome with an exhaustion that keeps spreading, multiplying like tentacles, strangling her with its countless fingers.

The streets are empty now, night has fallen, and the cold has stripped the streets of the sound of voices: people are walking lowly along in silence, hugging the walls, heading homeward.

Maria covers her bare arms with her hands, trying to hold in a little of her body's warmth. She trembles and staggers as she walks on, nearly falling.

Maria:

I never gave you any reason to doubt that I loved you during all the years that we were married, so why do you refuse to return? Did I ever force you to give yourself to me or do anything more than a man might normally ask of a woman?

I do not understand how you can still hold out after all this time. From whom are you receiving help? When you ran away from me, I confess that I never imagined you to be capable of such madness and thought it merely a whim of yours.

Nevertheless, I've done everything I possibly could for you, even exercising my legal rights over you (as my lawfully wedded wife). I am simply saving you from yourself.

Your husband

António

Maria tries to stay on her feet: her weary legs bend, her shoulders sag, and her breast is ripped open by the stabbing pain that tears at it, taking her breath away. Groping her way along, she finds a wall and leans against it to try to recover her strength. The silence closes in around her like a trap; inside it there is no one to help her. She feels cornered, and has no idea what possible weapon she could use to defend herself.

Maria:

Will I also be forced to endure the terrible experience of seeing you die?

Will your cruelty or your pride lead you to the point of preferring death to admitting your mistake and your foolishness in leaving your house and your husband?

There is still time left for you to return; I have been waiting for you all these many years and even today I am still waiting for the moment when you knock at the door to open it and welcome you, forgiving you for everything.

There is no other path for you to follow, no other possible way out.

Right after you first left I reached the point of fearing your return because it frightened me that I loved you so much, but now I am eager to make you mine again.

I am waiting for you.

Your husband

António

Maria is curled up in a corner, motionless, her eyes staring emptily into space. The heat of her blood lessens and pitilessly ceases to warm what little there is that still remains alive within her. She imagines that she is moving on once more, that she is running, fleeing, that she is finally reaching the place where she belongs in the world. 'Mas que lugar lhe cabe neste latifúndio?'*

Dear Sir:

Having been informed that my wife, Maria M., aged 29, is at present confined in the hospital of . . . , of which you are the director, and having also been informed of the seriousness of her condition, I hereby notify you that it is my intention to take my wife home with me, and that I am prepared to sign any and all necessary papers assuming full responsibility for her.

Yours respectfully,

António M.

Maria thinks she feels them grabbing her; she struggles and tries to escape once more, to run, but her body refuses to stand up, her eyes refuse to see, her mouth refuses to cry out. And it is not necessary to see for Maria to perceive, to be certain of his presence, to know that she is back in his house. And the panic that then overtakes her suffocates her, destroys the little life that is left within her.

Dear Mother:

I am writing to tell you that Maria is dead: she died a few hours after I brought her back home to occupy the place that was rightfully hers. You are well aware that despite your reproaches, I had long since forgiven her and that during all these

* 'But what rightful place does she have in this vast landed estate?'[32]

years I did everything possible to force her to return. Hence I feel no weight on my conscience; all I can do now is mourn for her . . . I beg you to pardon her too and remember her in your prayers. The poor thing was punished quite enough: she died a slow, terrible, agonizing death that was frightful to see.

What am I going to do with my life now, since up until today I have devoted it entirely to tracking her step by step with the one aim of leading her back to the right path and to her duty? And in the end, where did her terrible death get her . . . or my power get me?

Your wretched son

António

Game I

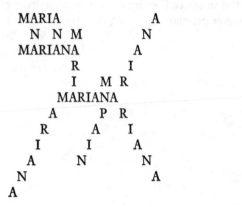

Game II

MARIANA MAEANA MEANA MINHA MEIA MIA*

* The literal meaning of this word game is: MARIANA MOTHER ANA MY ANA MINE MEAN MY. (*Translator's note.*)

Game III

```
MARIANA   MARIANA   MARIANA              A
EMASNEL   ENERMEN   ARENRAN
NALOTGT   UOUAAMO   LTLTTDT   MARIAN
ISALIAU             EIIEEOE   ENOLL
NIDDGDR             FFCRFMP   LASUT
AAAAAAA             IIAVAOO   EASSA
                    CCRACRS   CTPT
                    IIILTTT   ARAR
                    OOOOOO    SERA
                              TLVD
                              AAAA
```

Translator's note: Below is a literal translation of the above word 'game'
(to be read downwards):

```
MMWIADL   MYGRNNY   WTRIASP   DASICGG
AIRSNEO   IEUAUUE   IRENRTR   INILURI
ISAOCNF   NAIGRRA   TILTTUE   AALLLEV
DTTLIIT   ERLES R   CCIEIBM   M LUTAI
ERHAEEI     T E     HKQRFBA   OTYSITN
NEFTNDN     Y       CEUVAOT   NR TV G
 SUET E             RRAACRU   DARRAS
 SLD   S            AYRLTNR   CPOATTY
       S            F Y   E   HPSTEUO
                    T         AEEEDPU
                              SD D IR
                              T    DS
                              E    IE
                                   TL
                                   YF
```

A Proverbial Battle of Words Between Man and Woman

– What did you do with my tears?

I dried them in the war
They dried up in my milk

– What did you do with my wound?

I healed it with soldier's pay
I healed it by baking bread

– What did you do with my eyes?

I blinded them in your flesh
I blinded them with your staff

–What did you do with my sons?

I gave them death in skirts
I gave them death in arms

– What did you do with my hands?

I cut them off in my hunger
I cut them off in your hunger

– What did you do with my guts?

I brought forth my sons for you
I brought forth our sons for you

– What did you do with my bones?

I crushed them beneath a dead weight
I broke them to make them mine

– What did you do with my soul?

I gave it for others to hunt
I gave it for ours to eat

– What did you do with my love?

I wore it as adornment
Bed of evil and shame

– What do we do?

I hope to die wise
I hope to die without being killed

27.6.71

Magnificat

Letter from a Recently Married Woman, Named Mariana, to Her Unmarried Sister Joana

Oh, the glorious and wonderful footsteps of happiness, Joana! You may tell me that I abandoned many secret doors in order to allow this pregnant mountain of life to palpitate within my body. In the morning I allow the sun to alight on my arms, I bare my neck to it and warm myself in the colour of the blue carpet of wild lilies, the laughing exclamation points of the poppies, my relaxed hands no longer a part of me and my body growing rounder in the light, my flesh perfectly illuminated by the hills opposite, or weightlessly remembered, its curve joining the dusty line of the horizon that is softly glowing, the sun at twilight setting on my smiling mouth, that is to say, his eyes yesterday, his fresh mouth, the warm night, his hand on the curve of my waist as I sleep in peace and trust. I am certain, Joana, that if I were not a woman, the happiness that I am telling you of would not be this indistinct or this vague (like the sea). At peace and motionless, how clearly I see things! You will say to me: 'Is this love, Mariana?' and I will answer that it is something even more important: the world forming a perfect circle round about me. For what I receive and what is given to me by him (which does not seem at all peaceful, but rather a patient surprise at feeling as I do), my gift in return is my acceptance of it. I am calmly attuned to everything, I look at what is and find peace in everything, in there being birds and crawling snakes, in the massiveness of the cork oaks and the smell of the clean straw in the pigsty, in the squeak of cart-wheels and in bunches of grapes – a gentle harmony and wisdom. If this is not love, Joana, when he looks at me and through his hand and power brings this light of things that makes us glow and makes my body grow in size, what acceptance will I ever find? You will doubtless say to me in a sad voice: 'But don't you tell him anything about what you have learned in all your research, about how bad conditions are everywhere, don't you fight for our cause, Mariana?' and I shall answer that I say nothing, or very little that is not a vague *yes* that comes from my very flesh. I smooth my hair with my free hands if he is not there, I smooth my belly that is growing rounder and rounder and thus I live each day waiting in the smoothness of everything, smiling for no reason except that the swallows are softly swooping low. I have lost my rational view of life, Joana, and I know what fear this may cause all those who took me for an alert, sharp-tongued woman. I was an obstacle on the path of those close to me and now I am living these days putting forth fruit, the sap and the pulp quietly ripening. You will tell me that this is not a result of any power of his, but rather of the state in which I find myself. Try telling *him* that, Joana, when it's afternoon and he puts his arms around me, hiding his smile from me, as we lie face to face, the smile of someone who possesses me and knows that I am there with him of my own free will, the smile of someone who can cradle me in his arms, smiling patiently at the half-sleep, with my head drooping, in which I receive him, without having done anything, without telling him a word about my body's day, that is nonetheless full. Try telling him that this is simply the joy of the species at continuing itself, that I am simply the temporary place chosen by the species to renew itself. Because even though this may well be true, Joana, even though this egg of silence may shatter and I may give birth to a stillborn child, even though my heart too swells with the pleasure of receiving him and allowing him to smile at me without replying in anger, I also want to tell you that he too knows that what you say may well be true, but that he won't even listen to you, since through this grave and gravid thing, this mute and fecund embrace between us, this pregnancy of ours, which is taking place in my flesh but also in his arms and in the place of peace and in the contented body that he creates for me, we are living the harmony of the world, despite the bitter struggles the two of us have been through, or perhaps deserving rest and a meaning for our lives precisely because of them, I calm and quiet and he with a peace made to his own measure, losing his false pride and his tenseness, and with our eyes blind in the night, giving himself over to the movement within my belly, giving himself over to the flow of time, to generation, being able to sleep within me as he shall one day sleep within the arms of death.

I shall return, Joana, and how much pain and grief will await both him and me, will await all of us, when the City will again engulf us, and surely we shall all be misunderstood when we demand that it be just and wish each of us within it to be whole and meaningful, each with a name and a designated task, with a history and personal desires that are also shared with all the others. We shall return with another, a child, on which to inscribe these things, and some of the contradictory words and angry battles between him and me, between all of us, will have to be resolved. But this time, Joana, this unhurried period of waiting that we are going through, he shielded from the asperity of our former days there, since we are both keeping so many things hidden from each other, including our differences on this subject, I saying nothing about my reasons as an experienced, educated woman for believing as I do and relying instead now on my senses – this time, Joana, neither the memory of your serene loyalty to me, nor your beauty of glass, nor your wholeness of stone, you the virgin, can or will disturb us. This is another step, my sister, and though it was you who kept me company as I scaled walls and took to flight and laughed and cried because of hopes not yet fulfilled, only this, only he, gave me the chance to discover space, the vast expanse of sky in the afternoon, made in my image and likeness, the small and fragile but protected womb that is gestating, that contains us all. It is very little, my dear, aloof young sister, but at the same time it is so much, so much.

An affectionate embrace

Mariana

2.7.71

Letter by a Woman Named Maria, to Her Daughter Maria Ana, a Housemaid in Lisbon

Maria Ana

My daughter, you who will always remain my daughter, for you emerged from my body and were engendered within it, even though now I deny you and curse the hour in which you came forth from my womb and almost think that someone cast an evil eye on me while I was pregnant with you. The minute your father learned that I had given birth to a baby girl he said: 'She should never have been born, she's no good for anything; a girl is nothing but trouble to people.' And I answered: 'Shut your mouth, man, because what you're saying might bring bad luck,' but in the end he was right because you were never of any use to us and all you did was cause us trouble and worries, never showing any concern for us, and never hiding your scorn for us, leaving a deep wound in my poor heart that cannot stand much more, in fact it would even be a great relief and I would thank God if He would take me from this world where it has always been my lot to suffer without ever experiencing a single joy. And for that reason, and for your happiness, I put pressure on your father to let you go to Lisbon to be a housemaid when you wanted to and the rich lady asked us if she could take you with her to work in her married daughter's house, since they are respectable and decent people.

The fact is that you've never had any sense and a woman who is born to be unhappy can come to a bad end if she isn't careful.

Just yesterday your Aunt Ana told me bad things about you and I lowered my eyes in shame, without having the courage to defend you, and then she said to me: 'You're the one to blame, because you encouraged her to leave here, since if my brother had had his way that girl would still be tilling the fields we own and even if she didn't have luxuries, she'd have her honour. A woman without honour stains the honour of the family in which she was born and her kinsfolk can no longer hold their heads high.'

And I didn't tell her (I have my pride too) that it used to break my heart hearing you cry all night long and seeing you going out to the fields in the morning all bent over, not even looking at the things or the people around you, exactly like me, but you were so young, and with your whole life ahead of you. It was quite enough that I was already dying in this unhappy house.

You know that your father has had nothing but contempt for me ever since the doctor told him why I couldn't have any more children, seeing as how your father would give the very eyes in his head and his own flesh to have a son. From then on he treated me like a useless thing and humiliated me even in the streets, and so I stopped going out and here I am buried alive in this tomb, cooking for him, washing his clothes, without even a line from you, the child to whom I gave the milk of my breasts, the blood of my body. My daughter – you who are rejecting the mother that God gave you, the mother it is your duty to respect, you who don't even want to know about the grief you're causing me, who don't even care that you're being the death of me by leading the sort of life you are now – I hear things about how you're behaving every day, because bad news travels fast. You for whom I always set a good example, and took you to church regularly, and if I didn't send you to school it was because your father was dead set against it, being convinced that girls don't need to know how to read – and it's your father whose word is law – that's a woman's lot, my daughter, and all of us have our cross to bear, and if you at least know how to read a little bit and sign your name remember that I was the one who taught you how in secret . . .

When I saw you leave, I thought to myself: I hope she has better luck than I've had and may God help her and His will be done, but you chose to disgrace yourself, and if a person chooses the wrong path God's will is of no avail.

Just yesterday Padre José told me exactly that, and gave me a scolding for having left you helpless there in the city that he says in his sermons is the devil's domain and full of temptations.

So am I still the one who is to blame for your coming to a bad end?

Am I still forced to bear on my shoulders the burden of your actions, my daughter – you who never treated me with anything but bitterness and harshness, saving all your affection and all your laughter for the house of the rich lady, according to what I've been told?

Maria Ana, my daughter, if I am writing to you today, it is not because I think you'll listen to me or understand these outpourings of my heart that I'm setting down on paper as though they were cries of pain ... the purpose of this letter is to warn you against your father, who will surely kill you if he ever lays his hands on you, and so I beg you not to ever come back here, because he'll take leave of his senses and some further misfortune is bound to occur, and I've already had more than my share.

But I also beg you to write to me, Ana, even if it's only a few lines to tell me how you are. I still worry about you and grieve for you, and sometimes I want nothing more to do with you and at other times I want to take you to my bosom, because you are my daughter and you always will be, and I will go on loving you till the day I die.

Take care of yourself, my daughter. You know that you still have time to mend your ways and be what you once were.

People have short memories.

Love and kisses from your mother who cannot forget you and weeps many tears for you.

Maria

7.7.71

Text of a Declaration of Honour or an Interrogation, Written by a Woman Named Joana

I say:

A woman taken in adultery is still stoned to death today in Afghanistan and in Saudi Arabia.

(I ask:

Is the adulterous man also likely to be stoned to death in Afghanistan or in Saudi Arabia?)

I say:

In America, as in so many other countries, the law indirectly provides for a strange sort of 'death penalty' applicable to women, by denying them the 'control' of their own bodies, thus forcing them to resort to illegal abortions: 'It is estimated that between two and five thousand women die every year as a result of such operations' in America.

(I ask:

What are the two or five thousand men who impregnate these two or five thousand women who die in America every year doing?)

I say:

In Portugal, the majority of women are not purely and simply 'slaves' of men, since they act out their role of female object 'cheerfully' and with conviction, and it is not necessary for a woman to commit adultery in order for her to be 'stoned to death', to be destroyed ... she need only *appear in the public eye* and talk 'like a man'. And given the fact that abortion is illegal in Portugal too (since women, still as passive as ever here, are not fighting against this situation), plus the fact that information about the number of abortions that take place nonetheless is deliberately withheld by people who pretend to ignore what can no longer be ignored, plus the fact that everything thus seems to be going very well, in the best of all possible worlds where women enjoy their dependent and secondary role that limits them to being simply mothers and where even highly educated women choose marriage as though it were a profession though a non-remunerated one or one remunerated through the giving of their own bodies, and hence we find ourselves confronted with prostitution pure and simple ... And given the fact, finally, that all of this takes place in such a 'harmless' and benign way, to the general satisfaction of everyone, what other course is left open to us save joining battle?

(I ask:

Sisters, how many Anas or Marianas must still be brought back to life, or how many of them are there still living who are being put to the test, having their minds dulled, made weak and fragile through the workings of the law, the social proprieties, accepted beliefs, and religion?)

I say:

Let us refuse to be taken in by offers of help from males. We do not need men's help; or, to be more precise, we do not want to accept this 'Christmas present' in pretty gift wrappings concealing a bomb that is certain to explode once again in our hands, as usual. If we are the ones who want things, we must be the ones to demand them.

Let us put an end to mystifications and false modesty, let us cleave from top to bottom the waters we are drowning in, drowning in without being able to draw a single breath.

(I ask:

Hasn't the time come to share with each other, for example, the truths we know about our pleasures in bed, forthrightly denouncing the trick men are playing on us, by turning vaginal orgasm into a myth, by pinning the label of 'frigidity' on women who complain that they do not reach climax through simple intercourse? Once again, by falling into this trap of frigidity men have set, the woman unfortunately becomes the man's prey, his inferior.

Will we continue to remain silent?)

I say:

There will be those who, despite everything, will denounce as 'reactionary' the battle that will be joined along the long, exhausting path that the Portuguese woman will be obliged to travel all alone, with the meagre weapons at her disposal. And there will be those who will raise a great outcry, and keen knives and sharp lances will be brandished on every hand, and names like stones will be thrown at us; but whores or lesbians, who cares what they call us, so long as the battle is fought and not lost.

(I ask:

If we are offered no other alternative save outright war against an entire social system that we reject *in toto* and are forced to destroy everything, including our own homes if necessary, will we retreat?)

I say:

Ti-Grace Atkinson, a theoretician of the feminist movement who is twenty-nine years old, writes:

'Love is the trap, the barbed wire fence, the focal point of repression of women in a sexist world. What is love but need or fear?'

(I ask:

Can there possibly be any reason for a woman still to believe in love? Still to trust a man? Still to believe in her liberation if she continues to accept what has thus far been offered her: the role of companion and helpmate . . . in other words: the eternal dependent and domestic role in the world, coupled with the obligation to produce children and wash their nappies, and to accept the man who avails himself of her, either in bed or socially, using her to perform the worst-paid and least interesting tasks that he himself refuses to perform?)

I say:

Enough.

It is time to cry: Enough. And to form a barricade with our bodies.

Joana

7.7.71

Adultery : Conjugal Infidelity
(PORTUGUESE DICTIONARY)

What a narrow band separates us from Mariana, sisters ...
since the honour of man-the-husband is still situated in his penis
and our vagina, which he still has the right to use as he pleases,
and the right to kill an adulterous wife in order to take his
vengeance as a cuckolded male by stoning her, murdering her,
eliminating her, if possible, with the full sanction of the law,
with the agreement, the approbation of an entire society that
complacently condones this crime:

PORTUGUESE PENAL CODE
ARTICLE 372

(Adultery and the corruption of minors as the motive for an act of violence)

'A married man who discovers that his wife is guilty of adultery,
providing that said accusation is not contrary to the provisions
set forth in Article 404, § 2, and as a consequence kills either her
or her partner in adultery, or both, or commits against them any
one of the corporal offences set forth in Articles 360, sections 3
to 5, 361, and 366, will be banished from the country for a period
of six months.

'§ 1. If the offences are less grave, he shall incur no penalty.'

The law and justice, on the other hand, allow the woman to
take her vengeance for a similar offence, only if she (we) are
betrayed in our own houses, by the presence of a concubine
'possessed and kept' in it ... in the name of the defence of
established morality, that is to say, and not because of our name
or our wrath or our jealousy or our honour, the defence of which
is a right granted only to the man:

'§ 2. The same provisions will apply to the married woman, who in the act set forth in this article kills the concubine possessed and kept by her husband in the conjugal domicile, or the husband or both, or commits the aforementioned corporal offences.'

We will always be used as objects, as unmarried women subject to the will of our parents so long as we are minors, and after we have married, to the will of our husbands, who can always invent reasons for killing us and manufacture proof that will allow them to escape a prison sentence and punishment.

Will honour always be situated in our vaginas, our bodies, and not in the penis, the body of our brothers, who can do anything they please without deserving death in the eyes of the law?:

'§ 3. The same provisions will apply, in similar circumstances, to parents with respect to their minor daughters of less than twenty-one years of age, and to their corruptors, so long as the aforesaid minor females remain subject to the authority of their parents, save in the case in which the parents themselves have instigated, encouraged, or facilitated said corruption . . .'

(TRANSCRIPTION OF THE PORTUGUESE PENAL CODE)

10.7.71

Two Poems Found Among Joana's Papers – Written in Her Hand

I

To what precipice
pain
or what peak do I climb

to what richer
pain
or what darker pleasure

thinking that I am myself
and thus no longer thinking

or feeling that I give myself
while saying no to time

10.7.71

II

To what precipice
pain
or what peak do I climb

to what richer
pain
or what darker pleasure

In what pool do I swim in this time
of crystals full-formed
inside the wind?

10.7.71

Poem Found Among the Papers of Mónica M., Written and Corrected in Her Hand

O pleasure – O knife-edge
O peak more intense

my anguish banished from its terror
and my body opened through my belly in a sharper
thrust
as I come

not merely taken to be like you
as I overcome you
and mount you and increase you

ardently I am you
and I liquefy time

10.7.71

Letter from a Woman Named Joana to a Man Named Noël, a Frenchman by Birth

My dear Noël

I am enclosing some advice written by Paul Chanson, published in a book which came into my hands yesterday and which I found delightful reading.

We were lovers for so many months, taking our pleasure in bed together to the point of madness and sinking our teeth into sexual enjoyment to the point of wisdom; we are still lovers even now that we have gone our separate ways, and will remain so for as long as we both care to; we are lovers because of the freedom of what we know we enjoy when we are together; we are lovers because of the happiness that each of us finds in the happiness of the other's body; we are lovers through each orgasm that we built towards with each other, reaching climax time after time in long hours when nothing else counts and everything happens . . . We were and are lovers who have tried everything, holding back, prolonging each experience, each movement, each spasm almost to the point of pain . . . Nonetheless, you may not be as aware of this as I am . . . So note well the advice that I shall now copy out for you, and be duly impressed by this true wisdom with regard to the proper treatment of frigid women, the poor things, whom too hurried coitus keeps from reaching orgasm, when what is required is patience and persistence:

1. Never allow yourself to become nervous or lose your head. Remain calm and collected, as though the whole thing were of no importance;
2. Relax every muscle of your body as completely as possible – not forgetting the muscles of your face and hands;
3. Breathe rhythmically. Inhale rapidly, taking as deep a breath as possible;

4. Once your lungs are full, hold your breath for several seconds;

5. Exhale slowly, emptying your lungs completely;

6. Rest for a considerable time;

7. Then begin the breathing exercise again, as calmly as possible. Repeat it with the absolute conviction that you will thus overcome the difficulty; that is what your sense of pride, of self-respect demands.

Have you ever tried this?

Joana

P.S.   This is a very appropriate gymnastic exercise for a man to do in bed; meanwhile the woman, naturally, is simply masturbating herself when she allows him to enter her since his mind is so occupied with other things ...

14.7.71

Letter from an Accountant in Africa to His Wife, Named Mariana, Residing in Lisbon

My dear Mariana

How happy you made me and how proud I felt when I received your news! We finally have a baby! It's too bad that it's not a boy, because as you know, having a boy was what I wanted most, but it was God's will that it was a girl instead, and we must bring her up too amid the loving atmosphere of our house and the glowing warmth of our hopes.

A daughter, Mariana, a daughter who will surely be as sweet an angel and as pretty as you are, as quiet and gentle as you are and as you have always been – and that is why I love you.

May she grow up to be a good and virtuous woman: that is what we must teach her above all, because that is all she really needs to learn. And I hope, of course, that she'll be pretty, because beauty is important for a woman; you know how important it is for a creature whom we men wish to be the guardian angels of our homes and firesides, faithfully protecting us against moral anxieties, to have delicate features that clearly reflect the delicacy of her soul.

May she be able to follow your example, Mariana, one day offering to her life's companion not only a virgin body but also all the virtue of her spirit, all the tranquillity and innocence of a woman who has nothing to hide from her husband. And above all, may she learn to be forgiving! A woman who can forgive her husband for his faults, who is understanding, tender, and generous is a model to set before her own daughters later.

I want our daughter to be the very image of you, with the same sweetness, the same appearance, the same comforting smile at the most difficult moments in the life of her household; exactly like you in this respect too, a hard-working bee diligently caring for her beehive.

How proud I am of you when I see you in an apron washing the dishes, ironing my shirts, or making me the delicacies that you know I'm fond of.

I want our little girl to have all the spiritual riches and the thousand virtues that I have learned to recognize in you, a woman different from others in today's depraved world where the woman is forgetting her moral duties and her role, her important role as her children's guide. Because a woman is first and foremost a mother, and always will be.

If the great and grave decisions to be made in the world are the responsibility of the man, the woman is called upon to fulfil the glorious role of bringing up the men who will build this world.

No, I have no ambitions for our daughter to aspire to great and illusory achievements, nor to become a celebrity because of her brilliance of mind. I would rather see her be a self-effacing, sensitive woman, the guardian angel of her home who shares in her own heart and body all the torments and grief that may afflict her loved ones.

May God help us to bring her up that way, Mariana, with His protection and His infinite mercy.

I am anxiously awaiting the moment when I can take you in my arms and at the same time embrace our little girl, who in my mind's eye is a rosy-cheeked baby lying in her cradle like a cherub, wreathed in clouds, quietly sleeping . . .

Your husband who loves you very much and hopes to be able to kiss you very soon.

António

14.7.71

Sixth and Final Letter from Dona Mariana Alcoforado, a Nun in Beja, to the Chevalier de Chamilly, Written on Christmas Day of the Year of Grace 1671

Senhor,

It is not my intention ever to send you these lines to read, for their sole purpose is to be committed to paper. When I sent you words set down in the heat of passion and without restraint, I did not know that by putting them down in writing I was holding the reins of suffering in my hands, with the result that merely by grasping them my grief appeared to grow more intense, but in reality it was becoming more and more divorced from my true feelings through the very act of taking these reins in hand. But today I know that the love or the talents that lead one to pick up a pen and thus allay one's pain are of great value, for they put an end to what is merely transitory and enhance the real and enduring goods that are the only ones that merit being put into words.

I wrote you letters full of great love and great torment, Senhor, and after having had no commerce with you for so long, I began to love them and the act of writing about them more than I loved your image or the memory of you. I have penned many more missives than I have cared to send you, for this was a way of taking pleasure in the act of writing and hearing how my words sounded and of impressing my companions here in this house with my talents at composing elegant love letters. As others did embroidery, worked in the garden, or prepared sweetmeats for us to enjoy, or delighted us with their voices raised in song, so my task here, among those assigned each of us, was to set down in writing all the unusual hours that troubled this house or made it a happy place: I wrote of feast days and of sorrows that afflicted none of the others save myself, and composed letters for our Reverend Mother or for young novices to send on with their own signatures – thus taking hold of my life by letting myself go. I also read a great deal, as had always been my habit, though I now did so in order to learn from excellent teachers how best to tune my delightful instrument. And as for my grievous laments for you, Senhor, two years afterwards I no longer even remembered them, having found such pleasure in fulfilling these new duties assigned me, willingly performing a task that I had originally embarked upon for reasons quite contrary to my will. When one is puffed up with pride, one finds many sources of pleasure, and perhaps realizes only on his or her deathbed how vain such pleasures were, and hence only death takes away the joy of writing elegant or witty love letters – or of performing pious and charitable deeds.

And so it was that by writing and by reading works by our writers of old and even many Frenchmen (for I am allowed to read whatever I choose since my family and my superiors are so pleased to see how reasonable and well-behaved I've become) I came to understand, Senhor, that I had composed nothing that had not already been expressed, in other ways and in other times, in works that had touched the hearts of their authors' contemporaries and the hearts of many succeeding generations. And it was then that I began to smile at my sorrows, since what was really mine, really genuine about them I had never contrived to set down in words, and it now seems to me that for what is really true there are no words, only outcries as writhings in one's vitals, and two torments will have nothing in common save what is least important about them. Hence I am beginning to ask myself whether I ever really loved you, whether I ever really cared to discover who you really were, above and beyond your outward appearance, and to ask myself what attracted you to me. And the truth demands that I confess that I for my part found in you only the attraction of rebellion and gay abandon, in those days of mine as a young novice who had been deprived of everything and was by nature so given to both these feelings myself. You were adventure, novelty, the unpredictable life to which I had seemed forever fated. I thus did not love you truly, just as I did not truly love myself, and the only good and lasting thing that has remained in my memories of you are your silences and the seriousness with which you looked at me, as though you were waiting for something. That has been your legacy to me, a hope for after the love that I professed for you, for after the writings that I took such pleasure in, a hope for *after-wards*. It was as though in our love affair I had been the cavalier who gallops astride his cleverness and gracious manners and taste for adventure and you the lady entirely at peace with herself who is no longer offended or amazed at anything because she is so full of wisdom and virtue. Hence our commerce with each other was profound, Senhor, since everything that everyone expected of each of us became completely reversed. You ceased to be possessed and sought after, and I, with my calculated coldness of heart and my inflamed senses, was content merely to possess you and keep you at my mercy, thus behaving towards you as men customarily behave towards their women. You wanted only to die or to depart, and the one thing left for me to do was to continue to enhance my power and freedom in the same domains and in the same ways that I had once been so cruelly deprived of. You should see how respectfully my family and the clergy behave towards me today, how many people come to kiss my hand and to seek my advice, since they are impressed both by my fine style and my subtle wisdom, and I seem to them to be both someone who is acquainted with many authors' writings and ways of expressing suffering that others never speak of, and someone whose behaviour serves as an example of the seemly manner in which one's duties ought to be fulfilled.

I therefore write to you, Senhor, in order to humble myself by remembering your troubled smile, though I am certain that, however genuine my sentiment may be, I am again merely indulging in a vain exercise. The only real pain that I perhaps feel in my heart today is not knowing who I might have been had I not been born enslaved, had I been born a male. And even with my propensity for enmeshing myself in intricate lies, for allowing my vivid imagination to run away with me, and for indulging in flights of fancy that have served to make me feel sure of myself, I do not know whether, had I chanced to have been born a man, I could ever have displayed towards someone whom I had at my mercy, someone far more humble than myself, and a woman and a nun in the bargain, the same high-handed and heedless love as you displayed towards me.

I cannot praise God for the paths He has traced for my life to take, since I have never become resigned to them. Nonetheless I praise Him for my having found you along them, since if this had not come to pass, how would I ever have experienced such feelings as shame and deceitfulness on being extravagantly complimented for charms and talents that were worth nothing? How would I have discovered myself to be – though cloistered and a liar despite myself – someone who in the end was well-loved and lovable, the possessor of something worthwhile that you who were free did not possess?

I know that you have wedded a lady with few charms, though she is a cultured gentlewoman with exquisite manners, who is devoted to you and whose behaviour is most modest and circumspect. I have also heard tell of your sense of justice and your rigorous devotion to God and the pious works and reading of edifying texts that occupy you at present. Pray pardon me, Senhor, if I find it laughable that those whom great sufferings neither kill nor free find their lives slowly draining away in such a mediocre way.

Your servant, then, and your sister in the grace of Our Lord

Mariana

26.7.71

First Final Letter and Probably a Very Long and Disjointed One (I)

I could say that I was very tired and that would be true, but I couldn't say why. I might have said that I didn't want to say anything more and that was true and I couldn't have said why. I could have been discovering what I can and cannot do and disloyally be keeping it to myself. I *am* keeping it to myself, though the only thing I have discovered for certain is that I want no more of this. There is a place of horror that is also the place of the great rebellion that writing represents, which is not to be shared. And that is what I have gained from all this – the certainty of this, and the certainty that this is also the place where one slowly dies and where one loves. One lives and endures one's life with others, within matrices, but it is only alone, truly alone that one bursts apart, springs forth.

I have nothing more to say of the hours of myself that are snatched from me by everyone's hands, including yours; I have nothing more to say of the imbecility of living a meaningless life, wearing myself out, distracted by the little monstrosities of my life from day to day which is made up of friction, of dissension, and not of abjection or of rebellion or major insurrections that cannot ever be carried off successfully in groups. I do not want anything of anyone, not even of you, and even though that may be a lie, it is also the heavy burden that must be borne if the true image of things is to be set down in writing. Not because I feel a calling, a vocation to be as I am, not because it is a profession that I have deliberately chosen, for writing is not a profession – but because this is the outward form that my fury takes, and since it is not shared, I will never use the word *pain* to describe this rage of mine at the irrelevance and the unfairness of almost every effort I make or everything that I love, including this exercise of ours.

Neither a friend, nor a lover, nor sex, nor a commune will harbour what even writing no longer can – my silent phantoms that I carry on my hip and never write to anyone about, not even to you, all the stories I've never told, full of made-up words that are true: so be it. There is nothing more to lay bare. It is time to say *no*, a moment that not even the resolving of our bad tensions as a group or a good piece of writing can postpone. This exercise of ours is the reverse side of me, and I now divorce myself from everything contained therein. It is the harvesting of tares, seeing the ears of grain that I have imitated cut down one by one and ground to bits – a metaphor that along with so many others I dislike, having doubtless never liked anything save what is intangible and elusive, save meanings between the lines, the firm, sinuous line, the pure, steel-like water of real life, the life that lies beneath the surface, the life that is not yet, the life that gives the other life its incandescent glow, this absurd metaphor being the only one that seems really true and writing the only thing worthwhile, though everyone else appears quite content to live with the good angel of conviction perched on their shoulders, alongside their gestures, on the edge of words.

I say to you, then, 'Merry Christmas', for when I gratuitously attack myself like this and leave myself merely the indispensable as my heritage, then every day, even though marked on no one else's calendar, is Christmas for me, and I shall simply allow myself to exist now, abandoning this attempt at clarity that apparently does not tear others apart as it does me.

And from where I stand, I understand everything and choose very little, a single pact that I keep putting off fulfilling with this same unexpressed *no* that dwells within everything and everyone who is truly serious – the sort of endless waiting that day by day breaks off the conversation, *with no resolution*, while at the same time hope refuses to die. The difference between the sexes and others, the differences in the human condition (*ah, les gros mots*) create empty spaces where nothing happens. What terrific centrifugal force the wheel exerts, sisters. My place, one I did not deliberately choose, mind you, is the centre – temporary asphyxia. So then, we absent ones apologize for these and other interruptions in the family saga – the scheduled programme is about to be changed.

And let the deaf bury their deaf and celebrate their worlds.

Let no one tell me that silence gives consent, because whoever is silent dissents.

27.7.71

Ballad of Royal Pain

My Lord and king who keeps himself
from playing manservant or jester
who puts the bread upon the table
and cradles me in his hand

My Lord and king with happy smile
and with his countenance disguised
who wears the world around his waist
and lies down by my side

My Lord and king about to sail off
lightly kissing me goodbye
the house I have will fade away
the life I lead is thin

My Lord and king take up the power
of what you see deep in the grave
forever loving never being
slaves of earth we die

My Lord and king to keep you with me
the knife of tears is not enough
this weeping and this fearfulness
all you hear is moans

My Lord and king with crown raised high
wrought of sun   of mirth   of rice
a garment you have given me
made from your pain and sweat

My Lord and king I would have loved you
had not love's place become a desert
my arms would be too frail to hold you
my words would be too worn

My Lord and king of salt and cedar
turn your ship back to your people
come and tell them of your rebirth
here inside my bones.

2.8.71

Poem Signed by Dom José Maria Pereira Alcoforado Discovered Among Mónica's Papers

Of woman I do not say slow flowing stream
but wind

but sun
and sustenance

but wind

Of woman I do not say slow flowing stream
but time

but life
and its wonder

but time

Of woman I do not say slow flowing stream
but forever

but earth
and its heat

but forever

Of woman I do not say slow flowing stream
but wind

but sun
and sustenance

but wind

6.8.71

Poem by a Woman Named Mariana, Who Took Her Own Life on 11 August, 1971

How slow the body
of a woman sitting.
How easy the invention
of the unsure womb.
How yielding the sand
or how deserted the sea.
How lost the sun or the open cradle

How slow the body
of a woman lying down.
How mild the shoulders that then tighten.
How exact the fears
and how exact the gestures.
How mild the ships of lost defences

How slow the body
of the weary woman:
If giving birth is her voyage
and a wordless cry her only home
and the bread she eats is sown in rage

11.8.71

Love Poem that Resolves All Differences

your breasts of light and vigilance
chaste castles in water
most pure torso   beloved
live

my love kill yourself
why do you not kill yourself?

your hands a winged key
dark flesh kindled
to command (fingers of rope)
the moist cave
live

my love kill yourself
why do you not kill yourself?

your pubis lying in bed
rising to meet
your belly small
in the hollow my soul's cradle
live

my love kill yourself
why do you not kill yourself?

your teeth shining
yellow eyes lingering
oval face
live

my love kill yourself
why do you not kill yourself?

your waist soft curved
(flowing from back to belly)
your forehead fragile and the delicate
bone trembling beneath the weight
live

my love kill yourself
why do you not kill yourself?

your name given
that enormous none other
in the cry and the turning away
live

the sponge of your womb
your wavy hair
all these counted off one by one
live

my love kill yourself
why do you not kill yourself?

4.9.71

First Final Letter and Probably a Very Long and Disjointed One (continued)

Today I would like to praise solitariness, though dispassionately this time, without throwing it in your face, but simply cradling it in your lap. How beautiful things are now that we are expecting no one to tell us why they are! How intact the world is if we are not dying of loneliness because someone has left us. But who can laugh if he does not know that he is unique, that he is someone's favourite; who is self-sufficient and insists on remaining so; how many people experience for at least a few hours the glorious feeling of having no one or of lacking someone to hold us by the hand and nonetheless going on, as what we are writing goes on, as our bodies sustained by a wise hand, our own hand, go on – how many women, how many men have discovered the joy of doing what they are capable of doing all alone, all by themselves? How many women? For the upbringing we have had is that of overbred female setters, female pointers – specially trained to freeze in our tracks when we flush game. But men too are always having to climb to the very top of the ladder in search of a larger share of the spoils, having to kiss the king's arse or be arses themselves (the ass – what the royalty of others always sits on). We women are what men take us to be. Let the devil choose between the two images, and I, for my part, siding with Gil Vicente and Mariana the sinner, will choose to play the role of Mofina Mendes.*

I tell you, sisters, you with whom I have begun to be so secretly at odds – you are taking all these things too seriously – anyone who is self-sufficient is precisely that, though not all the time. If a person is not self-sufficient and he or she is tired of not

* Gil Vicente, the author of the *Auto da Barca* (*The Ship of Heaven and Hell*), created a character, Mofina Mendez, who resembles the proverbial milkmaid who stumbles and breaks her jug of milk as she dreams of all the things she is going to buy when she sells it at the market. (*Translator's note.*)

being so and doesn't like the idea of killing his or her spouse or superior, let him or her above all laugh (and above all laugh up his sleeve) until he or she *is* self-sufficient, because laughing at oneself is the only thing that can be done with true nobility; whoever acquires talents that will allow him to express what he has seen and heard, whoever writes and paints or makes his mark upon the world in some way other than the ordinary is belittling the ordinary and laughing at it. – Nor is there any other formula for liberation from anything except 'Suffer the little ones to come unto me', and since I can't kill myself because I am different from them, I shall give them such a hard and such a loving kick in the ass that they will never again be able to sit down comfortably on the rump of anyone else who seems to be supporting them. And we will only learn such things from the bottom upward, not vice versa.

And many men and women will be called to free themselves and few will be chosen to bear the curse of freedom, which consists of using savoury words, having an inquisitive mind, a carefree heart, and light touch (quite a trick that, since even the most skilful hand occasionally paws about clumsily).

So, my sisters, let us not preach boring sermons on the self-realization of women and their liberation from men. Freedom today, sisters, consists of persistent laughter on the part of anyone who can bear to laugh without making a wry face. Let the little ones kill each other off in their constipated womb-prison. Or do you imagine that you can infect them with these talents that we maintain are furthering the cause of justice and liberty, though they are really simply a sign that we are each playing our own little game, indulging our desire to be unique? Or imagine that what each of us is giving birth to with either of the others, or as three co-conspirators, is really intended for common consumption? The love of violating taboos as something that can one day be totally integrated within society is the truth behind this story and these crafty literary tricks of ours. If we are really what we appear to be, people whose profession is arts and letters, should the day ever arrive when men and women are truly equal, we would still cling to Mariana's example, not because she was a nun and a woman put behind bars, but because she was different. From the point of view of what we are really seeking, any law, even a natural law, is scandalous.

And we will still have very little to give in return, above and beyond the rarity of a really scandalous product, for what we are inventing is not enough for those who are hungry and more than enough for those who have a lord and master.

And then, besides that, beauty. But beauty does not lie in acceptance; it lies in suspending judgment and keeping one's distance.

Solitariness is never praised dispassionately.

5.9.71

Second Letter VIII

I think it is high time we visited our adolescence: young girls in our parents' houses, cut off from the world, our bodies used only by our own hands: the fever spreading up our flanks, the spasm fanning out from our fingers through our wombs.

Nonetheless, it is about childhood that I shall speak to you. How can I explain to you what things were like in childhood, sleeping in their glass jar?

Silence – I assure you – an enormous granite silence that I remember in the geometric gardens and the clipped box hedges, with statues outlined against the luminous, acid sky; a silence as dense to the eye as it would have been to the touch, and yet soft to the teeth and on the tongue. – A gentle tongue that I slowly ran over my arms, tracing on my skin shiny damp spots that later I let dry; far removed from everything and everybody, already falling asleep little by little, gone limp, with an enormous sense of well-being, totally oblivious to everything.

In the memory I have of my childhood, there stand out, towering over me, gentlemen with lazy expressions in their eyes and indolent mannerisms, their footfalls soundless as they wandered idly about inside the houses, in the golden half-light of the drawing-rooms. Expert horsemen, bull wrestlers, riders of women whose hands they subtly kissed.

In the memory I have of my childhood, there stand out women with soft, loose, wavy hair, in silk dresses clinging to their thin bodies, with long fingers where vague, hesitant gestures died away, as their strongest feelings died away in their eyes, scarcely reaching the surface, and the languid way they moved about, the way they lightly touched the gold or crystal objects where the light shimmered in iridescent colours. Women growing bored, slumping down, sinking deeper in the low easy chairs, slowly sipping the sweet wine in the glasses set out on silver trays on top of the tables.

One by one they were mine as I examined them, created them, destroyed them, moulded them in the silence, a barrier of hurt already separating us:

An abyss.

Yet childhood was also:

Mother:

her long legs, her smooth body, her dresses falling in soft folds and her blonde hair spread over her shoulders. Her porcelain eyes.

From a distance I watched, I spied upon her movements, her gestures that always seemed to be a kind of voraciousness carefully held in check.

Her distance.

Yet childhood was also:

Father:

the writing desk with its immense world of words, of knowledge, of solitude, of perfect order, a world that held me spellbound. – The books lined up on the enormous shelves that covered the high bare white walls; the leather armchairs the colour of honey, the microscope in its little varnished wooden case, that made me remember the case in which the statue of the Holy Family came every week to spend a day in our house, in the dark empty room at the back of the house. The room then lighted by the little vigil lamp with the flame of the wick slowly flickering against the oily sides of the low glass chimney.

When I knelt, I never prayed; I felt only the beating of my heart in my chest, and the gesture of humbly bowing my head and closing my eyes filled me with fear.

Yet childhood was also:

Mass:

with the enormous, immense, terrifying and threatening figure of Our Lord of the Way of the Cross, clad in His purple robe, with His blood and His crown of thorns digging deep into His torn flesh.

All my terror, sisters, all my unconscious terror of death and punishment and the end of everything, which even today this image gives rise to, suddenly overcoming me in the middle of the night, journeying deep within my slumber . . .

What path is left for me, with this trail indelibly stamped upon me by my childhood?

I think it is high time we visited our adolescence:

but we refuse to do this and I have also been avoiding doing so by speaking to you instead of my childhood. For telling others about ourselves is always difficult and sordid and ambiguous and lacks sufficient passion.

So once again we come face to face with passion, even when we reject its exercise.

10.9.71

Passing Ox

HEY THERE!

will I be able to pass beyond your name and your eyes, the
only current between them and mine, our rock, our father?
A suspension, this, that I know points towards some wisdom
where no one's face is veiled, or where all persons are equal,
lovable with a love such as that felt by someone dead or
someone truly alive who no longer hopes for anything save
pure hope, awaiting no one – a love that has merely existed,
merely been, without a focal point, freed of all its moorings,
a dry love of nothingness, without death – will I be able to?

HEY THERE!

I love you because of you, because I am your favourite, because I am wanted by you so much. Each moment at your
side is the restraining of gestures, the crying out to skin that
comes from the skin, and even suspending breathing, for there
is too much air between you and me, too much space. I hold
back my hand my wrist my arm my trunk, not even thinking of touching you, not even thinking – how hungry I am to
rid myself of this hunger for you by touching you – of what
name and limits the street, the earth, my expressed pain would
have, were I to touch you as though merely – though there
has never been any 'merely' ever since touching you long ago,
as I have never touched you again and never shall. I have felt
a throbbing pain ever since, so how could I touch you now
and have it be as it was before? I ache to my very fingertips at
the thought.

SO THEN?

know that this cold flows from my bones to my hands, though tears no longer flow from my eyes, and on the table of my speech I place a bread of horror, unleavened bread, I close my mouth with an acid fist and say nothing, everything was already said when we did not know – too long ago, when time went by more slowly or was much simpler. This was nothing to smile at, and we did not know it. Who will praise the children that we did not have, who will visit the perfect house on whose threshold we always lingered, who will call me the wife of all your wholeness, since I have been violated and by that very fact remain a virgin still, doubled over with nausea at the gate of the temple that neither you nor I had sought to enter, the two of us driven away and obliged to go about begging for the alms of the possible, as poor as the others, our hands outstretched, roughly handed a plate of food to fill our bellies, the inner blow on hearing children crying at the door of the room of a humble, peaceful married couple, children who might have been our children, a pain greater than ourselves that hence devours our vitals; tears and cold sweat when the hand is withdrawn, what use is it to beg for peace and receive only a partner?

VERY WELL THEN. WHAT ABOUT YOU?

what can I do? I see the lines etched into your face without your having attained ripeness, the acid mark stamped upon you at still too early an age. The sight has always made me feel ashamed, and turning round and round in a narrow circle, a filthy room   a well   a dawn, I dug at stringy meat with my fingernails, my own flesh, to find food for us and never found any way to say yes for us. Beyond us lies a place even more cruel, and yet my plea still has not died away. How to affirm or how to shout out what I yearn to? With what words? How to bear your weight and sustain you, the word 'we' is so great, greater than either you or me. Look at my grey temples and young bones, as though I were living in limbo and time and my years on this earth were passing more and more slowly – the centre of myself a tender man, too tender a man, lying pulsing in your childlike womb. Look at the veins of my wrists where no blood, not even that of a hearty embrace, healed me of the dull pulsing of your frail ones – a temple fell upon our heads and there is no place for our repose in the houses of the rich nor time for our agony in the houses of the poor. Look how a river of hope for everyone was born of the curve of your soft flank where I placed my mouth and never ever said anything save words of fear.

VERY WELL THEN. ARE YOU STILL THERE?

because I do not cry 'today', let it be today, because I do not take advantage of my rights as someone smaller, someone more frail, a female, dragging myself over the stones saying never again, this is not what I wanted, rather death than seeing our principles destroyed and all our bridges cut off, demanding freedom now, my eyes that knew they were the light of yours grown dim, my mouth shut tight. Look instead at how my hair still is, warm and full of fire even now, stretch out your hand and where you touch me there will remain a spot of blood the size of a flower and then after that our embrace, and who will be able to stop us? We will be equals, the couple, the kernel of the world and people will gather round us and bring their children and dance three days and three nights to celebrate the rebeginning of everything. Say just one single word aloud and I will give birth to the happiness of an entire people.

STILL HERE. HOW ABOUT YOU?

I see the cry flowing round about inside your mouth, your breast, the middle of you. Lean on me so as not to fall from the weight of this cry you are holding back. You know this, yet I nonetheless remind you of it, my hand hovering tensely just above the nape of your neck, which I do not touch. How beautiful you are because you hold yourself back, out of prudence or out of courage, disfigured only by the same hope that I borrow from you to sustain myself before you lose your stature and become mediocre. How I pity myself because you try to do more than you are able to do, you with your tiny little breaths, me holding back the tongue that anointed your yes: how I bless you for being little and how

I pant like an animal for you. Listen in my hard cheekbones to the secret gasp of agony of the legitimate animal that since childhood has been growing and dying at the mere touch of your transparent fingers that I did not know awaited me. Listen to my bones of a man crack to pieces before you as I stand erect.

ME TOO

So be it. Barren, with gentle, feminine senses, being gentle with you and light-hearted, as you wish me to be. And singing and telling stories of a time not yet come, dancing till a throne is created, stitching the shroud of what will not die, boiling water to cleanse the wound, allowing that bitter wine of ours to be suckled from my breasts, the sacred knot form-less but not undone. Can I not die, my love, after having been kept so long on the verge of life?

17.9.71

Finale – Dona Tareja[33]

Little girl chosen
by a lord from across the border
your body a mask
your speech a tempered cry

Knife worn in the garter
passed from father to son
in legend and song
grace and retribution for all
your face locked shut

Cunning fingers
fear of the royal flesh
the thorns of your wickedness
praised as goodness in others

Little girl without caution
who alighting in words spoken
in words written
shows signs of flying away

May your being be light
may your smile be set free
may the blue of your days be given
with grace
may your gaze be unclouded
for giving

24.9.71

Elizabeth Regina III

My Lady I free you from
sadness
and endow you with glory
not of book or office
nor of deed
(you the poor)
but of sweet laughter
and comfort to your measure
where you shall overcome wilfulness
and the need for a nest

My Lady for you I wish
a frontier captain more real
than a king
who knows the rhythm of the cradle
who understands crying in your sleep
in clarity of thought
to be master of the great world
of feeling and riding
and to hold you in as much esteem
in this farewell of rebeginning
as do I.

24.9.71

Second Final Letter

We eyed one another very cautiously. We acted like someone who, at a party among friends, is invited to perform a trick, to put on his own particular clever little act. The person gets ready to perform, clears his throat, adjusts his clothes, strikes a pose, is about to begin, hesitates, says: 'No, that's not right,' smooths his hair, and so on. That was how it was in the beginning, with little notes and verses to you and to me. A slight seventeenth-century turn of phrase, or give our words a Mariana-like patina; and the sentences tumbled out, wobbling first in one direction and then in another. And this obsession of ours that made us call each other 'little girl' (and certainly that is what we once were: 'Little girl, your mother is calling you . . .'; 'If little girls don't keep quiet and behave nicely . . .' and that is what we still are, since we are minors in the eyes of the law). And our continual narcissism. You, my one sister, a woman who looks upon her body as a separate thing, as her own erotic object, and not as her self (because the very survival of society is founded on this practice, the woman withdrawing from her body so that it may be used and explored without personal resistance: 'Who me, not me, I adore dressing up, and sex is men's obsession', and when women marry their body is part of their dowry, along with sheets and table napkins, being intended for everyday use and the production of children, and the husband and wife lie with their heads side by side on the pillow at night looking at the woman's swelling pregnant body; and because the man is searching for a womb for himself; and because it is the woman's body that brings forth the so-called fruit of a man's loins and of society; women are emerging from their long sexual hibernation but they still do not inhabit their bodies, they look at them, they speak of them as of highly prized animals). And you, my other sister, finding such pleasure in an 'intellectual adventure', that was not an adventure of the spirit but a playing with words full of *esprit*.

Oh how unbearable I found the two of you at times, when we were at first beginning these pages, and how unbearable I was too, with my pedantic rhetoric (I understand, you understand, he understands, we all understand the situation, in the beginning was the Word, and there we remained, waiting for the creative power of words, their power to change things, to come our way). Being tired of myself is nothing new, I am quite used to it, I am tired of myself at night, so I fall asleep immediately and re-create my self-respect. Hence growing tired of you, getting fed up with you was the greatest risk confronting me in this adventure. Was it the intimacy, the narcissism of telling you of my feelings, of my friendship for you (how moving, how generous an experience we were sharing, etc. etc.) that allowed me to overcome the nausea I felt during our first meetings? No, this undertaking of ours is not an evangelical one: quite the contrary. Christ vomited up hypocrites and ever since then (and even before) everyone has set a great deal of store by clear-cut truths, good and evil, yes and no, barriers, Maginot lines, totalitarian systems and their respective complementary polarities; and what is more, in totalitarian systems, anyone who thinks is automatically an intellectual, and even though he never possessed the sort of faith that would move mountains, Mohammed nonetheless came along and said that if the mountain would not come to him he could go to the mountain, thus setting an example not only for mountain climbers but also for social climbers, and if hens get fatter grain by grain (especially ones that range freely rather than being shut up in a poultry yard) and little strokes fell great oaks, and all that sort of received wisdom, a mountain of sand can also be levelled grain by grain (so long as it is taken for granted that such a thing as eternity exists): everything depends on how one goes to the mountain, on who eats and who spits, on what's good and what's bad, positive or negative, yes or no, because anyone who thinks makes distinctions – you or me, either/or, a barrier here a barrier there, with no middle ground allowed – here is not there, I am good and everything else is evil, and so everybody vomits everybody else up, and if a healthy revolution can digest a 'paradise', a 'paradise' that is badly planned can digest many intellectuals, all of whom have been vomited up. Because the basic principle of true revolution is: thou shalt not devour thy brother (for then you won't vomit him up); and so our vomiting turned out to be just dry retching, and we got past the risk safely.

And then the rest. The one of us who once frolicked with the other two as though we were all little girls, who danced in a ring with us and blew soap bubbles, suddenly turned serious and began to indulge in mystical outpourings about cavaliers. And metaphors about love as a floor, clean and freshly scrubbed, as simple as naphtha soap, and tales about lonely grass-widows. And she declares that we are as much fun to pal around with as young boys. And that the death of difference, the 'soil of revolution', is joyous, easy laughter. It is not because you laugh that your teeth fall out, but nonetheless there are those who are toothless. The soil of revolution is not the death of difference, nor does joyous laughter come easily. The soil of revolution is the death of the value of difference, of *all* differences, not only of those that you are thinking about, my sister; I even hope that 'intelligent' ceases to be an honorific title. Joyous, easy laughter – that *would* be nice, wouldn't it? But there are many people who still must learn to laugh – a revolutionary project, and the only thing that comes easily are stupid witticisms. The death of difference? Take back the words 'as much fun to pal around with as young boys' and stop pretending. 'I may perhaps speak to you of love or perhaps of death,' another of us said. Of both things; you wrote: 'Listen, my sister, the body. Now only the body leads us to others and to words'; '. . . you are the fruit, Mariana, the product, the prolonged moan of a symptom so often lost sight of, so often re-encountered, so often recurring all through the course of a pitiful story of powerlessness . . . oh fear and yet more fear, with nothing kept secret and no artful tricks . . . All rights of possession belong to males, Mariana, even today . . . A soft moan that escapes you takes possession of me, impregnates me, transcends me and kills me: my writing . . . I pretended to love you, to the point of vice.' Which of us did not gorge herself on your obsessive, narcissistic description – those long legs, those breasts, that vagina – how to explain to you, sister, how you reveal yourself, show yourself to be the object of your own self, bare your furious desire for your own self – my sister, anyone who can keep from being annoyed with you knows that you are to be respected; you were the one who exposed herself the most, and it seems to me that to expose oneself is to be true to oneself. And my grandiloquent anathemas supposedly penned by nieces and aunts, spontaneous burgeonings of a feminine lineage – and what do all of us women have left if we are not spontaneous, if we do not possess the foundation of revolution that our brother is still devouring?

(and I thought of writing a love letter to the man who will eventually come to be, do you remember? It is necessary to cure the man; to tell him both that his body is not sterile and that it is not only his phallus that is creative; to tell him that it is not always necessary to erect things in order to create, and that creating first and then building and raising can cease to be a woman's privilege alone. He must be told many things, but there is no way to say them yet that I know of.)

And then came the ramifications. You first, my one sister, continuing your 'pitiful story of powerlessness'. Fear and yet more fear, eternal love and death, constant melodrama, a host of characters, all of them crazy, were your creation, all of them howling with pain, always the same 'pitiful story of powerlessness', the father, the prostitute, the madwoman, the servant. How to imagine love in a world that is all awry? But how also to reject it? Only through death. You, my sister, the sister of death, of the flesh, say: 'Only the body, sister', and if it is of no use to us let it be a corpse. And then you, my other sister, who branched out by taking pleasure in the mere sound of the written word, nest/rest, mast/must – listen, my sister, it is not true that we are getting anywhere if we put two words together simply because they sound more or less alike; this will not ensure that the leap of love, and of death, towards somewhere beyond, towards a dream (yours) will inevitably be successful, even in the case of the young boy that you created for us, a 'guardian angel', an innocent man attentive to the harmony of sounds. And I, my sisters, who wanted to talk about the background, about barriers, about right versus wrong, a barrier here and a barrier there, was trying to say that mountains are levelled only by putting them under total siege and that probably the only great causes are those that actually touch us, and the parts I wrote were poor: the prison, the body. Listen, sister, the body: perhaps the love letter to the man who will eventually come to be is already written.

(and I thought of writing another text, on the couple that makes love, and then the woman afterwards, all alone in the house, leaning over and carefully remaking the rumpled bed, carefully folding the edge of the sheet back, bending over, decorating the nest or the altar – a priestess-victim? – as meanwhile the man goes about his 'masculine' business – mere usufruct. But how to write any more than what we have already written, which is very little, not from the point of view of quantity, but because we failed to follow the trail to the end, to trace the total pattern of the characters and its roots, whether rotten or not, and its tentacles, its waves that fan out in every direction, into others, into things, into the past, into the future – the father capable of raping his daughter and throwing her out of the house with a clear conscience for instance – where did all this come from, and where will it end? In bitter conflict, certainly, in exploration, but how far will it go, what new conflicts will it continue to create? We would never be able to follow the total pattern of the characters, of situations, to the very end.)

Let a bell be cast that can be tolled. From the body, the corpse of someone who was neither a man nor a child, you said.

The one who dreamed of Dom Sebastião; the one in Africa writing to his friend:

three centuries' distance is nothing, the men are there before us; words set men side by side and prove that they are ever the same. For you it is not simply a question of putting words together, I know that, my sister; I realize that you want to follow the total pattern of everything – there must be no gaps, the texture must be closely woven, must become denser and denser. So you then speak of the girl student attending the university, of the mediocre man, of the emigrant who's the object of a love that's all washed up and departs for foreign shores, and of the fiancé who's taken off for parts unknown. I know that you want to follow the total pattern, but you fail to show the difference between the prose you sweat over and that delicate, sophisticated, highly stylized lacework of words that betrays how distant the Other is from you despite your genuine concern; you forget hunger and those who are hungry all too easily, and instead ponder the possible compensations, the inner feelings, and the motives of the starving person. 'Little kings and queens sitting on thrones for sale'; to you protest becomes bullshit that sells posters. So you make games and rocking horses out of words. *Autant en faire, puisque c'est toujours pareil.** Haven't you made sheer garbage out of words? Will the threads running from me to you, from us to the others, be woven together in silence, in meek gestures, in delicate vibrations beneath the surface, or in action? I asked what words could do; we have filled reams of paper over the months, and what can we do, what are we doing? Words are not a substitute for action, but they can be an aid. They can be used, for instance, to outline the political background of the problem of the woman, for as long as that is missing, the problem will dissolve into one of which packaged soup to buy and 'how to satisfy your husband in bed'. And you are encouraging more people to kill themselves, Mónica: 'I give myself and deny myself' – but *qu'est-ce que je vais faire?*†

(and I also planned a reply to the Mariana who was pregnant, content, and as round as the world – but a round belly is not the world. The rightness of things, a little ray of sunshine entering your body . . . but so what? That's how it is when one is tired, and the feeling lasts only as long as one is relaxing. I planned a reply – because I consider it an urgent task to dismantle the mystique of pregnancy – but I've grown tired of words now that you insist on using them as a substitute for actions.)

And so in the beginning I was displeased. And I yearned to change things, to omit things, to elaborate, to take a blue pencil to precocities of form and content. But then I restrained myself. What is literature? And what is this experience shared by the three of us? Perhaps nothing more than squeezing a boil. Perhaps nothing more than telling each other aloud – out of courage? out of necessity? – about our discontents, our fits of rage, our refusals, and our fears. Anyone who writes omits certain things and dwells on others, in accordance with the rules of the time and the place, retouches his or her self-portrait to make it more attractive. Here and now, for example, certain liberties may be taken with language, but not others, the innovations that are acceptable are relatively few, and at the same time to be reactionary is to lose one's standing once and for all; we are all impeccable writers, alas, and our hearts are in the right places. So I didn't change things, I didn't omit things, and so on.

* What's the difference, since everything is always the same.
† What am I going to do?

Let our dialectic of women-born-and-raised-in-the-urban-middle-class-of-this-society-whose-values-we-are-all-too-familiar-with-and-hence-sympathize-with-all-exploited-classes-and-groups-with-the-heartfelt-feeling-of-belonging-to-the-exploited group-'women' come out in print then, let this contorted dialectic of ours unfold between us and the others, and not only between-our-selves or between-ourselves.

Am I evading my responsibilities? The writer who reveals himself by humbly and sincerely leaving himself open to slander and criticism – look, fellow citizens, what a likeable person! Either hung for a sheep or hung for a lamb, returning once again to accepted wisdom: the writer who conceals himself hoodwinks others, the writer who removes the hood and reveals himself tells truths that sell; and the whole thing ends up in little word games, O delights of culture! (Isn't that so, sister?) And in this final exchange of letters, this end we have reached, we once again come up against the original stumbling block. The best part was the middle, when we were so absorbed in our dialogue that we forgot even the possibility of eventual spectators. It is impossible to survive in the morass of self-analytical reflection; and so I disruptively break away; to hell with the whole thing; I'm fed up.

(and I still wanted to tell you of the sandbanks that surround us; each gesture we make is like a stone in the water, the waves come and go as they please, bound for heaven only knows where, some of them gentle and some of them wild, some of them washing in obliquely and some of them crashing in head-on; the sandbanks are always on the point of crumbling, as the water begins to soak through and we flounder about in it; 'It was all done with the best of intentions, I never did any harm to anyone,' the upright, irreproachable citizens say, but good intentions serve only as the goal, as the point of departure; once we have launched our gesture, passing it on to others, it is all a question of the right moment.)

4.10.71

My Poem of Love in the Manner of a Dedication

No one tells you
to stay
but I say

it is possible your eyes
are green

let it be the colour of the water
of your feelings
childhood and honeysuckle
you with me

A seal on the house that does not shelter
or a shining crack in the wall
apart from what you know
and apart from what I hide

I show you only your roses
not merely
your body that sings itself not claiming
to reach beyond the reaches of the earth
and my memory of you
in a thread of hard metal

No one tells you
to go
but I say

Insurmountable are the stones
of my feelings

Attentive I am
but not with you

10.10.71

First Final Letter and Probably Very Long and Disjointed (*te deum*)

This is goodbye, my dear ones, I've been trying to tell you so for two letters now, writing to you without having any news from you, yet a further proof of the spitefulness and arrogance involved in the act of writing. *La fin d'un livre? C'est un processus d'auto-défense de l'auteur. Il est fatigué.** I am not tired of writing, which I am now beginning to take up again as a lonely craft, the sort of writing that I have not done for a long time, perhaps because of what we took upon ourselves or what was imposed upon us – this exercise of passion by way of the written word and of compassion shared by the three of us, compassion for our own lives and that of others which we would like to see freer and happier, lives burdened with obligations and habits that are futile and of little value, and are so often felt to have no meaning at all. What will remain with me this time is not so much what I wrote about it, but what I received from it, the childhood feelings I relived in it, the heavy burden of each day that I hid from others and shared only in whispers, in exchanges of little secrets, the smell of baby's bibs and the bread and butter of a solidarity that was a bit frivolous but warm and affectionate, as legitimate as the solidarity of little children who search out secret hiding places or wide-open spaces in order to escape from grown-ups who do not understand them. This and what remained unexpressed, my talent and my torment, my talent that is a torment, sister. I must leave now. Because it is my feeling that with you, with each other, none of us ever ventured beyond the edge of many things, and above all simply hovered at the edge of this wild and solitary thing that love-writing is, which is not a thing that depends merely on circumstances, a thing that can be done only if and when the relations between men, the relations between men and

* The end of a book? It is a process of self-defence on the part of the author. He is tired.

women, the social-ethical-economic circumstances that determine them change, but a thing involving art, a thing involving a way of responding by asking questions – love in short, a permanent proof by the absurd that it is possible to say *yes*. For saying *yes* is already possible but it is so discomforting that it often very much resembles a *no* to everything that good sense or fairness proposes. We made our way through the territory of separation, the separation of Mariana and the chevalier, of mothers and daughters, of women and men, of masters and servants, of emigrants and those they left behind, of women friends and men friends: apartness.

> '. . . Who waits, stays behind and fails to choose . . .'
> '. . . Who severs, goes and reaps nothing . . .'

one of you wrote. And the other:

> '. . . of ancient moorings where we are secured separate from the others and so close.'

and also:

> '. . . Let no one ask me, tempt me, force me to re-turn to others' cloisters.'

*Il le faut, ma soeur.** It is necessary to hope, it is necessary to depart. Time is moving, and space. There are fixed points, but so far removed from everything, so hidden. And within all of us, men or women, burning with desire, there are empty spaces, spaces where something is missing, that no justice will be able to fill, no levelling of differences, for we are different by nature: some have too much and some too little. Even though everything were later to be changed – if men could give birth to children and women impregnate men, the time of peace would still not have come. Because the injustice done men and women in their very flesh, in their rights to property, in their occupations does not undo the injustice done them simply because they each know what they truly are. Different and separated.

* It is necessary, my sister.

Like the terrible difference between us at first, and then later, the fragile dawn of love that this book, this thing, came to be. A difference that was not healed, though our exercise was a sort of soothing balm that alleviated it somewhat. But it was a false relief, false because it was precarious and fragile. Look at the difference now, after working so hard for a unity we never quite succeeded in achieving. Look at how in these final pages we are again donning our masks – the masks that once upon a time fitted so well the sad little faces of the three little girls who did not know each other and yet went to the same matinee thirty years ago. Different and separated. Your mask that of someone serene and meticulous and strong and reasonable, my one sister; your mask, my other sister (exactly right for you), that of suffering, a suffering that in your case is very real; my mask that of someone who is intimately acquainted with the sublime and is saving it for a better time, the mask of someone who is sober, aloof, even-tempered. Masks of three women standing united and – what is of grave importance – really being so, but not always, and not always for good reasons.

And I said that the difference was terrible and the relief false, because I am playing with words in order to learn and in order to allow them to tear me apart. There is, then, a destructiveness in the game, but also an offering, there was an offering in the little trifle in the form of a book that I already gave to this City, there is an offering in my 'aesthetic' attitude towards this common undertaking of ours: you must believe that there is great sincerity behind my 'dilettantism', and I am tired of the sermons of the one of you who possesses a logical turn of mind that is more rectilinear than the life that she is so studiously avoiding.

Ripping everything apart now:

> I believe in the Other and know that it is I who am green and not the grapes
>
> I believe in the collective creations of all of us – even this one; they yield a few clusters of grapes that are not sour
>
> I do not believe in reason apart from the feelings of others and therefore I try to do a good job of being unreasonable and I am tired of trying to be like those who are reasonable, those who even

when they are on the verge of losing everything,
never lose their reason.
I believe in the individual creation of whoever (and
whatever) cannot exist in any other way. And it
is I who am green, etc.

But I haven't gone away yet because, besides the nun who
weeps and wails there have also been such recent 'unbalanced'
writers to keep me company as Mario Sá Carneiro, who committed suicide because he couldn't decide which of his selves
he really was, and António Maria Lisboa, and Herberto Helder,
and Florbela Espanca, in a big photograph that can be hung in
the hall; all relics. If we perchance have talent and capabilities,
they will die before your eyes, as this book is dying. Different
and separated. Unless we have loved and hated more passionately
than is indicated by what we have written and done, much more,
each one awaiting the other two, isn't that true, sisters? Isn't
that true, brother writers and readers?

I who have always been a Lego set[34] therefore leave you as my
legacy my (our) passing and this final game (why not?)

> O sisters, I feel
> It's fatal
> A defect that's natal
> To love a great deal
> In Portugal.

16.10.71

Poem of Contempt by a Woman Named Ana Maria

DISENCOUNTER

Tell me of your silence
the spaces it carves out
in our house   both of us
under its force

Two pitchers just alike
side by side
the bed made
without memory or shade

What meeting of years we have exchanged
for the fruit of the mouth that clings
to the glass of the word we used

It is abandoned – and far in the distance the body that evades
the fever of the half-light since we left it
and put on the listless habit of tenderness

23.10.71

Love Poem by a Woman Named Mariana, Who Died on 11 August, 1971

DESPAIR

I lost for myself in you
my own sustenance

Soft in the wind
are the gentle roses with which I nourish time

26.10.71

Finale – Isabel – Sister

I deposit, my companion
in you
my weariness

but in you – calm
clear, erect:
wholeness

your clarity
at the prow of this ship

your courage
its whole embodiment

7.11.71

Finale – Fátima – You of Roses

I treasure your ardour,
sister,
your fire

the fragile in you
the grief – the foetus

the velvet of your eyes
in the ultimate balance
of words

heedless words
that you use like roses

wounding – and pursuing
or wooing or consuming
the roses

or retrieving the roses
or putting the roses to sleep because they were

7.11.71

Three Fragments of the Diary of a Woman Named Mariana, Who Died on 11 August, 1971

INVOCATION I

I sicken for you in my silence.

I put down my cigarette and sit barely hearing your voice:

Why rediscover you now? This sudden fever that takes me: this plant that rooted itself in my belly and opens its petals, one by one, venomous and slow, vicious and sweet.

Spongy and sweet . . .

13.11.71

INVOCATION II

I fall back upon your image.

Your hands that move in circles in the smooth and fathomless glass of memory.

Your mouth that is still unknown to me, or already forgotten, or remembered only in my fingers

Desperate, perhaps, but so soft and slow, this vice of you that I now fall into.

That I take up again?

The sudden temptation of your tongue, as I ignore it and defeat myself.

13.11.71

INVOCATION III

What languid pools your verses . . .
   I sink myself in them (refuge?) and rediscover the wisdom
of the body. Of nerves. Of birds. The dizzying water envelops my
limbs, taking my mouth.
   What quiet suicide your eyes . . .

13.11.71

Poem Found in the Diary of a Woman Named Mónica

INTIMIDADE

Do you remember my love
when you undressed me:

your fingers running
slowly:
slowly unfastening and opening me

11.12.71

Third Final Letter

I am writing to you, sisters, because one of you urged me so insistently to do so.

I lack the will to tell you that we have finished and drawn certain conclusions from our experience, just as I also lack the courage to join hands with you to form a circle of laughter.

I also lack the will to accuse you (us), to use force, slowly driving words into your (my) skin.

What do we have left after all this? But for that matter, what did we have left before all of this? – A little bit less, it seems to me; much less, even.

Being alone with you, our comradeship that we did not weave on anyone else's loom, certainly not on that of any male, since we are fond of men (very fond in fact), but never in secret, and only if they are not expert horsemen (which is difficult, let us agree . . .), and in the end we laughed.

Oh, sisters, how we laughed!

And today (as so many other times), I confess to you my bewilderment at the world, my fear, my rage, my ravenous hunger for everything. O my love that is unflagging but futile!

Misunderstanding things and people . . .

And in all sincerity I say to you: we shall go on alone, but we will feel less forsaken.

25.11.71

My Text of Love, or Proposal of a Woman, in the Manner of a Monologue

Freedom or the urgency of death within my body: not necessarily without you, my love.

The death that is drunk out of voracious thirst; the death that is drunk like sweet wine, mellowed to a gold as transparent as glass. The death that is drunk out of torpor or indifference to everything, without our even caring to know why.

Let us cling to our vertigo, my love, lustfully, greedily. This eagerness to bite your wrists and your belly, your loins. This . . . eagerness to have you kiss my shoulders and slowly violate me to the point of ecstasy. This faint, delicate flicker of tenderness as I slowly run my tongue over your legs, your armpits, your testicles, so fragile and unprotected, so marvellously warm, covered with the soft velvet fuzz of fruits.

Urgently.

Let us plunge, let us fall to the very bottom of the vortex.

Of dizziness.

Let us make use of madness, my love. It is mobile, so mobile, and yet also so blind and so restrained, so certain to prove to be built on nothingness if you were to return.

And you take me.

I guide you by the waist and eyes. I control you through the fire in your veins: we who have so little will; creatures only of instinctive wisdom, immediate impulse. My earthenware and gold and linen and journeying.

Let us hasten the loss, the end, the beginning of everything that surrounds us; let us not listen to time. Let us deny persons: all of them, one by one; as long as women have long hair that touches their waists and paint their mouths and men have sharp-pointed weapons and fingers that fiercely clench these weapons in acrid and bitter hatred.

Let us forget, my love, let us forget. Even if we remain desperately lucid and the vertigo is nothing more than a dizzying imaginary fall, dreamed in a nightmare in some bed. I fall that way and think that I am killing myself, and as I hurtle downwards I curl up in a ball, in the wind, in the sun, in the soft stone of the air, in the forbidden wish to fly, enveloping myself in the fear of the weight of the body that is dragging me down and down and stripping me of my laughter, anchored fast to myself.

I cling to your neck like someone drowning as you swim against the tide of my death.

No, never . . . and I see you foundering and feel no grief . . .

Let us lean over the edge, let us fall to the very bottom, our feet touching the mud at the bottom of the cliffs. Let the soft plants of madness begin to wind their soft, pliant, heavy stems around us, sucking out our blood and its fever and its roots my love until nothing is left of us among others.

Let us listen to the silence, let us surrender: our arms to the needles that pierce our veins, and then slowly fall asleep, dreaming no bad dreams save those within ourselves.

They are waiting for us there beneath the trees.

The trees are waiting for us down there below.

I slowly descend on them; they are enormous, a brilliant green hiding the shady ground where our bodies will later rest, where our bodies will struggle, rather than above the trees that already are opening, already are parting to allow us to pass through:

wet, fertile, vibrant, nourished by the earth; by manure, by little animals that satisfy their hunger, kill their desire.

How really soft the burnt, crumbled, russet-coloured, quiet, warm stone is that welcomes me. This is death drunk like sweet wine, mellowed to a gold as transparent as glass.

An old wine that has been drowsing for centuries in bottles lined up in a row, with their heavy carved glass stoppers.

This, my love, is the death that in the end you do not belong to:

I descend all alone, eagerly, down through the dizzying vortex, and finally rest on the hidden steps beneath the trees:

huge steps of corroded stone, eaten away by the years, my head hanging downward, my hair, still warm, spread out over them. My hands clasp yours, and yours let go, allowing me to journey on to nothingness.

On my thighs I still bear the marks of your teeth, the mark of your mouth, the wet trace of your tongue, of your teeth.

I descend:

the ground that the trees nourish with their sap must be soft.

Freedom or the urgency of death within my body: not necessarily without you, my love.

25.11.71

Authors' Afterword

A description of the content of *The Three Marias: New Portuguese Letters* is scarcely possible without reference to the interpersonal dynamics, the day-to-day experience of the three authors while involved in its creation. WHAT is in the book cannot be dissociated from HOW it came to be. This is not the work of an isolated writer struggling with personal phantoms and problems of expression in order to communicate with an abstract Other, nor is it the summing-up of the production of three such writers working separately on the same theme. The book is the *written record* of a much broader, common, lived experience of creating a sisterhood through conflict, shared fun and sorrow, complicity and competition – an interplay not only of modes of writing but of modes of being, some of them conscious and some far less so, all of them shifting in the process, and all three of us still facing, even today, the question of *how*.

It all started when one of us said: 'What if we wrote a book together?' Our point of departure, which we decided on after the THING had already started: the seventeenth-century *Portuguese Letters*, first published in France – five love letters from a Portuguese nun, Mariana Alcoforado, cloistered in a convent in Beja, to a French 'chevalier' who had had a passionate affair with her and then forsaken her after his period of service in the Army sent to our country by Richelieu to support our recently regained independence from Spanish domination. Hence a number of motifs were already implicit in our choice of these letters as our 'inspiration': passion, feminine seclusion, and sisterhood; the act of writing; man and woman as strangers to each other; the couple; a national and personal sense of isolation and abandonment; hatred, separation, war; religious and moral prejudices and taboos; guilt; the pursuit of joy and pleasure; the community of the secluded; ingenuous love and sophisticated love letters; the constants of our national history . . . something of all of this. But also something having as its main focus certain key themes:

– three Portuguese women writers of today
– reworking together a classic, though possibly forged, work of literature
– written by another Portuguese woman, a supposedly educated nun, long since dead.

As for the accepted *rules* of our game, our research, our pact, or whatever one may choose to call it:

– as the THING gradually came into being, each of us was regularly to exchange letters with each of the other two;
– we were to meet for lunch, with no specific programme in mind, at a public place, at least once a week;
– we were to meet one evening every week and deliver to the other two a copy of whatever material we had produced that particular week.

And that is what we did. As the manuscript grew, we worked together, discussed each other's contributions, talked about our lives, and went on. We set ourselves no rules as to style, literary *genres*, quantity.

What we ended up with:

– poetry (mainly lyrical and/or erotic);
– fictitious seventeenth-century letters developing the Mariana Alcoforado theme;
– fictitious letters on such contemporary national themes as emigration, repression, war overseas, feminine and masculine roles;
– essays on the above subjects, the focal point of which, however, was always the condition of women throughout history;
– fictional sketches based on these same themes;
– and some of the letters each of us agreed to write to the other two, scattered throughout the book.

The other unifying principle of the book is chronological. Things in it are presented as they came, with no other criteria for their arrangement save our belief in their own (our own) inner development and unity, each piece dated but unsigned, the THING pulsing with a life of its own, from beginning to end, since otherwise we could and would have been engulfed by it, possessed by it, and in the end perhaps too tired, too frightened to carry it further.

The reaction to the book, however, has surpassed both our fears and our expectations. We knew that we were doing something disturbing and exciting. National and international attention is continuing to prove just how disturbing and exciting our work together was. All of which forces us to keep in mind, if ever we should be tempted to forget them, the words of Guimarães Rosa, the Brazilian: 'All I know is that there are too many mysteries surrounding books and those who read them and those who write them; one must be humble . . . Often, nearly always, a book is a far bigger thing than what we are.' Words perhaps even more true in the case of *our* book, one written together by three women.

MARIA ISABEL BARRENO
MARIA TERESA HORTA
MARIA VELHO DA COSTA

Notes

1. Maria Velho da Costa has written a novel entitled *Maina Mendes*, p. 25.

2. The sentence in italics is in French in the Portuguese text. (*Translator's note.*)

3. This poem, entitled *Brinco de Freira* in the original Portuguese, is based on puns, the majority of which are untranslatable. I have therefore substituted other puns in English, meant to suggest the sea imagery and the sense of linguistic playfulness of the original. This English version should hence not be regarded as a literal translation, but rather as a kind of re-creation of the whimsical original. (*Translator's note.*) Translated by Helen R. Lane.

4. The name of the town Beja is derived from the Latin *Pax Julia*. The law of Sesmarias established an alliance between the King of Portugal and the people against the nobles. (*Translator's note.*)

5. A province in southern Portugal. (*Translator's note.*)

6. Collin de Plancy, *Dictionnaire de Sorcellerie*, p. 87.

7. Ibid., p. 88.

8. Ibid., p. 89.

9. Ibid., p. 90.

10. Ibid., p. 91.

11. Ibid., p. 92.

12. Ibid., p. 93.

13. Ibid., p. 94.

14. Ibid., p. 96.

15. The Portuguese text is from an anonymous poet of the seventeenth century. (*Translator's note.*)

16. In Portuguese the word *marinheiro* means both 'sailor' and 'panderer'. (*Translator's note.*)

17. Heroine of Pierre Corneille's famous seventeenth-century tragedy *Le Cid*. (*Translator's note.*)

18. The phrases in italics in this letter are in French in the Portuguese text. (*Translator's note.*)

19. A reference to the title of a book, *Tristes Tropiques*, by the French anthropologist Claude Lévi-Strauss. (*Translator's note.*)

20. A play on words: *Três* in Portuguese means 'three' and *os três* means virginity. (*Translator's note.*)

21. Moravia, p. 147.

22. Ibid., p. 147.

23. Marañon, p. 149.

24. Inez de Castro (*d.* 1355), called *Collo de Garza* ('Heron's Neck'), was the mistress of Pedro, the infante of Portugal, who had married Inez's cousin Constança, with whom Inez had been raised at the provincial court of the Duke Juan Manuel. Rivals of the Castro family persuaded Alfonso, Pedro's father, that his son's alliance (and perhaps his secret marriage with her after the death of Constança in childbirth) represented a danger to the throne, and they had her murdered. Legend has it that Inez's dead body, crowned and robed in royal raiment, was placed beside Pedro's on the throne when he succeeded his father as King of Portugal, and the assembled nobles paid homage to her as to their queen, swearing fealty on the withered hand of the corpse. (*Translator's note.*)

25. Sebastião (1557–78) succeeded to the throne of Portugal at the age of three. As a boy Sebastião became obsessed with the idea of a crusade against the Moors, and was presumably

killed in Morocco in 1578 during an expedition against Larache. The Portuguese people long refused to believe that their sovereign was dead, and for many years legends circulated that he would one day return, thus assuring that the throne would not pass from the direct line of the Portuguese House of Avis. (*Translator's note.*)

26. All the texts in French in this letter are by Albertine Sarrazin. (*Translator's note.*)

27. The Portuguese title of this poem is *De Paredes y Flores*. It was partially inspired by a Peruvian nun named Marie Anne de Paredes y Flores, beatified in 1833. Offering herself in sacrifice to God during an epidemic of plague, a miraculous lily is said to have sprung from blood taken from her dead body; hence she is often referred to as 'The Lily of Quito'. (*Translator's note.*)

28. The first part of this phrase is in French, and the last two words in Portuguese. (*Translator's note.*)

29. The last words of *O Fim.* (*Translator's note.*)

30. The name of a small town in Portugal.

31. In Portuguese the word for 'notebook' is *caderno*, and the words for 'winter' and 'hell', *inverno* and *inferno*. (*Translator's note.*)

32. A refrain from *Vida e Marte Severina*, a play with a libretto by João Cabral de Melo Neto and music by Chico Buargie de Hollonda.

33. Dona Tareja was the mother of the first King of Portugal of Portuguese descent. (*Translator's note.*)

34. A set of plastic pieces that children can make a house out of, which they can then even throw out of the window if they like. (*Author's note.*)

Readers International is dedicated to making available, to the widest possible English-speaking audience, major works of contemporary literature from around the world.

Since 1984 Readers International has published some 50 titles representing almost 30 different countries of Latin America and the Caribbean, the Middle East, Asia, Africa, and Europe, featuring especially authors and works that have suffered political censorship or were written in exile.

INTERNATIONAL WRITING
BY WOMEN:
A READERS INTERNATIONAL SERIES

Rosario Castellanos, *The Nine Guardians*, novel (Mexico)

Victor Català, pseudonym of Caterina Albert i Paradis, *Solitude*, novel (Catalonia/Spain)

Agnes Hankiss, *A Hungarian Romance*, novel (Hungary)

Janina Koscialkowska, *Beech Boat*, novel (Poland)

Monika Maron, *The Defector*, novel (eastern Germany)

Monika Maron, *Flight of Ashes*, novel

Monika Maron, *Silent Close No.6*, novel

Cristina Peri Rossi, *The Ship of Fools*, novel (Uruguay)

The Three Marias, *New Portuguese Letters*, fiction/poetry (Portugal)

Marta Traba, *Mothers and Shadows*, novel (Colombia)

Linda Ty-Casper, *Awaiting Trespass*, novel

Linda Ty-Casper, *Wings of Stone*, novel (Philippines)